FOREWORD

ALL THE KING'S HORSES AND ALL THE QUEEN'S MEN

'A Soldier's Song'

I aged ten years because I spent three years of my life with the Colonel. I wanted to write this foreword to dispel a tendency you'll have to dismiss everything you read about the Colonel's life as impossible. If I hadn't traveled the world with him, I never would have believed any stories about him either. I watched this immense child, in a grown man's body, make heads of corporations, heads of state, world champions and window washers weep with laughter, none harder than I. With the charm of Valentino, the quick wit of Robin Williams and the likability of Jimmy Stewart, there is no person who has ever come in close contact with the Colonel who doesn't remember him. He leaves people better off than they were before they met him. He enjoys living, and looks at life, like no other human I know. 'No one ever lay on his deathbed wishing he had worked more,' the Colonel taught me.

Bob Sheridan gave his undertaker, Colonel Caggiano, a large escrow payment for his own wake. His instructions were simple. 'If anyone cries, or fails to get drunk, throw them out.'

In the spring of 1995, we were having dinner at a cafe in Vieux Lyon, France. Bob, who loves meeting new people, called to a street person walking a dog, evoking the Peter Sellers joke he used all week, 'Does your dog bite,' in a ridiculous French accent. The reply came in perfect English, 'No, he does not bite.'

The Colonel called the man, who appeared to be a little drunk, to come over for a glass of wine. After a few glasses of our wine the man became surprisingly belligerent. He poked the Colonel in the chest (big mistake). Bob, who isn't easily provoked, laughingly warned the guy off. The Frenchman retorted that all Americans were assholes (another bad move), whereby the extremely patriotic Colonel stood up and gave him a right cross that sent him down to the 500-year-old cobblestones like a cartoon character carrying an anvil off a cliff. The six loud people at our table were immediately silent, stunned by the sudden skirmish. Three long seconds went by and then the Colonel waved his arms across his chest and yelled, 'six, seven, eight.... I don't think he's going to make it....'

We've spent long nights, that seemed like joyous weeks, in Ireland. We'll be long remembered at the Quito Inn, in Ecuador. I watched Bob and other friends brawl their way across pubs in England, while coming incredibly close to putting down my beer and joining them. We ploughed through mountains of lobster in Baja, Mexico, as the Colonel became el hombre langoste, 'lobsterman,' in front of his seven-foot-tall bodyguard Pancho, the largest Mexican ever made.

I will never forget the times we've had, nor would I trade those memories for anything else I've ever been given in my life.

I met the Colonel for the first time on my first show with Don King, October 14th, 1994, in Mexico City. The event was the Carbajal/Gonzalez fight live from the Plaza del Toros, the world's most famous bull ring. After fifteen years producing and directing NBA, NHL and Major League baseball games, I was always leery of announcers. I considered most announcers as nothing more than life support systems for egos. I was especially concerned about starting a new relationship with an announcer who had been with Don King for nearly 25 years. I was the new kid. What if the Colonel and I didn't get along? This job could be over before it began.

I approached a large gent in the TV compound that I considered a likely candidate and asked, 'Are you Bob Sheridan?'

'Are you Mahtee?' (Boston for Marty).

'Yes, are you the Colonel?'

'Look, Mahtee, let's get one thing straight right off the bat,' at which point I rolled my eyes wondering what the hell was coming next. 'I'm in charge of the whores,' he cautioned, while pointing a menacing finger at me. 'I've always been in charge of the whores, I'm still in charge of the whores and I will always be in charge of the whores. Do you get that?'

'Absolutely,' I laughed. And I haven't stopped laughing since.

Marty Corwin
Friend, Boss and
Vice President, Don King T.V.

INTRODUCTION

On the eve of the 1997 Mike Tyson vs. Evander Holyfield rematch, I was recovering from my third heart attack in six years, and my fifth angioplasty operation on that same night. Faced with open heart surgery or even a heart transplant, I thought the Good Lord was telling me, 'You'd better write the book soon, buddy boy.' I honestly felt, as I woke up from my morphine induced state of euphoria, that there were two things I knew for sure: (1) I don't have long to live (unless I change my entire lifestyle - unlikely!) and (2) the Lord won't take me today because He'll probably want to keep Heaven on the peaceful side a bit longer. 'Today is not the day I die! I'm going to Heaven when I do!' Simple logic, but to borrow a line from Rene DesCartes (or was it Alex Hawkins?) - 'That's my story and I'm sticking to it.'

With full belief that I'm not about to check out for the big dirt nap, me and Pancho Limon, my 7-foot Mexican bodyguard, determine not only that am I leaving the Desert Spring Hospital by noon, but that we are not telling my producer and boss at Kingvision, Marty Corwin, that I just had a moderate to severe heart attack. Nothing will prevent me from broadcasting this fight. It is going out to more than one billion people worldwide, and my ego is salivating. There hasn't been a show this big since I did the Ali-Foreman fight with David Frost in Zaire back in 1974. 'When We Were Kings', the Ali story at Zaire with my call of The Rumble in the Jungle, led to an academy award for best documentary. Not only did I not receive an Oscar for my work, but I was not even mentioned in the award-winning documentary, and that pisses me off. But hey! Not nearly as pissed off as the producers will be when they find out they didn't have rights to my voice, and they owe my estate a shitload of gelt! And Lord only knows what historic event may take place at Holyfield-Tyson II, so I'm doing the telecast. If I fuckin' die, then I die! And if that sounds extreme, remember … I'm a bard, a storyteller, a singer of songs, a poet with poetic license, or (as the love of my life Annie called me) 'A FOOKEN LIER.'

So, here's that crazy night, and all the rest. Just as I remember it …

CHAPTER I

'I DID NOT HAVE THE HEART TO KEEP THIS ALL INSIDE'

I knew the indications. Ice-cold sweat soaking through my collar when it's 120 degrees outside. My left arm, minding its own business, feeling like it's being run over by a train. My joints and bones, achy at the best of times, all of a sudden oversensitive to the gravity in the room, as if they were plated in chrome. Yep, I knew exactly what this was. And the timing couldn't have been any fuckin' worse!

I carried on eating the 36-ounce porterhouse steak in front of me, chewing like I had a mouthful of glue. I probably should have thrown in the towel, but I respected cattle too much to leave the sizzling, boot-sized slab of beef uneaten. Not the wisest decision. By the time I had swallowed the last mouthful, my chest was heavy, and I was struggling to breathe. Somehow, no one sitting around the stacked restaurant table seemed to notice my situation, although it wasn't at all strange for me, on the night before a big fight, to be uncharacteristically subdued. I'm a professional boxing commentator after all, and I needed to preserve my voice to be ready to talk for four, five, six hours if required. Especially in Vegas, where the lights shone the brightest, and where I was required to be at my absolute best.

I could feel the color draining from my skin, and it was only a matter of time before someone in my flock noticed. That night I was with some of my nearest and dearest. I always liked to surround myself with close family and friends the night before a major global event. I wanted to be on top form, and I felt comfortable kicking off my shoes in their company, able to just relax. As a television personality, you often feel obliged to be 'on' at all times. In other words, to give the people what they want. And while I am a natural born entertainer, and I do thrive on the adoration of people, these were the moments to be silent and still, when I had to put away the clown suit for a minute and focus on what got me to the party in the first place.

To the left of me was my brother Jim, who is also Colonel Sheridan. To my right was Marty Corwin, my steadfast producer at Kingvision. And opposite us, guzzling red wine and putting away fantastic quantities of chow, was my great friend from New Zealand, the respected promoter and entrepreneur, Georgie Calvert. They were shooting the shit, talking it all up, mostly about the looming mega-fight on the strip. Everyone in town was talking about it. The air was thick with anticipation. You couldn't throw a stone without it getting lodged in some opinion or other about the alpha showdown. Remember, when Tyson and Holyfield had fought that previous November in arguably the most anticipated heavyweight collision since Ali-Foreman, it was a foregone conclusion that Mike would steamroller him - although I never saw it that way. To me, it was always a 50/50 type fight involving two great champions with something to prove. This time around, however, really nobody - but nobody - knew what the fuck was going to happen. Everybody was hyped; the excitement was at fever-pitch. But with the squeeze in my chest, the tight breaths, that piece of unfinished business was the farthest thing from mind.

I had to get to the hospital, and fast.

Georgie was eyeing up the dessert menu. 'I'm not feeling too well,' I said. 'I'm going to go home and get checked out.' Georgie looked up. 'Alright then, you fat fuck, go sleep off that entire cow you just swallowed!' Georgie laughed.

Sweating, I laughed too. Asshole!

As soon as I was safely out of sight, I picked up my speed and hailed a taxi. Then, jumping in, I said to the driver, my eyes wide as saucers, my voice sounding like a raspy singer, 'I think I'm having a fuckin' heart attack!'

For very good reason, the first heart attack is known as the widow maker. People are likely to ignore the warning signs, and the thing about a heart attack is - the longer it goes on, the more damage it does to the body's key organ. It kills millions every year. People who are too meek or too busy to get themselves looked at, well, the statistics speak for themselves. Thank God I had already survived a couple of these things, the first occurring six years earlier, when I was forty-seven years old and sitting at around 350 pounds.

Just like so many other ignorant dopes, I had turned a blind eye for nearly five days, too absorbed in my daily bullshit to attempt to save my own life, until I was curled up in the fetal position and communicating with the Holy Spirit. Well, I'm a fast learner. Fool me once, shame on you. Fool me twice, I'll pull the goddamn trigger myself!

My cardiologist, Dr Ram Singh, who saved my life on that occasion and once more in the interim, had drilled it into me: if you think there is a problem, don't be afraid to take nitroglycerin right away, and don't be afraid to go to the doctor and be wrong - as opposed to being dead. Well, his words were echoing in my ears as we raced to the Desert Springs Hospital, weaving through traffic and ignoring red lights at my urgent, croaky behest. As predicted, I was whisked away by medical staff moments after arriving for an emergency angioplasty - a procedure to widen the narrowed or obstructed arteries in hearts. Or more simply put, to unclog the fuckin' things! If you don't get this done, and fast, your breathing will diminish to the point of no return, and the undertaker's got yet another coffin to fill.

Well, mine got done. And believe it or not, I emerged feeling like a new man. You see, once they get the old banger working again at full capacity, oxygen floods the capillaries and you feel kind of lightheaded, but in a great way. You actually feel euphoric. There was only one problem: despite the 180 in how I was feeling, and my conviction that I would not miss a single second of the upcoming telecast (an event that promised to be the crowning glory of my broadcasting career), I was basically handcuffed to a hospital bed! Shakespeare himself couldn't have thunk it up. I was energized, I was mentally sharp, but the clock was ticking. It was imperative that they get all this bullshit done so I could get back and call the fight.

Dr Singh was uncooperative. 'You're not calling the fight,' he told me, under the impression that he was the one in charge. To give the doc his due, he had a point. Discharging myself from the critical care unit wasn't the brightest idea, nor was it a guarantee that I would even make it to the commentary desk. The consequences for carrying out my plan, I was told in no uncertain terms, could be catastrophic.

You see, the danger was not that I would have another heart attack. Most people make that assumption - and they're wrong. The danger was that I might pop my stitches and bleed to death on the spot. At the time, post-procedure, you were supposed to spend a meaningful period with a heavy weight on your groin, the incision having gone through the femoropopliteal artery in that perilous region. You then needed to be monitored vigilantly to make sure that it all coagulates, and that you're no longer at risk.

Well. I didn't have time for any of that bullshit. As far as I was concerned, I had already outlived my own expectations. The man upstairs is in charge, and anytime He wants you, He is going to take you. That was my attitude. Suffering my first heart attack, I learned that I had deteriorated physically - booze, whores, steaks, and having a good time. They told me I only had one solitary year left. Since that day, I had lasted a further six. Every breath now was a bonus, just a little extra credit from the bank to send me on my merry way. Because as far as my lifestyle was concerned, I hadn't slowed down one bit! My lifestyle back then was wild. I was a single guy, I was the biggest boxing commentator on the planet, people adored me every place I went, and I was taking full advantage. I didn't give the first fuck about longevity. Wine, women, and song. These were the only things I cared about - plus, of course, my broadcasting career.

Now, let's be clear about one thing. Spending fifteen to twenty weeks a year in Las Vegas can be hazardous to one's health - especially when you're a tinker like me! But we'll get to that aspect of my life a little later. For the time being, let's just say that doing what I did for a living, my fame was concentrated in one place, and I wore it like a mink coat. Why the hell not? Whenever I would be at a fight venue, in my black tuxedo and red tie, I was like Tom Cruise at a Hollywood opening. Not only due to people knowing me from the television, which would always generate a certain amount of attention. But because I was such a fun guy to be around as well. The average Joe just loved my company. And my being recognized was not limited to the United States, either. In fact, I stood more chance of going unnoticed 10 feet from my own doorstep than in some of the remotest locations in the world. As an international broadcaster, the fame I gained overseas far outweighed my status at home. Take Australia and New Zealand as examples. In those two countries, I have been on TV for over fifty years. Everyone there knows me. They don't know the Ian Darke's, or the Reg Gutteridge's, or the Harry Carpenter's, but they know the Colonel Bod Sheridan. No question about it. So as long as there were boxing people around, I was the center of attention - and I loved it.

But I was also running amok with my life.

Thankfully, Dr Singh had my full confidence. In addition to having saved my bacon twice already, he was also regarded as the top cardiac surgeon in Nevada - meaning that (without question) he was among the best to be found absolutely anywhere! Nowhere has ever had more heart attacks than the desert metropolis. Young and old, they flock to the glittering lights for four, five days at a time, their wallets brimming with ready cash, and all they have to do is whore, and drink, and gamble. Then whore some more. So what the fuck do you think is going to happen? They don't sleep, so by about the second or third day, the heart attacks start popping like a popcorn machine in a movie theatre. You want to know what's funny about Las Vegas? If you're at the craps table, and a guy's rolling the dice, and he drops down and dies on the floor right next to you, they don't stop the game. The first question on everybody's mind isn't whether the guy lived or died, but whether he made his press. That's Las Vegas!

I relished every minute of my time there. In the '70s and '80s, the media had a reputation for not picking up any tabs. Well, I did. To me, it was all part of the show. I figured, if I was going to spend $50 on a round of drinks, I might as well spend $500 and show everybody a good time. That was me. That was my persona. I didn't care about money. I was making fifty to a hundred grand per fight, which I had to pay taxes on anyway. Why not blow half of it in the bars and casinos, and have a great time, as opposed to giving it to Uncle Sam, and write it up as expenses? Plus, I couldn't help myself anyway. I was addicted to the adulation, to the ego-feeding attention of a crowd. My happiness came from making other people happy, from witnessing them having a great time because of me. And let me tell you something, it was all one big fuckin' act. Of course it was! I call Las Vegas the phoniest city in the world, and I love it there because you know what? I'm a phony too. A phony with the God-given ability to lift the mood of any room. That's my gift *and* my curse. When the camera is rolling, I have to perform. Unfortunately for me, the body can only endure so much fast living. The spirit may still be willing, but eventually everything else tells you to go fuck yourself!

I was back in a hospital bed, feeling the walls closing in around me. As I fidgeted on the hard mattress, I felt that not even the good Lord himself could make me waver in my conviction. You see, following the angioplasty, I was on an emotional high, and

I genuinely didn't give two shits that I was throwing the dice with my own life. This was the big one. No way was I going to spend it laid up in that shithole.

Remember, back then, Tyson was the most famous athlete on the planet; people couldn't take their eyes off him. The more he fucked up, the more magnetic he became. Nobody could draw a crowd like Mike. He was Jack Dempsey, he was Sonny Liston, he was George Foremen, all rolled into one. More than any fighter in history, his demeanor exuded the primal appeal of the sport. You didn't tune into a Tyson fight to watch a sporting event; you came to see carnage.

I knew Mike pretty well - and believe me when I tell you, the kid had a split personality. On his meds (whatever the fuck they were giving him), he was an absolute sweetheart of a guy. Off them, he was a straight-up animal, and at those times I steered clear. Especially in the lead up to a fight, when he was double mean and getting ready to hurt someone. Otherwise, he and I had a great relationship, and I always admired Mike. Remember, he was still just a kid when he won the title at twenty-years-old. A handful of years earlier he had been a mugger on the streets of Brownsville, abandoned by the world and forced to fend for himself. Then, practically overnight, he morphed into the 'Baddest Man on the Planet', showered with unimaginable wealth and acclaim. That would have been a cluster fuck for anybody!

In those early days, he had a layer of protection with Kevin Rooney, Jimmy Jacobs and of course Cus D'Amato in his corner, guys he certainly respected and would listen to. However, the problem always was this - they taught him to be a heavyweight champion, but never how to be a grounded human being who could mix well with society. Consequently, his heroes in life were guys like John Gotti and Sammy 'The Bull' Gravano because he was a street thug just like them. He admired those characters. If he ever met the Queen of England, I'm sure he'd be nice and everything, but he wouldn't have any proper protocol. She would just be another rich white lady that he couldn't relate to.

In this regard, I always had sympathy for Mike. And for all the bullshit he went through with woman as well. It was an absolute shitshow. When he went to prison (where he never should have been, by the way, because he was innocent) he told me himself, 'I fucked the broad, but I never raped her.' And he would have told me the truth because I was in his corner. Anyway, when he was locked down for those three years, every few months I'd like to send him a two or three-line note saying, 'Hang in there, champ, Won't be long till you're out, Don't let it get to you,' and things of that nature. And years later, when he was retired from boxing and doing some color commentary with me, he put his arm around my shoulder and said, 'Colonel, I really appreciated those notes.' So I always got on tremendously well with Mike. Although at the same time, I understood that Mike was habitually suspicious of people (especially in those early years) and had probably thought I was trying to use him - because everyone else around him was.

Those years in prison changed Mike as a fighter. He was never as fast. He never worked as hard in training. The trainers he employed, although good boxing men, were mostly just thrilled just to be working with him, so they never said no to him. And this of course led to the diminishment of Mike's abilities in the ring. He basically did whatever he wanted to do. He really didn't listen to anyone, and he certainly didn't learn anything. Guys like Alan Snowell, Carl King and Stacey McKinley, who were excellent trainers, ultimately had no more control over Tyson than the cat. Whereas in a camp run by, say, an Angelo Dundee or an Eddie Futch or an Emmanuel Stewart, none of that bullshit would have flown. Not for a millisecond.

However, the truth was he had fallen out of love with the game by then and was fighting purely for the Benjamins. So, with that in mind, you can't really blame the corner for anything. Were they the elite? Probably not … but they were also on a highway to nothing with Mike, who was clearly going through the motions.

Now, Mike Tyson going through the motions is still a more dangerous fighter than ninety-eight per cent of guys on the planet. And let's not forget, Evander had humiliated Mike in that first fight, standing his ground and effectively bullying the bully for much of the contest. For that reason, I gave the former champ a solid shot at turning the tables in the rematch - although I by no means made him the favorite. You see, having spent a significant amount of time in camp with Evander and his excellent trainer, Don Turner, I had seen firsthand how prepared they were for the fight. I knew that Evander was going to present a serious problem to Mike (yet again) and could easily spring a second upset. Sure, in my heart of hearts, I was rooting for Mike, but as a student of the game, I also fully understood the challenge that faced him. Evander was never a massive heavyweight, but he always got one hundred percent out of his ability. Always. The guy's desire to win was second to none. So when I called him a dirty fighter, I was saying it to be factual, first and foremost, but also as a cock-eyed compliment.

I had nothing but admiration for the man.

Not surprisingly, he took offence. Some years later, when we were recording an interview, he asked me straight out, 'Why are you always calling me dirty?' I grinned at him and said, 'Evander, Johnny Ruiz went to the school of Evander Holyfield dirty fighting, and he actually defeated you at your own game, and that's why I said it. Nothing derogatory, I just think you gotta use whatever you got. You used what you had, and I'm just pointing it out. You're a great guy in person, but you're a very rough fighter. Now that is interpreted as a dirty fighter, and I don't know what else to call it, because that's what everyone calls it. Therefore, I said it, and I stick by it.' And to his credit, he laughed it off and we carried on, because he always had that kind of personality. I admire Evander greatly. He was the 'Real Deal' in and out of the ring. I maintain, though, that he often fought outside of the legal bounds of the sport.

Anyway, back at the hospital, I was getting ready to discharge myself. As you would expect, there were plenty of objections, but I didn't give a rat's ass. I'm the Colonel.

I don't take orders, I give 'em! The only person who could prevent me from showing up at the arena and taking center stage was Marty - and he had no idea what was happening. Other than that, I had with me my bodyguard, Pancho, who was as loyal as a German Shepard, and that was it. Nobody in the place had any authority over me. And to reiterate, there was no fuckin' way I was going to miss the fight. I needed to be seen, to be part of the event. This was history.

It was also a massive payday.

See, I'd been out there gambling and whoring for weeks. My wallet was empty. Commentators are similar to the boxers themselves in this regard: if we don't show up on fight night, we don't get paid. So yeah, I couldn't afford to go to Las Vegas and blow twenty grand (which of course I was apt to do in those days) and not take a cheque home for fifty or a hundred grand. That was how I looked at it. And the reality was, I was ready, able, and willing. At least in my mind.

Knowing it to be entirely necessary, I said to Dr Singh, 'Doc, Pancho is gonna tell you, one way or the other, we're going …' And Pancho, his tremendous shadow darkening the room, added, 'As a matter-of-fact Doc, you're coming too.' Well, the doctor had little to no interest in boxing and dismissed the proposal quite rudely, until I told him, my eyes twinkling, knowing him too well, 'Wait till you see the pussy that's at ringside. You'll think you've died and gone to heaven!' Doc was on board. Equipped with a defibrillator and his medical bag, he was going to be at my side and attempt to keep me breathing should my condition suddenly go south.

The game plan was agreed. I would hop into an ambulance, call the fight preferably without bleeding to death (the Lord will protect me!), smile and wave to the Sheridan groupies, then get my ass back to the hospital before the strike of midnight. No problem! And of course, I would have Pancho with me as well, my great friend and travel companion till the day he took a bullet for me in bizarre circumstances and bit the dust. But that is another story for a different book. For now, I will say just this - with him at my side, I knew for sure nobody would fuck with me.

I used to joke that Pancho Limon was 'the world's largest Mexican.' A professional bodyguard hired by Don King after my first heart attack (referred to him by my executive producer, Chuck Haifley), he stood at seven feet two inches tall and weighed anywhere between 500 and 600 pounds - though without ever managing to get him on a meat scale, we never learned his exact weight.

Chuck, being concerned about my health, had said to me one day, 'I've got this guy Pancho - a huge former basketball star from Iowa - who is a real professional bodyguard and does a lot of work in Hollywood for celebrities. He doesn't push anyone around, he carries a weapon but never uses it, he stays close but doesn't try to get into pictures. He just turns up and does his job.' And it was all true. Pancho was a man of few words and had an ideal temperament for the profession. With that said, he was also an immersible, hopeless, despondent, depraved, drug-addled and incorrigible alcoholic, who was always looking for a good time. So we got along great! When Pancho and I used to show up together, people would say, 'Lock up the kids, lock up the dogs, put the babies away. These two fuckin' guys are coming to town!' And while I had some presence of my own, being a tremendous consumer of food and drink and a well-known personality, he looked and behaved like a king in command.

When he was around, you'd better believe people were on their best behavior. His head being the size of two blowing balls with a big full beard, and looking just like a grizzled sea captain, stinking of rum, he loomed like a natural disaster in waiting. Everybody in entertainment knew Pancho. He was mythical. For instance, we'd be in a production meeting with HBO or Showtime, and the executives would be holding discussions with the police department, deciding on how best to allocate resources, and someone would ask, 'How about the international side?' And they would reply, simply, 'Oh, they've got Pancho,' and say nothing more. That was the potency of his aura.

I guess the folks at the hospital sensed it, too. Pancho, at my request, commandeered an ambulance for my immediate transportation and led the way as we coolly exited the building. Then, along with two wide-eyed paramedics, we drove straight to the MGM Grand, crashing to a stop at the main entrance. People swelled around the hotel and casino like a body of water. Vegas is always in perpetual motion, whether Mike Tyson is in town or not; but as I disembarked from the vehicle, I could hardly remember seeing such a sea of humanity in one place. So soon after my brush with death, it was like being out in the world for the very first time.

Once there, I was more than capable of getting up to my room unassisted. Of course I was. But where's the spectacle in that? You know me. Once I'm in front of an audience, it's showtime again. So, with a few concise orders, I had the boys *lift* me out of the ambulance and *wheel* me into the lobby, as though I had been rescued from some Far-Eastern war zone only hours earlier. Cameras flashed and popped as me, Dr. Singh, Pancho and the two ashen-faced paramedics sliced through the throng. I couldn't have asked for a more stylish entrance. It was like something out of a movie.

Smiling from ear to ear and feeling the excitement rippling all around me, I was in my element, acting out a moment of true drama. Yet, as I neared my room, my elation quietly died down. It was now time to tell my bosses at Don King Productions that their star commentator, who they relied upon to carry their broadcasts to the full English-speaking world outside of the United States, was recovering from a moderate to severe heart attack - just hours from their biggest ever event! I knew they wouldn't be happy. A Tyson fight was wildly unpredictable at the best of times. Now, with the prospect of me dropping dead halfway through the show, the heat had been raised by several degrees. Marty, with whom I had dined the previous evening, nearly shit himself at the news. His first instinct, of course, was to hire another commentator.

'Marty,' I said. 'I'm calling this fuckin' fight, and if you kick up a stink trying to protect me, I'll let Pancho beat the living shit out of you!' Now, I would never have done that. Marty and I were friends, but I wanted him to know that I was serious. He yielded but had a couple of strict conditions.

Firstly, I would have to record the close for the broadcast *ahead* of time. That would be no problem for me. I was, after all, a battle-hardened pro with nearly thirty years' experience in calling world championship fights. And secondly, no messing about after the main event. I was to go straight back to the hospital and get myself readmitted. 'Marty,' I told him. 'That was the plan anyway!'

Filming the close was easy. Although it was still late-afternoon with not a punch having been thrown in anger, I knew just how to sell it. Planting my feet and clearing my throat, I invoked from my voice box the richest baritone I could muster, and with a beatific smile I declared, 'We could not have imagined the way this fight would end. What a night of boxing, something we won't soon forget. From Las Vegas, Nevada, I'm the Colonel Bob Sheridan, saying so long everybody, and don't forget what a fight you just saw. What a historic night it was!'

Kind of generic, but right on the mark. This was a Tyson fight after all. Something fucked up was bound to happen!

Don King was now in the building and had been apprised of events. He caught me as I was looking around for the doc, who was temporarily out of sight. I remember exactly what Don said to me, his smile as wide as the Grand Canyon. 'You are the Colonel Bob Sheridan,' he bellowed. 'You are the best. You're heading to the HOF. I knew I could count on you!' And he gave me a tremendous hug. He didn't mention my condition; why would he? With Don, business always, always came first. I knew that - I also knew that I was his number one. The priority was the show. And I was ready.

Showered, dressed, and prepared in 30 minutes, I headed downstairs to the venue. Suddenly a flick switched in my mind; no longer was I concerned about my health, only about my performance. I knew well how rapidly it could all go sideways on the air. Once the red light goes on, I'm 100 per cent focused on what I am doing. After all, at that moment, you are walking the tightrope. There are no erasers, no do-overs. On the air, you're fuckin' exposed to the world. They spend up to 50 hours producing the first 30 seconds of the show - with the music and the sprawling ariel shots of the location, etc. - then they turn you loose for the next four hours without so much as a page of script! You're bound to say something stupid. Talking to tens of millions of people around the world, non-stop. And the whole time, you're basically having to ad-lib. Easy, right?

Singh had it all set up. The oxygen, the medical supplies, the emergency services on standby. At boxing events, having ambulances on site is a legal requirement, for obvious reasons. Here, though, for the first time, a member of the media *not* engaging in a sanctioned fistfight had his very own!

Now it was showtime.

All the familiar faces were on display. Jack Nicolson, Denzel Washington, Michael Jordan. The beautiful people, adding to the glamor. Legendary fighters too, such as Larry Holmes and Sugar Ray Leonard, on tenterhooks, remembering the thrills and the agony of a championship fight. The noise in the arena was deafening, the excitement electric. Myself, I was perhaps a little lackluster in the early going; however, once Tyson and Holyfield had entered the ring and the iconic voice of Jimmy Lennon Jr began cascading through the stands, I felt my mind narrow into a ray of pure focused energy. Months of build-up, years of subtext, fascination and debate, with the clang of the opening bell, reaching a crescendo. Then, after three completed rounds, it was all over - with some of the most chaotic scenes ever witnessed in a boxing ring.

I fuckin' loved it!

Referee Mills Lane, as we know, disqualified Mike Tyson for twice biting the ear of Evander Holyfield, leaving chunks of his flesh chewed up and spat out on the ring apron and creating pandemonium. I remember having the sense, from my seat at ringside, of being caught in a stampede. And you know something? I couldn't have wished for a better outcome; it was pure Hollywood!

Once Mike got cut open I knew the fight was over.

Now, don't misunderstand me, I never could have predicted such an extreme reaction (who could have?), but the writing undoubtedly had been on the wall - especially to those who had been paying attention. Evander was fighting an incredibly dirty fight, yet again, and Mike finally snapped. He had trained hard - at least in his own mind - and yet another damaging foul from Evander, mimicking the dozens he had received in the first encounter, with no recourse from the referee, had caused him to erupt - the Brownsville coming out in him with the first trickle of blood. He went berserk - savage actually - baring his teeth and looking like he wanted to kill.

As a sportscaster, you can only call what you see. Initially, I didn't realize what had happened. All I saw was Evander's reaction as he yelped and hopped into the air, pawing incredulously at the side of his head. An ear-bite was the furthest thing from anybody's mind. Therefore, my first words were shrouded in confusion. 'Something strange has happened, look at Evander's reaction!' was all I could think of to say. Then, in my earpiece, I heard, 'He may have bitten his ear!' Marty and the other guys in the production truck quickly confirmed, and the rest is history.

Evander Holyfield won the fight by a disqualification that he created. That *he* created. This is very important to recognize. I am an expert in the game. I learned my craft in the most famous boxing gym in the world, alongside the all-times greats, and have called literally thousands of fights. My opinion holds weight, and it is my opinion that Evander knew - he *knew* - that his fouls would eventually cause Mike to go nuts. That he would either quit or get himself thrown out. And the plan worked. We can talk about the frailties in Tyson's psyche all we want, but the kid was raised wild, and his opponent correctly calculated that - with the right provocation - the 'street thug' would once again come roaring out of him. The outcome may have been the same regardless, but it was the easiest route to victory. God bless him.

It was time to go. The crowd had gone crazy, the corner men and hangers on were invading the ring and Mike was throwing punches everywhere. With Pancho leading the way, I grabbed on to his belt and we cut directly through the catastrophe of limbs and screaming voices. Honestly, I did not see much more of what followed after the end of the fight. Still, I was getting a kick out of the mayhem; this kind of chaos was the reason I loved the sport. With the ambulance only about 50 feet away, as the crow flies, Pancho got me there in 45 seconds flat without needing to put a hand on anyone. Singh had made it through as well.

But wait, there was time for one more bit of excitement. As I reached the ambulance, dazed by all that had occurred in the past 24 hours but feeling exuberant nevertheless, a girl who worked in the arena raced over to me and said, leaning in, 'Hey, you want a blowjob before you go?' Well, Doc just about exploded. I laughed, and said, 'Doc, she's not really gonna blow me. I'll have a fuckin' heart attack!' But I think he just wanted to see if she would actually do it! After all, it was his first fight night experience with the Colonel, and he was prepared for just about anything. Of course, though, he and I both knew if I were Bob Sheridan the local drunk instead of the famous sportscaster, nobody would be offering me free blowjobs. I understood exactly who I was and the fun it could bring me. Other than that, I really didn't care much about anything.

Still chuckling, we climbed into the ambulance, and they hooked me up to the intravenous fluid, giving me an evaluation at the same time. I felt a little tired, I'll be honest. A little drained. Emotionally as much as anything. But I was still able to wisecrack, I could still mess around. The engine rumbled and slowly we were led away by a procession of police motorcycles. Sirens and lights chaperoned the vehicle the entire way back to the hospital (where I would remain for the next ten days, requiring a further two angioplasties), creating one hell of a picture, one hell of a final act. Nobody could have scripted it any better. Remember, it is all about the show.

Every so often, I'm asked, 'Would you do it again? Would you risk your life again for the same crazy reasons?' My reply, always … 'Abso-fucking-lutely!' It was both the dumbest decision I ever made and the smartest. My name, my voice, my words, these will be forever associated with that infamous and truly unforgettable night, burnished in the history of boxing. I even coined the nickname, 'The Bite Fight'. This would all have passed me by had I simply stayed lying down in that white bed; had I listened to the learned doctors instead of my lavish ego and accepted my fate like I quite honestly should have. But from the moment the telecast was jettisoned, I was giddy as a schoolboy; nobody needed to tell me that I had done an outstanding job. I had just called the fight of the century, avoided disaster, and left the arena 100,000 dollars richer.

Not too bad for a night's work.

CHAPTER II

'THE SEED OF THE SHAMROCK
IS PLANTED'

Let's get one thing straight: Us Micks never always got along, but we absolutely hated everybody else.

The Dorchester section of South Boston was one of the most bigoted, most racially divided sections of the Birthplace of Liberty you could ever imagine. In Southie and Dot, the Irish of the U.S would comfort each other by hating Blacks and Jews more than the skinheads of the '80s, or the Klu Klux Klan of the '40s and '50s, when I was just a kid. The feeling was mutual. You see, all we had was our own community, no different to the Italians, the Polish or the Dutch, and while we might have feuded among ourselves, neighbor versus neighbor, father versus son, we understood the common knowledge - that when you're down in Hell, you'd better stick with the Devil you know. So that's what we did. We fell victim to human nature; we created our own vacuum. The only trouble with a vacuum is, while you are inside, the rest of the world keeps moving. Well, I determined very early on that I would not be left behind, that I would not be born, live and die within the same ten-mile radius.

It was this mindset that lifted me from the gray, stagnant waters of where I began. That, and a whole load of good luck.

Born on June 22, 1944, I had a happy, fairly typical childhood. Happy in that I was slick enough to often avoid my father's belt (he was fair but firm), and typical in that, while everyone around me was out of their damn minds, I knew no different. Nothing ever struck me as unusual. The vicious yelling, the casual swearing, the bloody fights, the rampant crime, the violent gangs, the desperate poverty; it was all just normal. More than that, it was fun! Only many years later did I realize that 'normal' was actually batshit crazy.

Trouble was never far away. Where we lived, tough guys and junkies covered the streets like menacing, unchecked wildlife. I quickly learned how not to be in the wrong place at the wrong time. This instinct might be described as having street smarts, I describe it as having plain good sense. No point in sticking around to take a beating (or worse), especially with good looks to protect. I was a funny kid too; I knew what to say and when to say it. It got me out of a hell of a lot of scrapes.

My parents, James L. Sheridan and Helen M. Doherty, came to America from Ireland in 1905 - both squawking infants in arms. My father, from County Longford on the County Caven border in the Republic of Ireland; and my mother, from County Mayo and County Donegal in the north and west of Ireland. I don't know too much about this period. Honestly, neither Mum nor Dad ever seemed comfortable in reliving the past. It was only from bits and pieces of overheard chatter that I learned they were childhood sweethearts - having grown up a few doors from each other - and that in the mid '30s they married and settled down. The world, though, had not been a friendly place for them. That much I do know. Persecuted, like so many others, for their immigrant status, they had to work twice, three times as hard as the rest of America to earn half as much. With few choices, and even fewer lucky breaks, they did the best they could while being kept at the bottom of the pile, trapped in Dorchester for most of their lives. Or, as my mother would put it, 'Hemmed in with the rest of the cattle!'

But life wasn't all bad. The place we affectionately called Dot covers six square miles in the city of Boston, split down the middle by Dorchester Avenue. Furious and fun-loving, we huddled together in the sawdust of the 'Irish Slums' in what was our little piece of the land. It wasn't much but at least it had an identity. A stealthily hard worker, my father would always put meat and potatoes on the table despite living from cheque to cheque (like most everybody else we knew) and having to be content with the bare, depressing essentials. Not that I or my older brother Jim minded. In fact, we have nothing but fond memories of the old neighborhood, the family crowded around the coal fire to keep warm, eating baked cabbage and pork sausages. Sometimes laughing, sometimes wanting to kill each other. Always as much affection in the house as there was anger - the way it should be.

We lived in what was known as a Three Decker, residences built in the 1890s to house immigrants near to the local factories. Cheap to make, they could easily fit three families, with each floor being its own apartment. Ours was a tired pointy-roofed dwelling that, with the exception of the railed balconies and long white pillars at the front, resembled a pale blue garden shed. Fortunately (and also unfortunately), we had the pleasure of the ground floor. This gave the family easy access to the little garden and meant we didn't have to climb any stairs. However, it also meant that our guts were chilled throughout the notorious New England winters by the bitter drafts. No one complained too much. No point. The house was old and shabby and permanently smelled of damp paint, but it was home. Aside from the wind chill, it was comfortable and well-ordered, my mother taking great pride in her abode. She worked miracles with an array of rugs and trinkets - and, despite having two young boys and a husband, she somehow kept the place immaculate at all times.

My mother was the sweetest woman alive. She was also a perfect lady and very loving. She spoiled the hell out of me. I remember on Sundays she would cook roast beef, slaving over a rickety stove from early morning. Her demeanor never once showed that she was overworked and most likely very overtired. She moved briskly and lightly and smiled whenever I poked my head in through the door, my stomach forever rumbling. A perennial battered apron tied around her waist, I remember her waving me into the kitchen and pouring me glasses of milk while I waited, the smell of the roasting beef filling my nose. She was a phenomenal cook and had a gift for improvisation. The alchemy she could perform with the most basic ingredients - lard, mutton, mountains of potatoes - was mind-blowing even to a kid. For this reason we ate like millionaires when, of course, we were anything but.

My father, on the other hand, was a gangster. No, he really was. At least in his younger years. At the time, there was nothing else he could be. Although he would ultimately become a very successful building contractor and provide a great life for us, like all Irishman who had grown up in 1920s America, he vividly remembered the slogan, *'IRISH NEED NOT APPLY'*. Well, those words had been seared upon his eyes. He understood the reality. Broader society viewed him (and everyone he loved) as no better than a dog, less than a dog in some households. But he'd be damned if he allowed himself to starve because of it.

Instead, he began working in the shipyards down in Rhode Island, schlepping for the Patriarca crime family - who overlooked his Irish blood in favor of his rough efficiency - doing whatever was necessary to stay afloat. Nevertheless, he wanted his sons to be law abiding citizens. And if my mother was sweet, he most certainly was sour - never shy with his belt or indeed the back of his hand. But I respected him more than anyone else. I recognized from an early age his desire to keep myself and my brother on the straight and narrow. The world had fucked him over, but he still had hope for us.

His 'business' partner was a grizzly Italian named Joe Leonardo, who was actually my religious godfather. I remember him having these thick wrists and enormous hands, as if they belonged to some kind of sasquatch - using them to pinch my cheeks. I'd scrunch up my face and grimace - I hated that more than anything! Still, I was hyped whenever he came by the house, for one reason only: always before leaving, he would slip me a five-dollar bill. To a kid my age, that was an incredible sum of money, enough to keep me in comic books and candy for two (or even three) months straight. Uncle Joe sure was generous! But of course, I was kept in the dark about most things, and I never knew exactly what my father and him got up to back then. Nor did I want to know. He took care of us, and I loved him.

As Dad got more successful, we moved from the Irish section of Dorchester to Lexington - a leafy suburban town that, while only 10 miles away, might as well have been a million. For me and Jim, it was a culture shock to say the least. Dot had been an incredibly rough and tough inner-city neighborhood where, like flies to shit, our young eyes had fallen upon gang-life and petty criminality. By degrees, we had been developing into hoodlums, always getting into more serious trouble. Mum especially could see it, as she regularly had to rinse the blood from our clothes, sighing into the bar of soap and biting back her tears. Now that we'd moved out to live among the 'nice' families, we were given a taste (for the first time) of lower-middle-class living and - truth be told - we had no idea how to act!

What we most appreciated right away was the extra space. Unlike the city, where everything had felt so piled-high and claustrophobic, not to mention unwashed, Lexington was open and spacious and noticeably fresher. The pace of life was a little slower too, and for the first time we felt as though we could breathe.

In school, I was a pretty good athlete. President of my class at Lexington High and loved by all. I was the Eddie Haskell of 'Leave It to Beaver' fame, only better at it! Butter wouldn't melt in my mouth. Parents, teachers, priests, coaches, the girls - they all loved me. But I lived and performed for my buddies. Nothing too heavy; farting during a quiet session in class, leading the boys to skip school for the St. Patrick's Day parade, and ball sucking teachers so bad in front of my pals that it was a howl. With all of their high education, they didn't even realize I was just shitting all over them.

High school was a breeze. As a natural born jokester and conman, I had fun every day I was there, shimmying away each afternoon as though I had committed a crime. The only problem was, by the time graduation came around, I had also conned myself out of an education! You see, the teachers all liked me so much that they never got on my ass about anything - especially my grades. I could read, write and count for sure, but not at the university level. Nowhere close. I felt like the smartest dummy on the green earth.

For a time, I thought I'd blown the whole damn thing. My dad had his heart set on my going to Notre Dame University on a baseball scholarship, it was all he talked about. Now, there was no chance of that happening. Along with the best athletes, they also wanted the brightest students. I was a dollar short.

For this failure, I had to attend prep school, a twelve-month isolation camp designed to bring up my grades. St. Anselm's College in Manchester, New Hampshire, to be exact. My father knew that if I wanted to play baseball at the University of Miami - which was now my dream - I had to learn to study. I would never make it without learning to read and concentrate at this secluded Benedictine monastery - situated on top of a mountain. A goddamn mountain! Looking back, I still can't believe that I actually went. From mid-November all the way through to mid-March, the temperature stayed below freezing, the air cutting like broken glass. My fingers to this day can still feel the shards that inhabited those gusts of wind. It was evil. But, like a good little jail bird, I hit the books relentlessly, often swotting till the early hours of the morning by torch light. I might as well have been a priest myself between Mondays and Fridays. However, just like everyone else, I lived for my weekends of freedom.

Thumbing rides, I came home every Friday, wanting to see everyone and cause a little ruckus - before returning to my mountain-top on Sunday nights. In the winter, we went to the ice hockey games, in the summer, the beaches and ballparks. Exactly like we had done in high school. Only now, we could legally drink, so the bars also became a nightly fixture. It was just the escape I needed to counterbalance my disciplined existence during the week. I worked my ass off, honestly, realizing what was at stake. I couldn't be just another fuck up from the neighborhood. My parents had broken their backs to give me the opportunities that they never had, and I wanted more for myself as well. Much more.

Spurred on by this thought, I studied and studied and studied some more until, in the end, it paid off. My work ethic had at last caught up with my intelligence, closing a distance that had previously been at least as wide as the Amazon River. With the loving support of my parents and the ill-tempered guidance of the priests, who called me out daily on my bullshit, I had accomplished my goal. I was off to the University of Miami.

Now, I've always loved sports. Physical games came easily to me, and to this day, I love the camaraderie of being on a team. All the way through school, I played ice hockey, football, and baseball tirelessly. Not to sound arrogant, but I was damn good at all of them - it was just a fact. I enjoyed the violence of hockey, with the numerous fist fights that broke out during a game. I loved the concussion of football, with our helmets constantly colliding. And I lived for the excitement of baseball, when the ball was in your hand, and you were right in the middle of the action. Once I got to the University of Miami, the Hurricanes took precedence in my sporting life, and baseball was on the front burner. I had the best ratio of less time on the field and more time in front of the camera than any scholarship athlete that ever roamed the athletic fields of the institution - and every second was a hoot!

Living apart from my childhood environment, my mind expanded. I became quite fond of a hot shit from Springfield, Massachusetts, named Seymour Margoulis, who was my first roommate. Sy was a gun freak who later became a jet jockey in the United States Air Force. Sy became one of my best friends. And Sy was Jewish. That's when it clicked - that my baked-in prejudices made absolutely no sense. I was just a knucklehead teenager trying to make his way in the world, and so too was Sy. There was no difference between us. From our first day on campus, all we cared about was having fun.

I was in charge of nicknames on the Hurricane baseball squad, and everybody was Irish. Even the Jewish boys loved the names I gave them. Jerry O'Reisman was our shortstop, Stanley O'Yanowitz played right field with Paddy O'Warren in left, and Tobe 'Darby O'Gil' Green was in center field. Our second baseman, Nellie Mitchell, was so small I just called him 'that little fuckin' leprechaun at second,' who was better at playing handball with a B-B up against a curb stone than a 4-6-3 double play. Those were the most carefree days of my life. I fell in love with a Hurricanette baton twirler named Nan Herring, who in the end couldn't live with my brutal honesty and my extreme emotion. I couldn't blame her. Since being freed from my monastic existence at St. Anselm's, I'd been on a rampage. Anything in a skirt had to be chased. Finally, of course, she dumped me for infidelity.

Nan was a beautiful girl from New York, well above the class of lady a mutt like me deserved. Back then, I was only looking for sex - and lots of it. My hormones were raging and staying faithful to one person - even to this girl who looked like an out-and-out Prom Queen - was akin to asking the wind not to blow and the clouds not to rain. I actually suffered an attack of conscience. Following an affair with a 36-year-old librarian with massive tits, with whom I thought I was in love, I confessed to Nan and begged for her forgiveness. She slapped the taste clean out my mouth and we never spoke again. So much for honesty! Turns out I wasn't really in love with my fling, either. I was just in love with her tits and the sex of an older woman. But hey, you can't win them all. My love-sick heart needed time to recover, and so for the remainder of my college career I focused solely on the Hurricanes.

Unfortunately, this shift in my attention would also lead to heartache. After graduating in 1966, the realization that I wasn't gifted enough to be a professional baseball player was briefly more than I could bear.

For most of America, the game of baseball is little more than a pastime. For me, it was my first passion. I remember going to Fenway Park as a kid to watch my beloved Red Sox. The sky deep blue and the clouds stretched apart like cotton candy, we bought our tickets and a freshly pressed program at the gate, unable to tell the players without their number. Dad got me ice cold Coca-Colas and hotdogs, while he nibbled on peanuts and talked shit about the opposing team. I couldn't stop smiling as I watched the players warm up across the field, gleaming in their white uniforms. Ted Williams was my idol, and when he struck the ball, the crack of his bat reverberated through my whole body. From that point onwards, all I wanted in life was to hit pitches with the same beauty and violence. For a while, I even convinced myself that I might actually be good enough to do just that - especially when, directly out of college, I was drafted by the Miami Marlins to play in the Florida State League.

Minor League Baseball!

It was exciting as hell. This was everything I'd been working for, everything I'd been visualizing and tasting for as long as I could remember. Yet in no time at all - roughly three months - my dream of being the next Babe Ruth had completely turned to shit. Facts don't care about feelings. The fact was, I didn't have the tools to be a Minor League ball player. Hell, I barely had the tools to excel at the university level. I was strong and I could hit, sure, but years of abuse playing football as a linebacker had destroyed my shoulder. There was no way I could have gone any further. Moreover, I was just a step behind the rest of the squad in every department. The coaches were trained to weed out players like me.

I was heartbroken but, in the end, sanguine - the wisdom I had acquired at St. Anselm's helping me through this period of disappointment in an unlikely way. Spending time with the priests, I learned to be spiritual, but also to leave the things I could not control in the hands of God. For these virtues, I love Father Steve and Father Joseph to this day. Now, onto my grandfather.

As a small boy, the Irish influence was indelibly scratched into my cerebellum by my grandfather, a Proddy turned Catholic when he married my grandmother, Annie Graham. I loved them both, and when I close my eyes, I can still hear their voices inside the old, yellow-tiled kitchen, ribbing one another and telling stories. My grandfather told me of a relative of his, named Uncle Nick, in Mountjoy Jail back in Ireland. I thought it was neat having an Uncle Nick Doherty in jail because he was an Irish patriot. I had no idea he was on a hunger strike with John Plunkett!

I was told never to mention 'Gramp's stories' to anyone, which was never a problem for me. It made me feel so close to him, and I loved the idea of us having 'our secrets'. In reality, though, I thought he was just a senile ol' son of a bitch telling me exciting bedtime stories. But he had a TV, and no matter what time my mother told him to put me to bed, he would always let me stay up to watch Friday Night Fights. This was the birth of my love affair with the fight game.

With Gramp's, I could carry on like the true entertainer that I was. Staying with him and my grandmother, sometimes for weeks at a time, the smile never for a moment left my face. I will always cherish the memory of those Friday nights sitting in the old living room, taking a few naughty sips of beer and learning about the sport. I was a kid who always loved baseball. Now, I was equally obsessed with boxing, up to speed with all the top fighters of the day, able to score rounds using the correct criteria, and as schooled in the nuances of a prize fight as any sports fan in the country. All thanks to my grandfather.

As an aging man, my grandfather was nevertheless a person of great character and passion who rose from the pig slop of Boston to become a very wealthy farmer and storekeeper in a place called Freedom, New Hampshire. He often told me, while I held up his gout-rotted leg on my five-year-old back listening to Irish Rebellion music on his old phonograph, that he chose Freedom, New Hampshire, because 'someday you must go back to 'the Old Country' to help ensure its freedom.'

My summers were spent at his sprawling farm in New Hampshire, where I roamed like a nomad in a new world. I loved his stories, I loved his horses, and to my surprise, I loved his cattle as well. Without a doubt my passion for veterinary medicine - in which I would later earn a university degree - and the great outdoors - where I spend most of my idle hours to this day - sprung from these times. My uncles Lawrence and Ray also had farms, and so over time I spent countless weeks with these thoroughly decent men, learning how to care for animals. However, the animals were only the catalyst. What I was really learning was this: respect, discipline, and ethics from these farmer relatives of mine, while I rolled up my sleeves and shoveled shit. Most of all, though, I valued the time I had with my grandfather.

Filled to bursting point with an innate love for his people, he bestowed upon me his passions, and for this I will be forever grateful. Stern at the brow when discussing the political history of Ireland and smiling toothlessly when reminiscing about the Old Country, his tongue resting on his lower lip as he chuckled, he was (alongside my father) my biggest idol and the figure I most looked to for guidance. As the years went along and Ireland became deeply set in my subconscious, Andrew Doherty succumbed to a coronary after Christmas during my late elementary school years.

I felt a strange yearning for the Irish. Luckily, my Aunt Kitty had a great Irish accent, and I could spend hours talking to her about the history of Ireland and about anything else Green. Then there was my favorite aunt on my father's side. She was a Sheridan, and she was a Sheridan who was proud to be a tinker. At that time, I thought a tinker was like some sort of rock star. I didn't know what great character that showed in my Aunt Evelyn, because she was married to my millionaire Uncle Ray and had seemed so privileged. Not until I eventually traveled to Ireland did I find out that the tinkers - by dint of their birth - are among the most marginalized and persecuted people to be found absolutely anywhere.

They are also the most mischievous. Me, I was a tinker through and through. And this pissed off my big brother, Jim, no end.

Two and a half years my elder, growing up Jim didn't want his snot-nosed brother hanging around all the time. He had his own friends, and my presence - I suppose - was like a fly annoying a wildebeest. Nonetheless, I always loved my sibling, but he's also a real Yank and has no passion for Ireland at all. He went to Ireland just once over a St. Patrick's Day weekend and was so drunk for three days he made the statement on our Aer Lingus flight back to Boston - in his hungover state of mind - that 'I will never ever travel with you again.' The rain in his head from drink, coupled with his bruised ribs sore from laughter, made this handsome hunk of a movie star-looking guy into an absolute heap of shit for the entire six-hour flight!

While Jim knows nothing of my life, he also has no idea how his seemingly normal older brother's tormenting of me would be etched so indelibly in my mind that it ultimately saved me from self-destruction later on. You see, as a child, I had an Achilles' heel, and the only person in the world who knew about this weakness and my uncontrollable temper was James L. Sheridan Jr., my brother. James knew he could set me off at any time by uttering just two words, 'Dipple Dipple'. For some inexplicable reason, these words would enrage me to the point where I once plotted to kill him.

One night, when we were around 13 or 14 years old, in our adjacent beds with the lights out and the bedroom pitch dark, he got on my case. I waited for some time in simmering frustration for what felt like an eternity. Then I crept up next to him, clenching my fists with premeditated fury, and I delivered a blow that I imagined would have knocked out Rocky Marciano! I held nothing back. However, just as I swung, he rolled away laughing, and my right fist - propelled like a fastball - shattered against his hip bone. The pain was excruciating, throbbing all the way through my arm, but I refused to let it show. I refused to let my brother know he had once again gained the upper hand.

I hated my brother at that moment and for the next several weeks, because our altercation had ended my eighth-grade season of my beloved game of baseball. Yet as the weeks passed and my hand healed, I realized that my mind must heal as well - that my uncontrolled rage was a blueprint for disaster.

My brother rarely fucked with me after that, and I stayed pretty clear of him until later years when we had a little feud over my getting drunk in Miami and coming to visit him in Boston. I embarrassed him in a restaurant. He turned into a real prick for a while and once again I was so sick of his arrogant attitude, I was going to kill him. However, my father was dead by now and my mother was broken hearted, and the Lord was telling me no. My temptation and violent thinking once again were kept under control and, thanks to my brother, these have never been a problem again. I thank God for that, and when I get too cocky, God will let me know. He's still the boss.

I needed a new direction for my life. So I started to teach gym at Cutler Ridge High School in South Dade County, Florida.

It was a wild twelve months. The overcrowded school was bursting at its seams, and the lunchroom and the overflow area - known as 'the bullpen' - were a horror show most teachers feared and avoided. Not me. You see, I loved the kids, and the worst dregs and outcasts of this migrant farm area they were, the more I wanted them in my class. At first, they hated me with such passion that my life was threatened by their juvenile gangs daily. But this was before zip guns and Saturday night specials, and I didn't have an ounce of fear. On the contrary, I liked their spirit, which couldn't be broken, and I realized that their aggression only needed to be channeled in the right direction.

So, me and my red arm-bannered storm troopers took over 'the bullpen'. This 'lunchroom patrol' gave the thugs a certain pride, because in order to become one of Coach Sheridan's LRP's, you had to pass a physical test that Navy Seals would have feared. No lawmaker in Education 101 would have approved of my boys, but I must say they became a crack unit of elite enforcers. What's more, they loved me, and I loved that.

By the time I was through with the idea of teaching and ready to vacate the premises, the lunchroom was more like Boston's elite Algonquin Club, and the 'bullpen' like a stroll on Dublin's Stephens Green on a Sunday morning.

THE COLONEL :

pacheco
98

33

CHAPTER III

'LIGHTS, CAMERAS, ACTION –
A NEW BEGINNING'

Being blessed with a tremendous lack of ability to play the game of baseball I love so much, and now working in public relations for the Miami Orioles, I decided to try sports broadcasting.

Teaching had been a stopgap, and I was restless when I failed the physical for Army Officers Candidate School with poor eyes, and a heart murmur. It didn't take long for the FBI to give me the same bad news. My pal Bob Neuman, who took the written test with me in Miami has had a fabulous career with the bureau and still loves it. Me, I was left at the starting gate.

At the urging of Bill Durney, the former road secretary of the old St. Louis Browns and then General Manager of the Miami Marlins - who also co-hosted a very popular radio show - I auditioned for WGBS Radio in South Florida, perhaps the biggest station in the state. To my astonishment, I was hired on the spot!

It was the Hall of Fame broadcaster Red Barber who gave me the thumbs up. Having agreed to take a look at me (as a favor to Bill), he was suitably impressed by my evident ability to talk and also by the easy confidence and charisma I displayed behind the microphone. Plus, I had a voice that was made for radio - deep, rich, and full of personality. From his perspective, I had all the right tools to be an outstanding broadcaster; and from mine, well, after the disappointment of my athletic career - which had cut me deeply - and the restlessness of my stint in the halls of education, I guess I was just relieved to have potentially found my true vocation in life.

Radio back then was in its heyday. A 50-thousand-watt station, WGBS operated out of a 10,000 square foot building and did huge numbers with its diverse programming. Everyone I knew was a listener, tuning in for news, talk, music and more. Since 1953, the station had also given plenty of airtime to intercollegiate sports. This began a nationwide trend, and by the '70s student athletics (under the regulation of the National Collegiate Athletic Association) had saturated the airwaves, drawing millions upon millions of listeners and propelling previously unknown college kids into the storm of athletic superstardom.

Now. The fact that I had *been* one of those superstar athletes, and subsequently a pro ball player (albeit briefly), gave me a real advantage. What I lacked in broadcasting experience (and yes, proficiency) I more than made up for with swagger and entitlement. My confidence was through the roof. However, due to my early success, I was also becoming a little too full of myself. Featuring on WGBS gave me phenomenal exposure and resulted in the kind of overnight fame that hits like the bubbles in champagne. But therein lay the danger. The fact of the matter was, without having come close yet to mastering my new craft, learning every day on the job, I was running on pure bravado. Basically, I was bluffing.

That can only take you so far.

Sports broadcasting is a trade like any other. Sure, it gave an extrovert like me the chance to show off. And sure, I was a natural in the sense that I had a visible effect on everyone around me. But if I really wanted to go all the way, if I really wanted to be the best, I had to learn the fundamentals as well. Right away I realized this. I realized, fast, that the profession I was striding into wasn't nearly so easy as it appeared.

Fortunately, I was a sports junkie.

Over the years, I'd probably listened to thousands of hours of sports commentary, my right ear burning against the hot tinny speakers. In many ways, listening was nearly as much fun as being at the games themselves. Guys like Curt Gowdy, who was the lead commentator for the Boston Red Sox, and Don Dunphy, who called all the big fights, I liked especially - because they both knew how to tell a story. That was really important for me. As a kid, I wanted nothing more than to be on the field with the players and in the ring with the fighters, living every moment. Their commentary seemingly did just that. With pregnant pauses, fluctuations of tone, carefully selected insights and descriptions, they brought the radio format to life. As such, it was through my experience as a listener, kept in a state of breathless excitement, that I could masquerade as a broadcaster in those early days, bending my voice to the same cadences, the same rhythms, and doing my best to be as engaging as my two childhood heroes.

As it turned out, I was a natural.

Teaching, public relations, these civilian occupations weren't going to satisfy me. Not in the long term. My dreams were larger, more unpredictable, a little more dangerous. Simply put, I needed some action. So, whilst teaching in South Dade County, I threw myself into the unknown and began presenting my own FM radio show. Hunting, fishing, camping. It wasn't massively successful, but here I cut my teeth.

Airing on WDER-FM, a small station in Miami, my Sunday morning show cost me $10 a pop for the airtime and served as my apprenticeship in broadcast media. Ultimately, it was a great springboard to my new position at WGBS and was where I learned my first key lesson in broadcasting: that you never, ever, admit to making a mistake on the air. I've carried this lesson with me for close to half a century, and in the nearly two years for which my little show ran, working with a highly experienced producer, I learned many more besides. However, it was still the minor leagues, and I was bred for the big time. Despite being still as green as my beloved Ireland, I was ready to move on.

My life changed overnight. Young, hungry and with an ego to rival anyone's (this perhaps being my biggest attribute at the time), I hit the ground running. Within the space of six months, I had been assigned to cover nearly every sporting event on the menu. I got a taste of everything - validation from the big wigs that they had supreme confidence in me and that I was talented *and versatile* enough to be a major player at the station. It was Ken Malden, though, who taught me the art of calling a prize fight.

Ken - aka Milton Toxin, from my hometown of Boston - was turf editor and loved the ponies, so he spent most of his time at Tropical Park, Hialeah, and Gulfstream, and his evenings at Miami Beach Kennel Club, Flagler Dog Track, and (our favorite place of all, with its Irish President, Jimmy Knight) Biscayne Kennel Club. I dabbled in racing, Ken dabbled in boxing. He was a great broadcaster with a gifted voice, but at that time he was my teacher, friend, and number one fan. I loved Kenny like a brother.

We sparked off each other. On the radio, you have a little extra rope to be creative if the action is lackluster. To take a dull spectacle and weave it into something more exciting, with a few creative liberties.

'Never let the accuracy of your commentary get in the way of a good sounding prize fight,' he told me. And he couldn't have been any more correct; about that and so much more besides. Ken was funny, quick, and thought outside the box, and I just really enjoyed working with him, especially at the fights.

We had so much fun together. You see, in those days, all the major fights were shown in movie theaters via closed-circuit television - the original par-per-view format, bringing global events to regional audiences. Well, since they already had in the line at the Miami Beach Convention Center, where of course we were also fully set up with our gear, Ken and I knew that we had a golden opportunity. Sat hundreds and even thousands of miles away, parked in front of a simple screen, we realized that we could easily create the *impression* of actually attending these events. So that's what we did! Known as a live remote, the practice in later years became very commonly used in radio broadcasting and relied upon a single disclaimer. That you told the audience you were calling the event from screenside. Therefore, once on the air, it was decided (unanimously) that we'd only ever say the word 'screenside' once. Once. And then for the rest of the show, we'd continue with, 'This fight is coming to you from London, England,' or 'from Sydney, Australia,' or 'from São Paulo, Brazil.' You get the idea. Our trick was to simply harness the power of suggestion, to keep our little charade going, saying things like, 'The air is stifling tonight in Brazil,' knowing full well, of course, that it would be.

As Ken would tell me, 'Treat the audience as if they were blind.'

'Paint a picture with your words.'

So, through watching him work, and listening to his advice, I became a better broadcaster. I learned to capture the atmosphere of a building. The temperature; the mood. Which celebrities were in attendance. How the fighters moved, how they looked, all the little quirks that they exhibited. Observations that, while not essential, would certainly enrich the experience of the listener. This was of course more necessary for radio, but as I crossed into TV, these sharpened powers of description only helped me.

That was one part of my education.

The other part came from working so closely with the aforementioned Red Barber. You see, every morning I prepped for my 6 PM show. The ol' Redhead would do the timely interview of the day and I would do the sports news.

Red taught me two very important things: 'Mr. Sheridan, you're a professional sportscaster. They don't ask bricklayers to put up walls for nothing, so make sure you get paid every time you speak!' and 'My young colleague, I'll tell you this just once, you can never be too prepared to go on the air. They don't put erasers on microphones!' These two tips have been priceless to me over the years, and I have followed them to the letter.

I soaked up the knowledge. My days were seminars in broadcasting excellence. Then, just for some added fun, it was off to the Miami Beach Auditorium for Chris Dundee's Tuesday Night Fights.

As ever, there was no masterplan. Yet when I look back at my early career, at the many wonderful opportunities I was given as a young broadcaster, it was the experience of going to these shows and calling the fights that persuaded me - assured me - that my future lay in the sport of boxing. More than anything, I loved the characters that it attracted. Being at ringside was like being at the most raucous bar you could imagine, surrounded by the most colorful people. Swathes of mad, wonderful folks just having a great time. I also realized that I must be some sort of boxing promoter freak groupie, because of all the people I've met in my life, Chris Dundee would have to be my all-time favorite. He was boxing trainer Angelo's older brother, and in the late '60s and early '70s, he was like a father to me.

Chris was a character to top all characters. He appeared to be a bumbling fool, like a cross between the Marx brothers and one of the Three Stooges. But like Don King of today, he was the boxing genius of his time. After relocating from Philadelphia to Miami to escape the clutches of the mob, he made Angelo learn Spanish so they could gobble up all of the great Cuban fighters coming to Miami - a stroke of pure genius which paid immediate dividends. Great fighters like Louis Manuel Rodriguez, Eddie Talhami, and Florentino Fernandez, and youngsters like Frankie Otero, were all caught in their net. The plethora of Cuban talent was unbelievable. There were terrific local fighters too, like Big Al Jones, Jimmy Ellis, Yama Bahama, Gomeo Brennan, Elisha Obed, and on and on I could go. A lot of these men were champions at a time when there was only the World Boxing Association (WBA) in existence, without the junior and super divisions of today. They all landed at the same place. However, if they'd expected a state-of-the-art facility, they'd have been dead wrong.

The 5th Street Gym in Miami Beach, Florida, although world-renowned, was actually a beat-up, dilapidated shithole of a place with only one shower. It was also brimming with the top talent of the day. I learned that you cannot rate the quality of a gym on the merits of its decor. Fuck the fresh paint and the shiny floors. Fighters came because guys like Moe Fleischer, Lou Gross, Chuck Talhami, and Max Goodman, some of the best and most experienced trainers around, were all fixtures in there and could be utilized. The place may have been a dump - a rusty crown on top of a drugstore - but it oozed class.

That first day, between the moldy walls, as I entered with my college roommate to see what a real pro boxing gym was all about, I saw Angelo Dundee, the head trainer of then Cassius Clay (and soon to be Muhammad Ali). Dr. Ferdie Pacheco, Ali's personal physician and future HBO commentator. And Louis Rodriguez, a Hall of Fame middleweight whom I idolized. It was a thrill for me just to be near them. I never dreamed that day in the fall of 1963 that, within five years, my career as a fight broadcaster would begin.

I soon realized that no fighter alive could resist the place. It was Chris Dundee, though, who spotted the talents of a young fighter from Louisville, Kentucky, named Cassius Clay, and it was he who engineered the Louisville Group that held Cassius Clay's contract to hire his brother Angelo to train 'the Louisville Lip'. The rest is boxing history.

I'll never forget my first time there. When I saw the place from the outside, I thought I must've gotten lost. After double-checking my directions, I finally climbed this creaky old staircase that barely had any light, must've been like forty or fifty steps, and it felt like my legs were gonna give out on me. When I got to the top, breathing harder than I'd care to admit, I was greeted by Sully. 'Fifty cents, please,' he said. 'Press!' I told him. 'Press my pants!' he yelled back, showing me this half-full jar of jingling change. I gladly handed over the money. This old-timer was a real character, the kind of nutjob I couldn't help but love. And once I got past him, I saw some of the top boxing talent in Miami, all packed into one place. Fifty cents for admission? I'd have paid any price!

Just picture what I got to be around. Mere feet away from a young Muhammad Ali, looking up through the space between the ring apron and the bottom rope, I watched as he chirped and clowned, as he jived and jousted, as he ranted and riffed, all the while giving the press boys so many dream quotes that they swooned like groupies. Then there was the physical artistry on display. The dancing feet, the swiveling torso, the whirring fists, each distinct movement chaining together like exquisite choreography. It all looked so effortless, so graceful, that you were left with the impression that the kid had not learned how to box, but rather he had been gifted with the sublime ability from birth.

Of course, that was the idea - to make people think that he barely broke a sweat. The truth was, he absolutely did. You see, Muhammad did all his serious training behind closed doors, with his assistant trainer from Cuba, Luis Serria. It was during these sessions, away from the glare of the media, that he labored to achieve a level of conditioning that set him apart from his rivals and could make him appear superhuman. Head and trunk suspended over the side of a bench, I watched him do a thousand sit-ups while Luis rubbed oils into his belly, exhorting him to finish. Believe me, the man trained harder than anyone when his mind was focused. How else could he have absorbed the blows of George Foreman?

Gene Kilroy, Muhammad's closest friend and advisor, who ran his training camps, knows this fact better than anybody. Ask Gene, and he will tell you just how incredibly fit and strong he was, and how none of that was by accident. One of the sweetest men alive, he had some trouble when his friend got mixed up with the Nation of Islam, unable to convince Ali that he was being used by the extremist group and in particular by Herbert Muhammad - the son of Elijah, leader of the organization and known charlatan, who regarded Ali as his personal cash cow. But the problems really came in the latter stages of Ali's career when the great man seemed to be fighting only for money and ego. It was then that he began to take terrible beatings, both in sparring and under the lights, and the rest of the story is known. Gene was loyal to the end, however. Nobody could tell Muhammad anything, and he always insisted that he had no regrets. But the way it all played out; I know it broke Gene's heart.

I always was glad that Muhmmad had at least one guy in his corner who genuinely cared for him, and who wasn't just there hitching a ride on the gravy train. I had seen it for myself, in those early years. It was before they moved him out to Deer Lake in Pennsylvania that Gene really got the best out of Ali. During those times, I never once saw him slack or complain, and it was clear that he was totally in sync with his environment. The 5th Steet Gym, I maintain, had a special aura, a certain magic that brought the best out of fighters. You saw that not only with Ali but with a host of legendary champions.

The gym itself was as basic as it comes. There was one big mirror, a speed bag, and a heavy bag. The heavy bag immediately got my attention. I was frozen by the sound - the feeling - of the thuds that emitted from it. It was like standing next to a brass band and being kicked by a mule at the same time. George Chuvalo, the perennial heavyweight contender from Canada who twice battled Ali, was working it, feet dug into the floor, a succession of dull, devastating hooks. I couldn't fathom how anybody in the world could stand up to the impact of those punches. In later years, I would see guys like Earnie Shavers and Ron Lyle in there, who almost broke the bag in half. Being so close to these displays of such awesome power, I gained a respect for the sport that borders on the reverential. This respect extended to the trainers as well.

Moe Fleischer was my favorite guy to annoy. In the twilight of his career, he was an assistant trainer, matchmaker, and talent scout who in those days was a permanent fixture in the gym. He and the Dundee brothers were great pals. Once a successful promoter, Moe famously sold out twenty-three shows in a row in the New York area, earning the nickname 'Sellout Moe'. In his younger years, he had trained a string of world champions - including Kid Chocolate and Sandy Saddler - and had been involved in some of the great promotions at Yankee Stadium and the Polo Grounds in Upper Manhattan, which seated over 100,000 spectators. Talk about having direct access to a living legend!

The Dundee brothers weren't too shabby either. Angelo and I got along fine, although he was all business and I mostly tried to keep out from under his feet. His older brother, on the other hand, I found irresistible. Chris at first seemed like a crotchety ol' bastard, half deaf and half dead. Believe me, though. Chris was anything but half dead. He was a character, to be sure, and sharp as a razorblade. One time on a telephone call in his office, Bill Daily of Puerto Rico was on the other end of the phone asking Chris Dundee for money. 'I can't hear you, Bill.' Then he hits the phone off his desk a couple of times. 'I can't hear you.' The operator comes on the line and says, 'Mr. Dundee, he says he wants ten thousand.' Chris doesn't miss a beat and says, 'If you can hear him so well, you give him the ten grand!' When it comes to heavyweights, Chris Dundee (in his heyday) was king of the heavyweights.

He made it all happen. I like to compare him to the guy behind the curtain in The Wizard of Oz, pressing dials and pulling levers. Because without anyone knowing it, he controlled everything in the sport. Nothing in boxing happened without his authorization. In later years, Don King and Bob Arum took up the mantle, followed by Cedric Kushner and Lou Duva, and today by Oscar de la Hoya and Eddie Hearn. However, back in the '40s, '50s and '60s, Chris was, without question, *the* guy.

Here's how we met.

In 1964, when I was in my sophomore year at the University of Miami, Chris (who never switched off even to take a nap) had put in a phone call to our football coach, Ron Fraser. A consummate hustler, Chris had wanted half a dozen kids to sell Coca-Cola at his upcoming promotion. As it turned out, a pretty damn big one! Sonny Liston, the brooding heavyweight champion of the world feared by all, was coming to the Convention Center to defend his title for the second time … against some skinny loudmouth by the name of Cassius Clay! I couldn't believe my luck. I'd never even been to a boxing match before, much less a heavyweight championship fight. Of course, I leapt at the chance.

To my surprise, I actually did pretty well as a salesman. A bottle of Coca-Cola back then cost a nickel, so in the space of about an hour - zipping around the arena - I made roughly three dollars, which I handed over without qualm. That day I didn't care about making money; my payment was purely to be in attendance. The stands filling up, I moved to about fourteen feet from the ring and took in a sharp, shallow breath - the excitement in my belly crackling. I then sat down on my empty crate (in Ali's corner) and silently took it all in. It was unbelievable. All the beautiful people were there: Frank Sinatra, Elizabeth Taylor, Robert Wagner, schmoozing and smiling for pictures. 'What the fuck is this?' I was thinking, not knowing that in roughly four years' time I'd be calling fights for Chris Dundee in this very same arena. At that moment, as I moved my head from left to right like an antelope on the plains, I felt my senses collide in a crunching pile-up and all I could think about was how exciting it all was. How different an experience it seemed to be from any other sport. Then there was Liston and Clay and the fight itself. I remember being in awe of Liston as he entered the ring, appearing to be surrounded by a lethal, brooding energy. At that moment, I didn't believe a man alive could lick him.

How wrong I was.

After six completed rounds, I realized two fundamental facts of life: that no man is invincible, and that everybody gets old in the end. It was as one-sided as a fight can be, a blowout, and without knowing it at the time, I had witnessed in live action one of the most iconic sporting moments of the 20th century - the moment that a twenty-two-year-old kid named Cassius Clay, against all the odds, 'Shook up the world!'

That was my introduction to Chris. Years later, when asked by my paymasters to see whether I could negotiate a deal with the mercurial promoter for the station to cover his weekly boxing shows, I was fairly certain he wouldn't remember me. Nevertheless, I decided to approach him as though we were old friends, saying, 'I work for WBGS Radio. We'd like to broadcast your Tuesday Night Fights every week and do the entire fight card.'

Chris peered at me through his glasses. I gulped. Then a quick smile curled his lips. 'That'd be wonderful. We'd love it.'

And that's how the radio station gained the exclusive rights to broadcast Chris Dundee's Tuesday Night Fights, held at the Miami Beach Auditorium, and etched into pugilistic folklore; and how me and Ken - over the coming years - ended up calling the action for literally thousands of fights. It was that simple.

The shows got excellent ratings. How could they not? Boxing was a booming sport, and this was boxing at its most raw and exciting - brought to a mass market. The Auditorium itself was pretty much how you'd imagine: a dusky, smoke-filled hall seating around four thousand people, with about two-thirds of the spectators being regular attendees. This gave the feel of a cult-like spectacle. Though ultimately it was the quality of the shows that kept people coming back - the bang they got for their buck. Miami was teeming with great fighters and Chris wasn't shy about matching them. I've already mentioned how, if required, I could embellish a sporting event to keep things interesting. Well, I rarely if ever had to perform that trick while calling fights at the Auditorium. Making my way there, usually on foot, I was the happiest guy in Florida. When I started turning up at the venue with a blonde on each arm, I was the happiest guy in the country! Remember, it's all about the show.

That was the glamorous side of my job. However, it was back at the old gym where I really learned about boxing. The trainers, most in their fifties and sixties, were all savants of the game. As a kid still in my twenties, being around these figures - each of whom possessed a world of knowledge - was daunting, to say the least. But at the same time, it was also one hell of an opportunity. I soon realized that these old-school grunts were actually some of the nicest gentleman you could ever come across. Even with all my fancy education, I clicked with them because deep down, I was just a street kid from Boston. So, making friends and fitting in was a breeze. Thereafter, I simply watched and listened ... perhaps for the first time in my life.

It was a great education. I didn't want to be another Howard Cosell, the ABC broadcaster who actually knew jackshit about the sport. I thought that would be a disservice both to the fighters and to myself. So, I set about learning the craft of boxing - the fundamentals of technique, the fine detail of strategy, the diversity of styles - all the stuff that would eventually become second nature to me. But I had to study, visiting the gym three, sometimes four times a week, as focused on learning as I had been during my calculus-filled days at St. Anselm's.

And it paid off. Today, nobody in the media can analyze a fight like me. Because nobody has done what I have over the last fifty years.

For me, calling 8 to 10 fights every week, from 1968 to 1973, had me ready for the big time. I had done over 3000 fights on radio and local TV during these years, so I was prepared when Hank Schwartz and Barry Bernstein of Video Techniques came looking for someone to handle the blow-by-blow of a lightweight championship contest between Ken Buchanan and Frankie Otero. The fight was being telecast back to England, Ireland, Scotland, and Wales. I was good, and I knew it; moreover, the producers liked my work. From that day to this, I never had a contract, but I was the lead commentator on every single fight Video Techniques ever telecast.

Of course, I had help along the way. In showbiz, connections and word of mouth are paramount. It was at the request of Chris and Angelo (who told anyone who would listen that I was the best commentator in the world) that I was given the opportunity to call the Buchanan-Otero fight - my breakthrough job. Actually, I'd had a word with Chris about my desire to do that particular telecast. I knew that it was being shown over in Europe and, being the incorrigible showoff that I am, thought it would be a great opportunity to wave to my mates in Ireland. That was honestly the height of my ambition. Yet at the back of my mind, I also knew that it could be the start of something big.

They actually had Cosell in mind initially. At the time, he was one of the most popular broadcasters in the history of American television, doing his double act with Ali. But to me, he was always a bullshit artist, a so-called expert who didn't know boxing from Adam. What Cosell had was a fantastic ability to recall - the unique ability to parrot back something pertinent at exactly the right time. Now, most of the fights, Howard didn't do. He'd do a replay of the big Ali fights in the studio a week later, and that's how he and Ali used each other for their own fame. Howard used Ali to get famous, and Ali certainly used Cosell, since he was such a polarizing figure. Half the people couldn't stand him, and to the other half of the people it wasn't an event until Howard Cosell was doing it.

Anyway, he was their first choice. At the time, he was probably the right choice. But with the push I was getting from the Dundee brothers, and after having met with me themselves over lunch (I guess just to see what all the fuss was about), they decided to take a chance on a young kid with stars in his eyes. Suffice it to say, I smashed the ball out of the park. Opportunities are there to be taken, and I certainly took mine.

When Hank Schwartz and Barry Bernstein went in another direction, Don King took over the fight game and I've been with him since the inception of Don King Productions. I've been blessed with great producers like Jack Murphy and Mary Vee in the early years, David Fox for 12 years, and till the present day, Marty Corwin, the brilliant talent over from a career in the NHL, NBA, and Major League Baseball. All of these people have been great boosters to my career and all of them became close and intimate friends.

I had my years anchoring the local sports for TV-6 in Miami, covering the championship golf tour that hits South Florida every fall and winter, great horse racing, University of Miami football, Florida State League baseball, and covering the Miami Dolphins championship years of the early '70s. But more on that incredible period a little later. The point is, I could have gone in whichever direction I wanted.

However, something about the spectacle of prize fighting, and the chaos that surrounds it, had me hook, line and sinker. I chose boxing to be my sport. I loved the hustle, I loved the con, I loved being in the spotlight of the great championship fights of my time. I loved the travel, I loved the fighters, the trainers, the celebrities, the whole ball of wax. To me there is no more pure form of sport than boxing. Two finely conditioned athletes all alone and it's always sudden death. Remember, the simple object of the sport is to render your opponent unconscious. Still, it's never quite as simple as that. While boxing is filled with enough drama and angst to fill a Hollywood script, all the cards are on the table. The world isn't pretty, and neither is boxing. At least boxing is blatant about it.

For me, that's always been good enough.

"WAIT... I'M NOT LOOKING FOR A FIGHT!
I'm here to broadcast the BRUNO Fight at Wembley!"

CHAPTER IV

'THE LOG'

The 'log' was a collection of notes which actually got that title for the lack of a better name. It was a loosely kept diary of events which took place during the 1971 summer vacation of four very different, but truly unique, fun-loving but extremely bright individuals, whose conduct in no way reflects their moral fiber while serving as citizens in good standing in the United States of America.

Basically, if it wasn't for sex sins, these boys possess great character and loyalty. They are all very honest and sincere characters, and no court will ever convict any of them. After all, there is a whole lot more to morality than the sex lives of healthy red-blooded American 20-something boys.

The feeble foursome spent late July and early August tripping around the European continent. It is of great importance that the reader of this transcription understands that the actions of the members of the travel party were undertaken while the individuals were in foreign lands, seeking leisure and relaxation.

The log was intended for the amusement of the traveling party and no pictures, descriptions or accounts of this trip were intended to be published without the express written consent of the CIA and Major League Baseball. However, since neither organization has a commissioner — Fuck 'em! On with the log.

Disclaimer: In order to spare their blushes, the members of the travel party – with the exception of yours truly – have been given alternative names. However, everything else is told exactly as it happened.

*

July 20, 1971: Bob Sheridan and Mike Shwartz departed Miami for Nassau to catch a flight to Luxembourg. Moe Murphy, the third member of the party, met Shwartz and Sheridan at Nassau. Sheridan wasted little time getting started giving the group a preview of what was to come by asking the barmaids in the Nassau airport bar to feel the size of his prick...this they did with surprising pleasure. On the plane to Luxembourg, Sheridan and Murphy served as bartenders for their section of the plane, passing out drinks. Sheridan and Murphy themselves consumed two six packs of beer, two large bottles of wine, two large bottles of champagne, and half a fifth of scotch. The second half of the scotch bottle was confiscated by the stewardess.

July 21, 1971: Sheridan made friends with the pilot of the plane and landed in the cockpit with the flight crew. Upon landing in Luxembourg, Shwartz, sporting long hair and beard, was the only member of the party to have his luggage checked. Bob wasted little time in becoming a European travel guide. He stood outside the airport directing passengers to the various means of transportation. It was here that Bob first began use of his newly created universal language which spawned by the end of the trip such words as "lufthieden," "zieten" and "oofenzy."

While waiting for a train to journey from Luxembourg to Amsterdam, the group ran into an Italian musician who they told they would make a big star in the United States. He was a little hesitant to believe the story that was told him, especially because he couldn't understand a word of English and was relying on his hippy girlfriend from New York.

Sheridan exhibited his broad knowledge of animals on the train to Amsterdam by sighting a group of what he called "large field pigs" grazing in a track-side pasture. The field of pigs turned out to be shaved sheep.

The group arrived in Amsterdam late in the afternoon and by a stroke of luck ran into Jack, the owner of the Hotel Post, which as it turned out was one of the finest lodges on the continent. The price of the room, which included breakfast, was $3.50 a person. Breakfast was served by a good-looking broad with a pierced nose containing a blue, sparkling butterfly. Our room, the size of Bernie Rosen's office (very small) contained three beds. The bathroom was down one flight of steps, and the shower was one flight down, then four flights up. By the time you climbed the steps to the shower, you needed to rinse your body because of the sweat. As far as the bathroom...it was rather small, and it was a pretty smart rule to place a fifteen-minute entry embargo on the quarters after one used it to give the fumes a chance to clear. The finest facility at the Hotel Post was the lobby. A room containing a beer bar, a slot machine, a television, a well-stocked juke box, and a much-played pinball machine.

The lobby was also the main operating quarters of Sean, the smoke master. Sean, the owner of the largest pipe this writer has ever seen, would go around collecting guilder from the guests and then take his scooter to town to purchase hash for the group. This was fun to watch but we were all holiday alcoholics. Sean was only about five-foot-seven but possessed the best conditioned lungs anyone in attendance had ever seen. At the opening night party, we got shitfaced while they got ripped in quick fashion, especially the two Irish hooligans who charged out on their first visit to the red-light district.

The group then visited a Sex Show. The main attraction was a girl attacking a large paper machete prick. One of the funnier scenes in the district was the Salvation Army band of women marching and singing through the streets knocking down prostitution.

When the group finally got back to the hotel, they found they were locked out. Shwartz had to climb through a window into the lobby to get their key. Sheridan and

Murphy eventually went back down to the locked lobby to play the pinball machine and drink beer at three in the morning. They pissed in beer bottles and on the floor to relieve kidney calls. Then the two "big" Micks got great pleasure from sealing two bottles of Heineken and returning them to the "frig." Needless to say, we didn't drink any "Heinies" at the Post Hotel the next day!

Very little done during the day. At night some of the lads got drunk again, then took a trip to the Dam Square where they picked up a beauty from Stockholm, "Helga." The group retreated to the Post Hotel where they proceeded to get further fucked up and further naked.

July 23, 1971: Another day for Bob and Moe in the red-light district. The pair were averaging about 70 glasses of beer a day and were becoming very popular on the streets because they would buy the bar a drink wherever they would go. Sheridan wound up being dubbed the mayor of the red-light district. He is said to be loved by all of his constituents because of his heavy support of the economy.

July 24, 1971: This was the day for the group to leave as a group to go to London. The group did leave, but not as a group. Shwartz was first to fly over the channel. Getting slightly hammered does not have the morning aftereffects that getting seriously drunk does. Bob and Moe saw a sex movie and got laid twice before leaving for London where the group met Hank Shapiro at the Churchill Hotel. The Churchill is one of the high-class inns in London and the group was a little out of place walking through the lobby.

The group met Angelo Dundee and his wife, Helen, for drinks at the Cumberland, and in the process saw one of the greatest built broads ever put together. It goes without question that Sheridan and Murphy had to have her - and they did! Shwartz and Shapiro forged on to the Playboy Club where Hank admitted for the first time that he was a sick gambler. It was at the Playboy that Hank fell in love for the first time during the trip. The first love was Tonie, the blackjack dealer. Bob and Moe showed up at the club for a few drinks and Bob told us the story of when asked by the immigration inspector at London's Heathrow Airport why he was in England. Bob's answer was "to fuck around." Bob and Moe then took off to get more drunk and hook up with their new, larger breasted beauty Sheridan called "Bambi." In the course of getting drunk, the pair wandered into a clip joint where they were charged $14.00 for a pack of cigarettes for their honey. The pair got pissed off (this is never a good omen for any establishment). Bob tipped over a table, Moe punched the waiter, and Sheridan then threw a champagne bottle into a mirror. When Bob and Moe got back to the hotel around 3:00AM, they were still jacked up, so they attacked Shwartz and Shapiro in their underwear with pillows.

July 25, 1971: The group began the day by goofing on an Italian waiter at a London restaurant during lunch. The group also visited a betting parlor. Hank was touted off the horse he liked. The horse he liked won, the horse he bet…lost.

The group also visited the Miami Beach Tourist Development Authority. The TDA has as bad a reputation in London as it has in Miami. Walking back from the TDA, a lady glanced at Shwartz, who was wearing his newly acquired bush hat and his great beard and said, glaring at him, "Look at that one." The statement shook up Shwartz a great deal. He went back to the hotel and shaved off his beard.

The group went to the Luis Rodriguez fight at night and sat in a box. Sheridan had a little trouble fitting his fat ass into his seat. Rodriguez had his brains knocked in, while Sheridan gave us the blow-by-blow, which was far more entertaining than the fight. Murphy and Sheridan are Irish hooligans to be sure, but they've got to be the funniest two on the face of the earth! After the fights we asked a taxi driver to take us to a good bar. The cab driver complied by taking us to the same bar where Bob and Moe had their tussle the night before. Of course, the two Irish lads were all for fight number two. Instead, we were taken back to the Playboy by Hank, who wanted to feed his illness and see his new love. The following is Hank's ode to Toni, the blackjack dealer:

ROSES ARE RED, VIOLETS ARE BLUE
TOO BAD THE CARDS HAVEN'T FALLEN
THE WAY I HAVE FOR YOU.

Obviously, Henk (as he was called by Toni) dropped a bundle of pounds at the Playboy club, and I don't mean the fleshy kind. It was only a matter of time before Sheridan and Murphy got the bum's rush for grabbing a bunny's tail. They didn't go easily either, or they left a trail of bloody, fucked up bouncers in their wake. It's something about them being Irish and being in England, because usually, as drunk as they get, we'd never seen them as rowdy as these few "daze" in London.

July 26, 1971: Hank got the day off to a good start by being called a "Hooligan" by some lady after he pushed Shwartz around in the street. The group then visited Buckingham Palace. There they watched the changing of the guard, having timed their visit quite by accident to perfection. Hank, meanwhile, stood there barking off his chain of commands which he picked up in the Army.

In the late-afternoon, Bob and Moe departed for Ireland, while Shwartz and Shapiro stayed the rest of the night in London and went to the rock version of Othello called "Catch My Soul." July 26th to July 30th were rather uneventful except for Shapiro's addiction to gambling.

July 30, 1971: Moe and Bob were greeted in Copenhagen as they arrived on the afternoon train from Amsterdam. They missed an earlier train because they were kicked off a plane from Ireland. The reason...they were drunk. Bob and Moe, however, spent the previous night in Amsterdam with another group of broads. They took turns with one girl, while the other sat in her window, inviting in more girls! Sheridan told us how he was thrown in an Irish dungeon for pinching an Irish Bunratty entertainer's ass. He had to sing "When Irish Eyes are Smiling" to get out of the dungeon. Sheridan also told us about banging a Jewish hooker the night before in Amsterdam and dedicating his efforts to his pals, Shapiro and Shwartz.

Bob and Moe treated Mike and Hank to a night at the Club Venus, a sex club in Copenhagen. It cost $18.00 apiece. This included membership, admission, and all the beer you could drink. The show started with movies, then a participation strip, then a beautiful blonde got on the bed and played with herself, aided by a battery-powered dick. She was then joined by another good-looking broad and the pair proceeded to eat each other out for about a half hour. Next came a cartoon, "Snow White and the Seven Lovers." The record player in the joint broke and we had to go next door to another club. Sheridan commented that they ought to put on shows like this at baseball games to liven up the sport.

The action continued at the club we were moved to. The first activity was a man and woman going the "69" route and then throwing a long fuck. Sheridan.... "A great halftime show for the Orange Bowl." A girl came out next and tried to give an older guy a hard on. She pulled on "it" for about 20 minutes, but to no avail. Some lady sitting behind Shwartz was heard to say, "She's doing it all wrong." Next came another audience participation strip. A sassy brunette came over to Hank and asked him to take off her bra. Hank tried for a few minutes but could not remove it. She went over to Sheridan who got it off in a matter of seconds. Hank was very embarrassed. Sheridan refused to go on the bed with her, but Moe did. She sat on his face, and Moe went to work with his tongue. She then tried to expose Moe, but when she tried to get his zipper down, he resisted. She asked him if he was small. Answer...: "Yes." Moe was so shaken up he walked into the ladies' room in the Hula Bar. There was a great fight with two broads beating on each other outside the Hula Bar. Sheridan delighted at doing the blow-by-blow commentary for the boys.

July 31, 1971: The foursome took the North Sealong tour. Hank introduced Shwartz to the people on the tour bus as the "tooth fairy." The tour stopped at Hamlet's Castle, and everyone went to the castle except Bob and Moe, who were seen going in the opposite direction towards a public house. Still, we all visited Tivoli Gardens at night. Bob and Moe really dug the games and bumper cars. During one stretch, they spent an hour and a half on the cars — a good $20.00 worth. They took great pleasure in knocking the shit out of anyone and everyone with a British accent.

Hank, Bob, and Moe went to another sex show. Shwartz went to the hippy van colony and got his sex in the back of a van. At the sex club Sheridan spit beer through his teeth to wake up a guy who was snoring. Bob, Moe, and Hank got a cab driver crazy with their "fuckenzie...suckenzie" expressions. The cab driver was talking in their language to other cab drivers. Shwartz invited one of his hippy friends to come back and sleep on a couch in his and Hank's room at the D'Angletere Hotel. Hank got pissed off at Mike. All that did not last too long because once "the hooligans" found out we were in truly lavish digs, it was only a matter of time before the shit would hit the fan! But in Denmark the humor of the two was great fun for everyone in the entire hotel. We were out of England and these two funny bastards were at their best!

August 1, 1971: Hank, Moe and Bob went for a sex massage...love affair number three for Hank. Forgot to mention, he fell in love with one of the lesbians at the Club Venus. The latest love affair was with Mary Ann, his masseuse. She also fell for him and gave him some extras. She was married and her husband was supposedly a producer of the movie "Song of Norway." That didn't stop Hank though and she's expected to visit him along with Toni sometime in the fall. Shwartz, meanwhile, was off to Bohemia again at a party that was thrown in a couple of vans. Included were a bunch of Canadians and some German chicks. The party wound up a wild orgy in the back of the vans...much German and English was flying about.

Bob, Moe, and Hank went to the Bonaparte Disco. Hank liked a girl there who had a date. Moe offered to throw her date through the window to get rid of him. Bob and Moe definitely showed some serious signs of liking to fight during the trip. Bob told us how they beat up on drunks in Ireland.

Later, the lads took the liberty to send Bunny Toni a postcard from Copenhagen of a couple screwing. They wrote on it, "Hope this will be me and you when I get back to London" and signed it Hank.

August 2, 1971: We were supposed to leave for Oslo this morning, but Bob, Moe and Hank were too hung over from their night at the Bonaparte. Shwartz was not hung over from the sex party. When Sheridan was asked if he wanted to go out for breakfast, he said he "hadn't finished throwing up yet." Hank was still drunk at noon, and Moe didn't know where he was at one. Moe finally sat up and said he wasn't going to do anything all day but take a seventh inning stretch.

Hank took another trip to see his dear Mary Ann at the sex massage. Elsewhere, Bob and Moe ran into a topless, very full-breasted girl passing out leaflets on a shopping street. You guessed it! Sheridan and Murphy ended up with her in their room! Finally, as we were leaving for the train station late in the day, we ran into Mary Ann, who was leaving her office, rubbing her heavily calloused hands. Hank kissed her goodbye in the street. After the farewell was recorded in the log, Hank added in the book, "Shwartz showing definite signs of heavy sex addiction." Shwartz's answer, "So what!"

We got sleepers on the train from Copenhagen to Oslo. Bob and Moe stood in the hall of the train in their underwear having a pillow fight. They soon stopped whaling on each other when two Aryan beauties caught their attention. It wasn't long before Irish-Viking relations were improving by the minute. The hooligans were so charming it sickened Shwartz and Shapiro.

Early in the morning, a Norwegian immigration and customs inspector checked Shwartz's bag and found a bottle of "Excedrin" which caused him to become very suspicious. Finally, after checking out the suspicious drugs, he returned the bottle.

Moe was given the duties of travel master for Norway since he'd been there before. Moe led us on a wild goose chase. Carrying our bags through town was quite a sight as we tried to find the Hertz car rental office.

Moe was impeached from his office by unanimous vote within 15 minutes of our arrival in Oslo. We finally hit the road and within ten kilometers, Moe had taken a wrong turn. On the trip we stopped at a small roadside store. The lady inside almost went into shock when we entered and began talking English, which she didn't understand. Sheridan tried his own language which didn't help much. After getting up into the mountains, we stopped several times for snowball fights, pictures and just to utter such adjectives as "magnificent," "ah," "oooh," and "oh," etc., etc., etc.

Moe was impeached for the second time during our stay in Norway when we almost got off a ferry at the wrong stop. Shwartz was already off and almost left ashore. Moe did an overall excellent job of driving. We were nearly involved in only one to four what could have been fatal accidents.

Sheridan, in checking how many kilometers equaled a mile, asked what country we were in to figure out the ratio. He was surprised to hear that kilometer values don't change from country to country like the money. (He knew better but his sense of humor kept us with sore ribs from laughter for days.) He never stopped his running commentary, and we never stopped laughing.

After an 11-hour ride, we finally arrived in Bergen. It doesn't get dark in Bergen during this time of the year. A fact that was brought up numerous times by members of the troop. We stayed at a dorm at the University of Bergen. Sheridan had talked for about 14 hours straight during the day, carrying out his duties as entertainment director. He only stopped to fill his mouth with food, and beer.

August 4, 1971: We spent the morning trying to find Moe's missing money which was wired from Nassau to Copenhagen and was supposed to be transferred to Bergen. As it turned out the money had gotten mixed up because the names of the sender and receiver were switched around. Moe misunderstood the cost of the phone call from Bergen to Copenhagen by 174 Kronen.

Moe took us to a restaurant where no English was spoken. Sheridan ordered his 23rd case of beer of the trip. We took the beer to the top of a mountain where Hank echoed Lou Gherig's farewell speech at Yankee Stadium... three times. Very effective. We then went to dinner on top of another mountain. We were the only people dressed like slobs. We had a busboy for a waiter — 45 minutes between courses of the meal.

August 5, 1971: Left in the morning for Munich by plane. Hank fell in love again. This time with an SAS stew. He called Mary Ann "a jerk off artist." How soon love does fleet from Hank's heart.

We were delayed in Copenhagen on a flight to Dusseldorf because of a German air traffic control slow down. Hank and Bob panicked and wanted to stay in Copenhagen. As it turned out, the plane left in fairly short order and if we ever tried to get our bags off the plane, we would have only found them in Munich. Hank's hate for the Germans heightened when we got to Munchen, and he found that Lufthansa had ripped his garment bag. Moe and Sheridan convinced Hank it wasn't the Germans but rather the British ground support that ruined his bag. Hank was pretty tired but still decided to go with us to visit Dachau. We rented a V.W. and found the way to the camp pretty easily. After the visit to the camp, we stopped at a carnival. Bob, Moe, and Hank rode the bumper cars, and then Bob and Moe almost cleaned a guy out shooting rifles. It was obvious the Irish pair were very familiar with the handling of small arms.

We ran into a hailstorm on the way back into town.... "un-fucking-believable." Bob and Moe got drunk after drinking many beers in the Haufbreau House. The pair went to another bar where they ran into a Nazi yelling "Heil Hitler." Moe grabbed the guy by the tie and Bob whacked him in the jaw adding, "without your fucking machine guns, you ain't worth a shit."

Earlier in the evening, we listened to the Belmont Stakes on Armed Forces Radio. Hank did a recreation of the broadcast at the Haufbreau House.

August 6, 1971: We visited the Olympic site in the afternoon and then prepared to take a night train to Paris. Moe stayed in Munich for the night, then split from the group to go to Berlin. Hank and Bob held a big pig out with some New York girls and a Roumanian on the train to Paris. It was most important to Sheridan to let all these "Nazis" know it's D-Day plus 2 months, and he was off to free Paris. The Germans were totally offended, but they were not about to fuck with this bigger than life son of Erin.

August 7, 1971: Spent the day shopping in Paris. At night Bob, Hank and Mike attended the French version of "Hair." Hank made this addition to the log: "Tooth Fairy" danced with girl on stage with the "Hair" cast during the show and had two curtain calls for his Bush Hat." Shwartz then took Hank and Bob to the "Pigalle" via the metro. Shwartz left Bob and Hank in the red-light district and went to Orly to go back to New York.

August 8; 1971: Shwartz was frisked at the airport before boarding the plane while Hank and Bob carried on for their last few days in Europe. The pair ran into Robert Vaughn from "The Man from Uncle" at the "George the Fifth Bar." Sheridan's father "Big Jim" was in Paris and took Bob and Hank to a strip show at La Sexy. Ironically, this was the same joint that Shwartz had gotten taken in several years back. Sheridan Jr. said he thought the strip was good but that they had a lot to learn from Copenhagen's Club Venus. For Bob Sheridan it was a most memorable three days whoring around Paris with his Dad, who died of heart failure later that summer.

August 9, 1971: Toni took Hank to the airport for his trip to Miami. Bob flew to Ireland to continue the festivities among his fellow Irish. And Moe went back to Nassau. Toni said she may be visiting Miami in the fall with her flat mate. It was a fond farewell to the continent for Hank. As he admitted upon arrival in Miami, his last day in London made the trip. For all of us, so did the first, the second, the third, etc. etc. etc. What did we learn on this trip?

"You only live once!"

Here, my dear, lets rehearse
the opening again

CHAPTER V

'PERFECTION, DIVINE GUIDANCE AND THE MIAMI DOLPHINS'

On January 14, 1973, the Miami Dolphins of the National Football League completed the perfect season with a 14 to 7 win over the Washington Redskins. The perfect season, 17-0, is a football team record that stands to this day and may never be broken. Why? Because to achieve 'perfection' far more must fall into perfect place than simple talent, hard work and desire. In my observation of life, the *real* key ingredients are in fact 'divine guidance' and a lot of 'just plain good luck!'

In my personal life I considered things just about perfect. I was a healthy young man doing with my life exactly what I wanted to do. In the late 1960s, I was developing my skills as a broadcaster, working with the likes of Red Barber and Mel Allen. I was building a relationship with my childhood hero, Curt Gowdy, as his spotter during Miami Dolphin football games for NBC Sports. And much to my delight (and indeed surprise), I was also very close to the Dolphins head coach, Don Shula, who I could clearly see was a driven man bound for glory. I felt that with his work ethic, Shula was surely headed for the Football Hall of Fame. I never dreamed Don would break the record of George Halas to become the most winning coach in the history of pro football.

There were only a couple of areas in my life over which I had no control, and which I found very upsetting. By early 1970, I had learned that my father was in dire health and probably would not live much longer. Simultaneously, I was rocked to my center by the bloody war that had broken out in Northern Ireland. To numb my pain, I did what I'd always done in times of distress: I threw myself into work.

By 1970, you could see that the Miami Dolphins were on the move. Although much of my time was spent covering the University of Miami football games on WGBS Radio, without question, the big story in those years in Miami was the Dolphins. I was extremely close to the team and attended practice nearly every day. I had the same knowledge concerning the team that any of the beat sportswriters possessed. Eventually, this led me to doing a nightly sports talk show called 'the 710 Sports Line'.

Now, this was the brainchild of Ken Malden. Then program director, he had the feeling that talk radio, strictly on sports, just might catch on. This 50-thousand-watt powerhouse in South Florida was way ahead of its time. We were the first major market radio station to go to this all sports format. Ken and a lawyer and judge by the name of John Gale had the idea, 'We need to duplicate this format on television.' They attempted to purchase Channel 6 TV in Miami with full expectations of doing just that. Potential investors thought the format would 'never go,' so Ken and Judge Gale couldn't raise the six million dollars necessary to purchase the television station. The station is now worth about 300 million dollars, and I ask you, 'Do you think ESPN has been a success?' Boy, oh boy, if that acquisition had ever taken place, what a difference it would have made for me, Judge Gale and Ken Malden. It was just a matter of divine guidance and a whole lot of bad luck!

Thankfully, at the time, I had little comprehension of this missed opportunity and my climb up the career ladder continued unabated - spurred on by my insane work ethic and by a sudden abundance of sporting talent in Miami. It's kind of strange, but in the very early years of the Miami Dolphins I had built up an extraordinary relationship with the team. I was dating Claudia Sims on the 'QT'. Claudia was the coaches' secretary and the personal secretary of Charles Martin Callahan, the public relations director of the franchise. Charlie Callahan was from my hometown of Lexington, Massachusetts. He had gone to Notre Dame and later became the public relations director for the 'Fighting Irish' during the great years at the Golden Dome. Notre Dame football had taken a turn for the worse by the early 1960s and Charlie's heart couldn't take that. So, Dolphin's owner Joe Robbie brought Charlie in as the new public relations man for the resurging Miami Dolphins.

I mention Charles Callahan and Claudia Sims because with the great relationship I had with the public relations staff, nothing could happen with the team that I didn't know about. I had begun to develop close personal relationships with all of the front office staff. I became friends with the coaches and especially the players, who were all about the same age as me. I learned I could not use all of the information I was exposed to on my nightly radio talk show; however, what I could use, always was more than enough. No matter what the local newspapers were saying, or the competitive Channel 4, with hard driving sports producer Bernie Rozen, I always had the 'inside scoop' on every story. Needless to say, this gave me tremendous confidence as a young sports talk show host.

My daily routine consisted of doing the early morning sports on WGBS Radio, taking a nap, and getting up to the Dolphins training camp by noon. Then I did the late afternoon sports show back at the WGBS studios, following an afternoon trip to the 5th Street Gym in Miami Beach, or a visit to the University of Miami to catch football practice. I did the sports show every night except for Tuesday nights, which was fight night at the Miami Beach Auditorium.

During those years, I would broadcast all eight to ten fights on the card along with Ken, the experienced pro who taught me all of the necessary nuances of calling live sporting events. I was getting pretty good at this fight business because I was calling so many fights. I've always said, if you don't improve with experience, you've got to be an idiot. However, it wasn't just the sheer number of boxing matches I was calling; I was really beginning to love the sport as well. You talk about perfection? What a perfect life for a former sportsman in his late 20s. And of course, the local football wasn't too shabby either! As the Dolphins headed back to training camp in 1970, there was great optimism in the air.

Shula was now the head coach.

Immediately, he surrounded himself with great assistant coaches, reshaping the team as if it were a hunk of iron and he the blacksmith. General Manager Joe Thomas funded this endeavor, making deals to bring Nick Buoniconti, Paul Warfield, and Mary Flemming to Miami, among others. By this time, Shula had already turned his players, the owner, the press, and, most importantly, the fans into believers. It was 'Dolphin mania' by the summer of 1970 in Miami, a storm of jubilation covering the streets that surely sprinkled a little fairy dust onto the players themselves. Bob Griese was developing into a great offensive leader. Larry Little and Bob Kuechenberg were opening holes for the likes of Larry Csonka, Jim Kiick, and Eugene Mercury Morris. Paul Warfield was flat out the best wide receiver in the game, and with Jim Mandich and Mary Flemming at tight end, this offense was developing into a solid force.

Bill Arnsparger was the genius behind the defense. With a leader like middle linebacker Nick Buoniconti (who should be in the Football Hall of Fame) and a supporting cast of intelligent men who loved to hit, the Dolphins had a formidable defensive unit. Place kicking was handled by a guy named Garo Yepremian, who remains my great friend to this day (Garo, too, deserves to be elected to the Hall of Fame). In my eyes, this was a team of destiny, akin to the 1967 Boston Red Sox, who made it to the World Series, or the 1969 New York Mets, who beat the mighty Baltimore Orioles to win the World Series. The same indefinable momentum seemed to be at their backs.

A tremendous season ended for the Dolphins against the Oakland Raiders, when a ball sailed past the outstretched arm of defender Charlie Babb and into the endzone arms of a Raider. It ended hopes of a trip to the Superbowl for Miami, yet for the first time in a long time a contagious sense of optimism far outstripped any disappointment. You could feel it coming. The breakthrough.

The following year, the Dolphins once again fell just short, retreating for another summer to lick their wounds. On the other hand, I still had one more game to think about: Super Bowl V was in Miami, and I would be at the Orange Bowl to cover it.

On that day, once again, I felt the intervening hand of divine guidance. The game was just about over, and I was preparing to do the post-game interviews with the victorious Dallas Cowboys for WGBS Radio. I was selecting my first player to collar when, all of a sudden, a ball thrown by Craig Morton sailed into the arms of Mike Curtis, whose 13-yard return brought the ball all the way to the Cowboys' 28-yard line, with under a minute to play. I realized this was a tremendous turn of events and the Baltimore Colts had a chance to win the Superbowl. I could use the winning field goal on my morning sports show with my call. Talk about being in the right place at the right time! The whole play was taking place directly in front of me in the closed end of the Orange Bowl.

I turned on my tape recorder: 'This will be about a 32-yard field goal for Jim O'Brien. Talk about pressure, five seconds to go, there's the snap, the ball is down! The kick is up!........It's good! Jim O'Brien has done it, the Irishman prevails, and the Baltimore Colts will win Superbowl Five!' The final score was Baltimore 16, Dallas 13, and I loved my call. That was my first and only call of football play by play action. I did pre- and post-game shows for the Dolphins on radio. I did color commentary on the University of Miami football games on radio and TV, but I've got to be the only sportscaster in the world whose only call of a football play was the winning field goal for the Superbowl championship!

I loved my job, and I loved the fact that I was so close to the team. Hell, in my mind, I was as much a part of the team as the coaches and physios. Though I was having one issue. While my association with head coach Don Shula (ultimately) was one of great mutual respect, it's true to say that we didn't immediately hit it off. You see, in my personal life, events were taking place that felt much bigger than coaching a football team - such as losing my father to cancer. Frankly, this guy Shula was no hero to me. Besides that, I loved George Wilson, the first Dolphin's coach.

I had a wonderful relationship with Coach Wilson and his entire family. The day he was fired, I was the only reporter who got a personal interview with him. I actually reported back to the 710 Sportsline of WGBS Radio from his home. No matter how I felt about the change of coaches, this was great reporting, and I knew it.

I also knew, in the end, that Coach Wilson needed to be replaced.

Time showed I was wrong in my emotional attachment to Coach Wilson. I learned that the proper business decision, as cold and calculated as it was, was the best decision, and that Joe Robbie had made a brilliant move in luring Shula to the Miami Dolphins. I was on hand at the announcement. I held an old-fashioned two-way radio by the microphone for what seemed like an hour, so the listeners could hear the live press conference. But, going forwards, I had no relationship with Shula. We just didn't get along. He was all business, with his chiseled chin. He never seemed to loosen up. He was a control freak, and from my perspective, he was a prick. I hated him! Of course, by the start of the 1971 season, I learned my intuitions about Shula were altogether wrong.

I learned to respect the man. While I may have initially harbored some fear of Don, leading to a bit of friction between us, I quickly dismissed that. If you wanted to experience fear, just take a walk through 'the Murph' (an Irish section of Belfast) during the Marching Season. In contrast, walking through the Dolphins' locker room after being summoned to Shula's office was a cakewalk. I did, however, modify my behavior on certain fronts, such as never confronting him in a press conference. If I had a sensitive question, I would ask it when I was alone with him. He appreciated that, and soon enough, I felt the hostility cool and a more friendly disposition begin to emerge. I knew Don liked me, and I knew why. Firstly, he knew I wouldn't let him get away with trying to control me. Secondly, he knew I worked extremely hard at my job, and he respected that. And lastly, he knew I was as much a fan of the Dolphins as I was a reporter covering the team. After all, some of my closest friends at that time were players.

My closeness to Shula and his staff, the members of the team, and even team owner Joe Robbie, ensured that I never missed a sensitive story concerning the Dolphins. No matter what the story might be, as busy as Don Shula was, I'd always get a call back from him. Though I also understood that my relationship with the Hall of Fame coach was strictly business. You didn't sit around and chit-chat with Don Shula. Get to your interview, have your camera crew ready, don't ask hypothetical questions. Keep the conversation to football and don't get too chummy.

But Shula was not a completely humorless guy.

I remember doing an interview with him outside his office one day. Some fan walked in front of the camera asking Shula for an autograph while I was conducting the interview. In one motion, keeping it strictly business, I smacked the guy right on the nose with the microphone, causing his nose to bleed, and went right on with my next question. Shula began to smile, went into a full grin, and then a full-bellied laugh. Finally, I had managed to crack up the chiseled-chin iceman!

From that day on, I knew Don Shula was actually a human being and my relationship with him became very close. Don was a guy who only lived for football. He had a single purpose in life and worked his ass off to prove it - driven by a frustration at his own limited talent as a player. He couldn't control the ability God gave him to perform as an athlete, just as I couldn't regarding my own failed athletic career. I could relate wholeheartedly. Shula always said, 'You can't worry about what you can't control.' This, in my mind, was his most profound statement, and I've learned to live with this thought in my mind since first hearing it so many years ago. When people ask me about the Don Shula I knew, I always say he is a man that got 100% out of his own ability, asked the same from his immediate family, demanded it from his players and assistant coaches, and lived his entire coaching career in fear of failure rather than in the exuberance of winning.

And yet, Shula was not the insensitive man he seemed. His oldest daughter, Donna, once said, 'He was never the kind of father who could tell you he loved you, who would hold you or kiss you. It was real awkward for him.' However, when his first wife, Dorothy, died after struggling with cancer, it was the first time his kids ever saw their father cry. You see, Dorothy was able to get Don Shula to laugh on a regular basis - the same thing I was able to accomplish only once. Following the death of his beloved wife, Don was totally devastated, wandering around in a sort of lonely stupor. Two and a half years later, Don married Mary Anne Stephens, and from what all of my friends who still cover the Dolphins tell me, this was the best thing that ever happened to him. Somehow, this man, whose only passion was the endless pursuit of winning football games, learned that there is actually more to life than the National Football League. Although, in his mind, given all that he accomplished, perhaps not anything quite as exhilarating.

You see, in 1971, the Dolphins were on their way to their first of three trips to the Super Bowl. The 1971 season was a mixed bag of emotions for me. There were challenging times in Ireland, and my father succumbed to cancer in October of that year, a loss that I still feel to this day. Yet, the Miami Dolphins were playing great football, and following the longest game ever played on Christmas Day, they outslugged the Kansas City Chiefs, with my pal Garo kicking the game-winning field goal. I was thrilled, but it was a long day for me. I had flown up to Sebago Lake, Maine, to spend Christmas Eve with my mother and brother. It was our first Christmas without my Dad, and it didn't seem like Christmas at all. I had to be in Kansas City the next day to cover the Dolphins' playoff game, and it began to snow like hell around midnight in Maine. I got a short nap after our little Christmas Eve get-together and left for the airport in a blinding snowstorm at 3 AM.

I had mixed emotions as I alternated between crying for my father and singing the Christmas carols that were on the radio, while trying to concentrate on driving in the blinding snowstorm. It took me three and one-half hours to make this two-hour trip, but I made my 7 AM flight to Kansas City. I was just about the only person on this Christmas morning flight, so I finally got some sleep, and woke up at my destination in plenty of time to make the team bus to the old Kansas City Stadium. The game was sensational, and Hank Goldberg and I worked as spotters during the game for Curt Gowdy and the TV crew from NBC. As excited as we all were, the players were exhausted and so was I. The trip to the airport for our Eastern Airlines charter was fairly quiet. After a few beers (and the Coors were plentiful) the party began. It was wide receiver, Howard Twilley, along with Larry Csonka's birthday, and by now the magnitude of the win was beginning to sink in. This turned out to be one of the best parties I ever attended, and it started all over again when we arrived back in Miami. Over 30 thousand fans turned out at the airport to greet the team. It was party time, magna cum laude! The troubles in the North, the Dolphins on the way to the Superbowl, the death of my Dad, and Christmas Eve with my grieving mother - what a goddamn few months.

Our first trip to the Superbowl on January 16, 1972, was a great experience for the team and the City of Miami. And it was extremely exciting for me to be covering a team that was in the World Championship game. New Orleans was a fun city, and for the first couple of nights there was no players' curfew. My pal Garo, Doug Swift and Strat Zammas from Channel 4 in Miami took full advantage of the great spirit in the French quarter of the crescent city. It's tough for any team to win in its first trip to the Superbowl because of all the effort to get there in the first place, coupled with all of the distractions leading up to Super Sunday. The game is almost a second thought. Not so for the players. But when Larry Csonka fumbled in the first quarter, it was kind of a foreshadowing of how that great Dallas team was going to play that day. The Cowboys held the mighty Dolphin offence to just 80 yards rushing and went on to win the game 24 to 3.

The two things I remember most about the immediate aftermath of that game were how vocally pissed off Mercury Morris was about not getting enough playing time and how 'beside himself' Don Shula was at becoming the most losing coach in Super Bowl history, 0-2. Despite Shula bringing two teams to the Super Bowl in five years, there was an undercurrent of thinking that he couldn't win the 'big one'. He was humbled in defeat and pretty quiet when asked about winning the big game. As far as Mercury Morris was concerned, Don put an immediate halt to any speculation of a revolt from any of his players when he made it absolutely clear to the press that he 'wouldn't want a player who was satisfied with limited playing time.' There was a lot of disappointment at losing the big game by all involved. The momentum of the previous twelve months had run aground, and heading into the next season, you might have been forgiven for thinking that the team was now a busted flush. How wrong you would have been. Time after time, the Dolphins did remarkable things.

I believe the second-half comeback against the Minnesota Vikings was the key to their extraordinary performance. The Dolphins were 16-0 heading into the Super Bowl on the fourteenth of January 1973. More than 90 thousand fans were on hand to witness the Miami Dolphins manhandle the Washington Redskins. The game was nowhere near as close as the final score ended up. As a matter of fact, I believe the Lord sent a message to Coach Shula when Garo Yepremian fired an errant pass following a misplayed field goal attempt. That little place kicker put the ball into the hands of the Redskins' Mike Bass, who returned it 49 yards for a Washington touchdown with just two minutes remaining. However, the defense played a perfect game, giving up no points to the mighty Redskins. Nick Buoniconti quarterbacked the defensive effort, while Manny Fernandez played the game of his life at defensive tackle, and free safety Jake Scott turned in the game's MVP performance. The offense did what it had to do, simply scoring more points than Washington. This was something they managed to do all season against every single opponent, with aplomb.

Beating the Redskins 14-7 and winning the Super Bowl made it a perfect season, 17-0. This was a feat that no other team had ever accomplished in the history of the

National Football League and to date has never been duplicated. Don Shula and his 1972 Miami Dolphins had attained perfection. And yet, despite being so close to that remarkable team, my own life during this period felt strangely out of control.

Publicly, I really enjoyed the reputation of being a bounder, a cad, a womanizer, and a happy-go-lucky bachelor sportscaster, tooling around in a red Corvette. On the outside, I was a loud, extroverted show-off, but inwardly, I was nothing like that at all. When I was alone, I was deeply spiritual. I often cried in my red Corvette because I missed the guidance of my father so much. Then, to ease my pain, I would take out a tattered, stained, and yellowed bit of paper from my wallet, and I would read this prayer:

Lord, make me an instrument of Your peace;
Where there is hatred, let me sow love;
Where there is injury, pardon;
Where there is doubt, faith;
Where there is despair, hope;
Where there is darkness, light;
Where there is sadness, joy.

I couldn't tell you where or when I originally found this prayer, but the words may be familiar to many of you. They were written by St. Francis of Assisi . . . it was the perfect prayer following a season of perfection.

CHAPTER VI

'I WANTED TO BE SUCCESSFUL, NOT FAMOUS'

I don't want to sound egotistical - although I am - but I'm fully aware of my fame. You can't be in my position, enjoy my status, and not know. After all, for close to half a century now I've been at the pinnacle of my profession as a sportscaster. My voice, my style - which is to give zero fucks about anything except the audience at home - is as synonymous with championship boxing as Mike Breen with championship basketball, or Kevin Harlan with championship football. Except for one catch: in the good old US-of-A, outside of the boxing fraternity, I'm basically a nobody!

There is a good reason for this. While I have been calling championship fights for decades (and have been prolific in my output), not a single minute of these telecasts has ever been aired in America. With the exception of those moviegoers who came across my commentary in *When We Were Kings* (which remains a sore topic), my fellow Yanks, quite simply, have never had the pleasure of my company. For all the major fights of the last half century, they've instead been offered up the likes of Howard Cosell on ABC Sports, or Al Bernstein on Showtime, or Jim Lampley on HBO, while me - well, I was outsourced by my paymasters to the rest of the globe.

The international telecast.

Since the mid-1970s, when I started working with Don King and Kingvision (and in later years with Bob Arum and Top Rank), this has been my exclusive outpost. Meaning that, if a network in any country outside of the United States wishes to broadcast a given event, say a heavyweight title fight, its viewers will instead get my voice layered over the action. Same fight, different commentary team. Now, in this way I have been breaking records in the world of broadcasting for decades - surreptitiously! The very definition of a quiet storm. This has probably cost me in terms of fame and wealth, but, honestly, I can't complain. What I would argue, though, with justification, is that my binary experience of fame - aside from making me the most famous boxing commentator in the world *not* known in the United States - has granted me a unique perspective.

You see, there are two types of people that work in radio and television: ex jocks, and those groupies that love being as close to the stars and celebrities as they can be. Well, I was a good enough athlete *myself* not to be obsessed with professional athletes, and when you work in entertainment for a few years, you begin to realize that most celebrities are spoiled, self-centered assholes. In my public life as a sportscaster, I've had my share of celebrity friends and acquaintances. That's just par for the course. But I can honestly say that I was fond of these guys not because of their status (which in the world of entertainment is so often the defining feature of a person) but because they were good men who just so happened to be celebrities, whose paths just so happened to intersect with mine. I never, ever got dazzled. To me, their shine was all plastic.

I'll admit, I have been starstruck. Mickey Mantle, Joe Namath, Ernie Banks, Jack Nicklaus, Arnold Palmer - these are some of the names that I have loved interviewing. However, any idol worship I may have felt - any excitement - I always kept it hidden, masked behind a natural confidence that, to this day, allows me to mingle with the rich and the famous. Of course, sometimes being a fan just strikes. Especially in the beginning. But in my line of work, anyone worth his salt will soon overcome this kind of vertigo and plant himself on solid ground. It just cannot be any other way. Basically, you need to desensitize yourself as quickly as possible to extraordinary sights and experiences, so that one minute you're saying, 'Holy shit, that's Steve McQueen!' and the next your saying, 'Holy shit, I forgot to eat lunch!' Once this happens, you'll instinctively find other stuff to get excited about - in my case, the thrill of being ringside to call world championship boxing - and you'll effortlessly fit into your new shoes.

Secondly, you realize that you're a professional. Know your worth. Pay-per-view events go on for fuckin' hours. Knockouts are nice when they happen, but of course they don't always materialize. It's a lottery. More than anyone or anything else, it's your voice that is needed to carry the show. Rarely does a card produce more than three or four really good fights anyway. That's just the nature of the business. Think about it: a twelve-round stinker will endure for nearly an hour, clogging up the air like a really stubborn fart. That's a terrible prospect for a producer. A good commentator, with enthusiasm, creativity and skill, will generate drama where none exists. We are - and I cannot state this enough - an integral part of the show.

And thirdly, self-image takes precedent. Mine is my masterpiece. You've probably heard the saying before that perception is everything. Well, in my world, perception is exactly what I make of it - *especially* when I'm charming an audience. In my career as a self-proclaimed (and proud-of-the-fact) phony of the highest order, I've learned to control the narrative, the emotion, the satisfying crescendo. The whole goddamn experience. Because that's what I want to give people, whether they're Joe Bloggs or Joe Frazier - an experience that they won't soon forget.

As far as the celebrities I encounter, I want them to feel as though they're meeting me, not the other way around.

Creating a self-image is akin to sculpting a rock. Looking back at my life, I can now say that the best thing that ever happened to me (professionally) was when my producer - a guy by the name of David Fox, who had been very successful over in England working for the BBC before coming to the States to work for Don King - asked me one night at dinner, 'Hey, Bob, what's all this Colonel shit?'

'What do you mean?' I answered, all innocent.

'I mean, why do I keep hearing you being addressed as Colonel?'

'Because, cocksucker, that's my fuckin' rank!' I then picked up my fork and jabbed it into the cornea of an imaginary eye.

Of course, I was only having some fun. But it was a fair question to ask. At that time, I had never thought to mention my association with the Ancient and Honorable Artillery Company of Massachusetts. It was an entirely sequestered part of my life. The only reason it had come up now, around the dinner table at a swanky restaurant, was because joining us that night for filet mignon and champagne, happened to be my superior in the military ranks, General Bob Marr.

Oblivious to the key role he was about to play in my career, his presence would ultimately set in motion the creation of my new identity on the world stage. That weekend, he had flown over to Vegas at my invitation to attend the world title fight at Caesars Palace, immediately inspiring reverence and intrigue from all in my flock. The General could drink like a fish, and during dinner, the bubbles had made him a touch more mischievous than usual. Tipsily, he eventually announced to the table, with a face solid as stone, 'The Colonel is a war hero. He's killed more men than smallpox!' And then, as those words hung around the room, he went back to his hundred-dollar steak, chewing and swallowing with the confidence of a despot.

I guess everyone believed him. I sure as hell didn't argue, silently chuckling at the General's deadpan delivery. Of course, whenever I'm asked straight out, I'll tell the truth - that while my uniform is awash with ribbons, making me appear like some third-world dictator of a banana republic, not a single one pertains to valor! I'm very upfront about this fact. I even have a few Purple Stars that I don't wear because, frankly, I agree that they would look ridiculous.

But thanks to David's insistence - who deserves a tremendous amount of credit for his commercial instincts and powers of persuasion - my name would no longer be simply Bob Sheridan. No no no. From that point onwards, whenever I took to the air, I would instead be known as 'the Colonel' Bob Sheridan. Larger than life military veteran and weapons aficionado!

The moniker has slowly but surely subsumed my identity. For all intents and purposes, I now regard it as my real name, with Bob being the guy I was before I became 'the Colonel'. Not just *a* Colonel, either, but *the* Colonel. That's very important too. Because to my ear - and I would imagine everybody else's - it sounds imperious, like *capo di tutti capi*, the boss of bosses. This was where my own creativity came to the fore, where I really took the bull by the horns. The character was conceived, and I ran with it, as if holding a baton. And forty years later, I'm still running with it.

But I'm also lucky to have preserved a sense of perspective.

From the outset, I've known that people treat 'the guy' who is on television or radio, calling the games or reporting the news, with admiration. I've also known that it really doesn't make any difference if 'that guy' just so happens to be me. I see fame for what it is. Of course, I am aware of my status and all the doors it can open for me, and I'm grateful for it. But at the same time, I realize that in the grand scheme of things, whatever I do or attempt to do is small fry compared to so many other events in the world. Better than anyone, I understand that the nature of my 'rinky-dink' TV career is utterly trivial. Therefore, through an awareness of my place in the universe, I have learned over the years to enjoy my celebrity without being consumed by it.

Or, to put it another way, without turning into a complete prick!

I regard my sense of humor as having been the key to achieving this. Namely, my ability not only to laugh at and make fun of the world around me, but to laugh at and make fun of myself as well. To me, that has always been the Holy Grail, something to never lose sight of. Honestly, I'm the most self-deprecating son of a bitch you'll ever meet. Why? Because making yourself the butt of the joke puts you at the same level as everyone else; it keeps your ego in check. I'm no better than the next guy, believe me - I'm just a street thug from Boston with a big personality - a big voice - who caught the right breaks. I never, ever, try to act like a bigshot - unless, of course, I'm in a room full of 'em! Otherwise, there are enough assholes in the world already.

And on the subject of assholes, let me tell you a little story.

This is a story about the biggest asshole I ever encountered in my time as a sportscaster. In the mid-1970s, when I was the lead broadcaster on all of the big Muhammad Ali fights, I worked with all kinds of Hollywood types, including Frank Sinatra, James Brown (the Godfather of soul), Redd Foxx, Jack Palance, and Kris Kristofferson, just to mention a few. In those days, the producers used me as the lead commentator and hired a celebrity for the movie marquees, to add a little extra glamour to the event.

Usually, I wouldn't have minded. Brown and Foxx had been a hoot - mostly because when they showed up, both were as high as the Empire State Building! Brown, the man who summoned electricity to flow through his body while on stage, had been slowed to the pace of a slug by quaaludes, slithering over to my side with a far-away smile. Quaaludes, for those of you who don't know, are real downers, and he probably had about five of them. Suffice it to say, he didn't offer much to the telecast - but he was funny as hell! Foxx, on the other hand, had been blasted on cocaine. He was a tsunami of energy at the desk, as out of control as he was hilarious. While you do encounter this kind of thing regularly in the showbiz world (guys whose pupils are larger than tax discs), when he said to me, 'Man, Bob, it seems like those punches are landing before they even throw 'em!' I knew the game was up! His contribution had also reached its end.

Thereafter, I'd had a real good experience with Kristofferson, who said to me off the bat, 'Bob, my agent got me this gig. I don't know too much about boxing.' Etc. And I said to him, 'Kris, don't worry about a thing.' I knew right away that he was a real gentleman. Humble, funny, extremely bright. So, throughout the fights, I lobbed him as many softballs as my arm could manage, and by the end of the broadcast he had completely come out of his shell and was even giving *me* a run for my money.

Those were really fun few hours, I think for both of us. Then, a few fights later, along comes Sinatra - with four or five of his flunkies. What a difference a day makes. I'll never forget it. It was during the Ali-Larry Holmes championship telecast in Las Vegas, and I'm sitting there doing my final preparations when I hear from somewhere above me, 'Hey kid, grab me a couple of seats for my guys.'

Of course, me being Irish, well, I don't take to Italians too well anyway. Where I came from, in South Boston, we had a big-time rivalry with the greaseballs. I'm also a stickler for good manners. I felt the rage coming up through my toes. This prick had come at me all wrong.

Now, Sinatra was not a very big guy. Without his voice, in a crowd he could easily have been mistaken for an arm or a leg belonging to someone else. 'I don't even know who the fuck you are,' I say, 'but you get your own seats! Then squaring up to him, I add, 'And you're not sitting with me!'

God, the stretch I got on those manicured eyebrows!

Wrapped in his cotton wool existence, who knows how many years it had been since someone spoke to him in that way. But I didn't give two fucks. He was in my territory and needed to know it.

'Who are you?' he manages to say.

'Why don't you ask around to find out who I am, because I don't know who the fuck you are, so obviously I'm more famous than you!' I threw back at him.

Well, he just shook his head and walked away.

In my mind that had to be said. 'To hell with the show,' I thought, getting ready to do the broadcast solo. However, to my great surprise, he actually came back and took a seat at the desk. Never apologizing, never saying anything. And you know what? I didn't help him out one bit. I left him hanging out to dry like a shit-stained pair of underwear. He was a terrible guest who didn't know a thing about boxing. No personality. No smarts. He was just Frank Sinatra, someone who had been treated like a God - bowed at and groveled to - for far too fuckin' long. But why should I be impressed?

The fact is, he thought he was a tough guy because of his mob connections. Willie Moretti was his godfather and the underboss of the Genovese crime family, but those guys were just using him to frontline in different hotels. They made him famous, and the truth was, he was nothing but a little wise ass - the type of guy I would have beaten up at school and taken his lunch money probably. With that said, he was a tremendously talented singer and I happened to really like his music. But in person, a total fuckin' asshole. I'd be embarrassed to bring him home to my mother. That's why you should never meet your idols. You're always going to be disappointed.

Well, almost always. There were some good eggs as well, shining amongst the rotten ones. While I've made it abundantly clear I'm not a jock sniffer or celebrity suck up, I was genuinely fond of the Miami Dolphins' Garo Yepremian and Nick Buoniconti, because both were great guys. Sometimes in life you meet people who are just the same as you - who reflect in their personalities your own quirks and sense of humor. For me, that was Garo and Nick. And practical jokes were our thing. Together, we perpetrated a campaign of terror that would have met the standards of Al Qaeda. Looking back over those years of mischief, we might well have been responsible for more anxiety in team locker rooms than inspired by athletes' foot and staff infection combined!

Those were personal friendships. On a professional level, outside of the world of boxing - which is filled with the sweetest, most down-to-earth people you could ever hope to meet - my experiences with the big stars have been hairy to say the least. Of all the celebrity sidekicks I had on all of the big fights, most of them were egocentric assholes, with the exception of Kristofferson, who is genuinely a terrific guy. I know if I lived in the L.A area, Kris and I would be great friends, not because of who he is but because of the kind of guy he happens to be. Frankly, as soon as I discovered he was a military man, I was like putty in his hand. I wasn't in the least bit surprised to learn that he had served. Kris was so damn polite and respectful, only the armed forces could have been responsible. If only Sinatra had stopped singing into his hairbrush for a minute and picked up a gun himself, maybe he would have learned some manners as well!

Needless to say, I was relieved when the 'beautiful people' stopped showing up at my desk. I thought it was gimmicky anyway and distracted from the fights. My commentary was more than sufficient to keep the folks at home entertained, to keep their eyes and ears glued to the television set. After all, that's why they pay me. If anyone's attention does ever drift away from me, and I catch wind of it - even when I'm off the clock - you'd better believe I'll say something. Not that I'm the kind of guy who's confrontational at all. I just delight in the company of others, and it's reciprocal. I entertain, and my audience reacts. That's how it's always been. Only when I feel as though I'm not commanding a room with my presence, my voice, do I get a little testy.

All I ask for is everyone's full attention.

So, with that in mind, whenever I'm on stage at a black-tie event, and I can still hear a few murmurs of conversation, I'll bellow to the back of the room, 'Hey, if you're not interested, get the fuck out of here, or else shut the fuck up!' Then, if that doesn't work - and this has happened on multiple occasions, especially at corporate events where you reliably find a few saggy-eyed workaholics unwilling to put down their cell phones - I'll tell them, 'Hey listen, this isn't working out. I told them to triple or quadruple the sound in here, they didn't do it, and I'm not going to try to outshout a room full of a thousand people. So, I'll come around to your tables, I'll sit down and have a couple of drinks at every table, we'll have a ball, you can take pictures, do your selfies, whatever you want, I'll sign whatever you want, then I'll eventually get around to all the tables. But I wouldn't want to be at the back of the room, 'cause when I get there, I'll be fucked, and I might throw up on you!' Laughter erupts and I continue, a shit eatin' grin on my face. 'Short of that, ladies and gents, we'll have a good time.'

And they always lap it up.

These events are great because I get to rub shoulders with the people who really want to see me and meet me and talk to me, and it doesn't matter whether I'm in Africa, the Middle East, or Tokyo.

Speaking of Tokyo. Here's another quick story - about my fame in nearly every country in the world outside of the United States. Me and Sugar Ray Leonard, one of the greatest and most recognizable fighters in history, are having a drink together in the Tokyo Dome following an event. Ray and I often did commentary together and afterwards we'd find somewhere to puff on a fine cigar and sip some good whiskey. Aside from being a legend of the sport, 'Sugar' is also a sweetheart of a guy and one of my dear, dear friends. He is also fantastic with the fans, which in my experience is smart, because I'll tell you this: if you fuck with the fans, they'll fuck you up sooner or later. But if you're good to them, the word of mouth is unbelievable.

Anyhow. We're sitting there making artful clouds of smoke and reflecting on our night's work, when along comes a guy who recognizes me. Me! He doesn't even notice the boxing royalty that's perched to my left. A mass of nervous energy, he starts jabbering in my direction, his English sounding like it's going through a wash cycle. But it's all smiles and handshakes, the kind of conversion I'm used to having on my travels. However, after a couple of minutes, I even began to feel a little awkward. Sure, I'm a big deal, but I'm no Ray Leonard. Ray probably never felt like more of a potted plant in his life. Thankfully, he had a grin on his face and was content to keep sipping on his bourbon. Usually it's him who they recognize. He probably was relieved!

Finally, I interject, saying to my new friend with a stroke of my arm, 'Would you like to meet Sugar Ray Leonard?' And the guy looks at Ray, then looks at me, then looks back again at Ray. I'm wondering now whether he's even a boxing fan at all. Then the bolt of lightning strikes. 'Oh Sugar Ray!' he says, shrieking in excitement. And within the next 60 seconds he probably repeats his name a further 20 times, filling the lounge with his chirpings and descending on the ex-champ like a bird of prey. If he hadn't recognized him before, he sure had now! But the funny part was this - with his accent, he pronounced the name (with radiant innocence) Sugar L-A-Y! So of course, from that day onwards, Ray Leonard has always been to me, whenever I see him, Sugar Lay!' 'Oh hi, Sugar Lay,' I bellow as soon as I catch a glimpse, usually at the fights.

'Colonel, remember that day?' he answers me.

'I'll never fucking forget it. That motherfucker didn't want to talk to me anymore once he realized it was you.' And then Ray says, 'Yeah you prick, you walked away because we couldn't get rid of him!'

You suffer from your own fame.

That's the relationship I have with fighters - they're both the biggest of names and the smallest of names. I'm not impressed by names; I'm impressed by people. Most of all, though, I'm impressed by the wealth of good-natured humor to be found in the world even when the applecart is toppling. The fighter who can crack a joke after being knocked senseless; the family member who can find a moment to chuckle on the day of a funeral. Therefore, the most exciting thing about my celebrity, to this day, is not walking around being a bigshot - that kind of thing has an expiry date. No, it's being able to get my buddies, or even a perfect stranger, to laugh and have a good time because I'm right there with them. I really enjoy that. It makes it all worth it.

CHAPTER VII

'HOME SWEET HOME'

'Bob Sheridan likes the women, but he *loves* the cattle.'

A friend of mine once said this; and you know what? He was bang on the mark. From spending all those summers on my grandfather's farm, caring for animals and breathing in the flora and the flies, I had within me a real, enduring love for agriculture. So, when an opportunity arose for me to acquire my very own piece of land - in Ireland no less - to distract and busy myself, I grabbed it like a pair of tits.

By the mid-1970s, I was well on my way to being the best boxing commentator in the world. I had already covered The Rumble in the Jungle and The Thrilla in Manila; I was the highest-paid local TV sportscaster in the South; I had been with the Miami Dolphins during the great Super Bowl years; I had covered the World Series, Olympic Games, Stanley Cup, and NBA Finals. But, having achieved so much in such a short space of time, by age thirty, I was practically burnt out!

Moderation may be for cowards, but excess can make your gums bleed. I could not keep this up. I needed to make a change - a drastic one. So, while I continued to broadcast the big fights for Don King, I decided to purchase a small farm in Bunratty, County Clare, in the Midwest region of Ireland - the idea sweeping me away like a candy wrapper in a gale.

Friends, colleagues, they all thought I was crazy. To them, the notion of someone jetting back and forth over the Atlantic every other week and splitting their life in two simply didn't make any sense. But I was deaf to their objections. I knew what I was doing and why I was doing it. Sure, there would be some logistical hurdles to overcome, but those were just details. I knew that the smell of dung in my nostrils - out in the crisp country air of my new property - and the serenity of rural life among my fellow Irish, would make it all worthwhile. I sure as hell wasn't concerned about a bit of jetlag. Hell, it was too slow for me anyway: before it could set in, I was usually back in the same time zone already!

Aer Lingus did all the heavy lifting. At one point, I did eighteen straight weeks of flying out on Thursdays from Shannon Airport (on board my 'Shannon Shuttle') and coming back on Sunday nights. It was a crazy routine that to me felt perfectly normal. I loved the double life: the glitz and glamour on the weekends, and the humble (and anonymous) existence wedged in between. It was just the diversion I needed to let my mind cool, to keep myself grounded and energized, so that the train could keep moving.

Bottom line: I was becoming an ever-better announcer with some distance between myself and the circus.

I decided not to tell anybody who I was. Not through modesty - I always want to be the center of attention - but through circumspection. I believed that, should the locals learn of my celebrity status, it would be damn near impossible for me to buy cattle. It just didn't make sense getting into that side of my life. Remember, I'm a businessman first and a showoff second! Already, they regarded me as an exotic American interloper - probably with some wealth. If they'd known I was a world-famous broadcaster to boot, I more than likely would have been criminally overcharged at the auctions.

The fact of the matter was, I liked buying and selling my own animals. However, about five years later, while I was rodeo riding in Minneapolis, Minnesota, the truth about who I was finally came out - courtesy of a sensational newspaper spread. It blew the hat, glasses and moustache clean off my secret identity.

Published in The Sunday World (one of the most widely read newspapers in Ireland), the article detailed everything Sheridan - from boxing to bulls. The revelation was a bombshell, a testament to how successfully I had kept myself to myself in those years. But in reality, nothing really changed. Though I had to put up with a few strange looks, the folks in County Clare turned out to be more curious than judgmental, with about half of them thinking the story was complete bullshit - especially the part about my high-flying television career. To them, I was just Bob Sheridan the cattle farmer; the idea that I was some kind of celebrity in disguise, living a double life in their little corner, was frankly ridiculous.

They all knew me so well. Appearing one afternoon like an alien from planet Yank, I embraced the country life - and my community of people in Bunratty (in the New Market-on-Fergus Parish of County Clare) - wholeheartedly and with due reverence. I loved being there - especially in those early days. Everything was new and exciting but in the most profound way. Including the nightly booze ups! All other things revolved around these. After all, when on their deathbed, nobody ever wished that they'd worked harder and enjoyed themselves less! Unsurprisingly, this behavior served to complicate the following mornings and actually made them a giant pain in the ass! At least in the beginning. You see, in choosing this new life of a farmer, I had given myself plenty to do; the demands never stopped or slowed, certainly not for a hangover. And they required plenty of physical effort too. As I quickly discovered. But rolling up my sleeves, I was only too happy to meet the challenge.

It was actually deeply satisfying work. Despite the modest size of my plot on the Hill Road - around ten acres - I managed to set up a very profitable little operation, keeping about fifty head of cattle in the winter and about twice that many in the summer. This too was run at my convenience. For example, feeding hour on the farm should have been an early morning affair. However, since I was often still bladdered come sunrise, I gradually taught them to leave me the hell alone until noon, pushing their mealtime back about fifteen minutes a day so that I could sleep off the booze. Then, in unison, they'd make their way up to the fence and start bawling, creating a tremendous racket.

Early on, my neighbor, a defiant but endearing fellow named Peter Haynes, who was about 30 years my senior, would come over at 7am every morning and attempt to rouse me. 'You gotta get up yer lazy bastard!' he would yell into the seashell of my slumber, keeping at it until he got a response. 'Petey, I just got in,' I yelled back. 'My cattle will eat when I eat. They'll eat at noontime!' And that's exactly when they did. God bless Petey, who actually taught me more about cattle farming than I absorbed even at agricultural school some thirty years later; but he quickly learned my ways. Bunratty was an introverted little place that just had to get used to my personality. For my part, I probably had to learn to be a little quieter. But like all decent fish out of water stories, it all came good in the end!

Livestock farming, it turned out, is actually pretty easy - with the right smarts. You just have to seize the opportunities when they present themselves, like my buying the quaint (if neglected) little farm in the first place. Believe me, I'd never planned to throw down my life savings on a vegetable patch some 4,000 miles away. Back in the States, I'd been living a fast paced and fully metropolitan existence, with almost no free time. But the moment I realized that Ireland was in demand for its purebred cattle, that the market there was piping hot, I pushed all my chips into the middle of the table and prepared for my new life as the Bunratty Cowboy!

Here's what happened exactly. As a radio broadcaster in the late '60s and early '70s, I covered an event called The Irish American - an annual greyhound race that pitted against one another the best dogs from either nation. Held in Miami, it was an occasion that attracted both high society and the basest gamblers you had ever come across. And I fuckin' loved it. Mingling with just about everyone, from the royal guests to the royal fuck ups, I had become very friendly with a guy by the name of Des Hanrahan. Des, in addition to being the chairman of the Irish Greyhound Board, was also a drop-dead alcoholic. So we hit it off right away! Eventually, he invited me to come to Ireland - my maiden voyage - and here I fell in love with the land of my heritage for real. I was completely blown away.

A thoroughly decent old drunk who really loved me, Des had seen the wonder in my eyes and promised to take me all over the country. Just nine days into the trip, without a shred of trepidation, I then bought the farm. The equation for me was simple. I loved Ireland. I needed a break from my schedule. And I had a chance to make some serious dough. The decision was a no-brainer. Knowing it was the right move to make, both emotionally and financially, I signed the deeds for the property with such enthusiasm that the pen in my hand nearly snapped in two. Eight short weeks later, I was both a proud resident of my ancestral home and knee deep in cow shit! It all felt like a dream. Fortunate that I never had any problems with Mad Cow

Disease, Brucellosis or Bovine Tuberculosis, or any of those diseases that affect cattle, I soon established my daily routine.

Though far from fit, I managed to condense my key chores - putting out the fodder, changing the water, and carrying out general maintenance of the property - into just a few hours. Thereafter, I was free as a bird to embrace my surroundings and, more often than not, chose to spend my afternoons going to cattle auctions. These I relished, because in the cattle business, you learn that money is made on just two days: on the days you buy and on the days you sell. And I made plenty of money. You had to be a real crafty son of a bitch and I loved it. Why would I waste money on hiring a cattle agent? Instead, several times a year, I'd take 100,000 punts and go buy some weedlings for the best price. Quite honestly, I savored the challenge, using my intellect and charm to outhustle the hustlers and make a few bucks in the process. That kind of thing gave me endless pleasure and really put a spring in my step. It also killed some time before I could respectfully announce myself at the pubs!

I was in my element. A stone's throw from my house, I had my local watering hole, Six Mile Bridge, where I drank quantities of Guinness that would have made a sailor blush. There, I exerted myself far more than I ever did carrying out the duties on my farm - the smile on my face masking my deep exhaustion! And let me tell you, due to the famous dark stuff being closer to a meal than a beverage, the result was that my underpants - come morning - would regularly have more streaks on them than the landing strip at Shannon Airport! Still, while I adored my little local and its wonderful patrons, the best evenings I spent getting 'fucked up till the wee hours' actually took place about a mile or so down the road.

Bunratty Village was a surprisingly lively place to be. It is home to the famous Bunratty Castle, an imposing 15th-century fortress which overlooks the Raite river; and also to Bunratty Folk Park, which takes you back in time with its thatched-roofed cottages and turn-of-the-century shops and markets. I adored being there. My favorite place to go was a pub named Durty Nelly's, one of the oldest and most visited watering holes in all of Ireland. I couldn't get enough of the place. Especially in the summers. At the end of each day, people bundled in through the doors like fans at a soccer game, with one side being for the locals and the other for the tourists. However, at around 10 PM every night, like the demolishing of the Berlin Wall, this imaginary partition would inevitably tumble, and we'd suddenly be a mass of humanity having singalongs and getting well and truly blitzed.

I did, though, have to tone down some of my bravado. In Ireland, tipping isn't the custom, and neither is being a big shot. Well, I was an offender on both counts. They actually thought I was a bit of a fool and, rather than being thankful for two or three extra whiskeys, would seem slightly embarrassed on my behalf, pulling faces and clearing their throats. I soon learned my lesson. Back in the States, I remained as grandiose as ever, but in the earthy pubs of County Clare, I learned to follow the correct protocols. How to be sociable yet restrained; or, as the locals phrased it, how to be 'in company.' This crash course in Irish propriety served me well, and never more so than when I met screen starlet Maureen O'Hara.

I had been invited to attend her 80th birthday bash at her home in County Cork. By this time, I'd long since repatriated to the States but returned often to see friends and to feel at home. I missed everything, especially the early morning dew and the low drifting fog which could not be replicated. But it was a buddy of mine from Boston, Doc Arcidi, who actually wrangled for me the invite. He was very friendly with Maureen because she had been spending her winters out in Saint Croix, in the Caribbean Sea, where Doc had a place too. As neighbors they had hit it off. And after learning that he was going to be in Ireland later that year, when she would be back home, Maureen insisted he drop by. So, along with another great pal of ours, Mike Berocki from New jersey, off we went.

Now, my companions both are used to traveling in style. Doc owned a chain of luxury rehab centers across America and Mike, who came straight out of an episode of The Sopranos, was one of the principles in BFI Waste Services - perhaps the largest waste management company in North America at the time. But they had made an error in judgement. So far from home, they opted to delegate the travel arrangements, without reservation, to yours truly. Neither could have expected such a cockeyed outcome.

I'd known just who to call.

Gerry the German was referred to as such because he had such a strange fuckin' accent. Something between the ramblings of a hobo and the bleating of a lamb. Nobody could follow a word he said. But aside from being my hapless neighbor, he had also been my de facto driver throughout my years in County Clare. I always like to repay loyalty, and to tell you the truth, I missed the goofy bastard - in a whimsical sort of way. Gerry pretended to be a bit of an eejit, but I was never fooled. The man had a thousand private jokes contained in his eyes, and I was adamant that he come along for the ride. Only when a chuntering Ford Grenada pulled up in a cloud of fumes, the red paint all but washed off and the hubcaps peppered with rust, did Doc and Mike realize that they were slumming it for the day.

Poor Gerry actually was a terrible driver. He couldn't find his way across the street with a map. But he got us there eventually - with only a few minor altercations taking place between the passengers!

As we rumbled in from the open road amid a plume of dark smoke, we arrived at a large country manor that looked every bit as stately as its owner. Its long driveway lined with ashes, silhouetted against the greens and browns of the surrounding countryside, the place was a mixture of traditional style and modern excess. We parked up - with some further difficulty - and a sour faced woman of about fifty answered the door to us, who turned out to be Maureen's daughter. She requested that our chauffeur, Gerry, please stay in the kitchen, while the rest of the guests were entertained in the parlor.

Well. To me that was impolite, bordering on cuntish! But I bit my tongue, remembering where I was. Instead, I just stayed in the kitchen as well, while Doc and Mike - without a moment's hesitation it appeared - strode on through.

For the next 45 minutes we sat while notes from a piano, muffled by the sound of distant laughter, drifted down the hall. Half-full when we arrived, a now empty bottle of fine Irish scotch idled in front of us as Gerry and I, nursing hurt feelings and a growing alcohol-drenched sense of injustice, contemplated our exit strategy. First, though, I needed to take a leak, and just as I stood up to find a bathroom in that hotel of a home, in through the door came an older lady draped in a magnificent dress - jewelry hanging from ears and limbs. It was Maureen O'Hara! 'Oh hi,' she said, slightly startled. 'How are you doing?' More noise came in through the open door, clobbering us while we sat on the breakfast bar stools. I said: 'This is Gerry my neighbor. Your daughter said that Gerry had to sit in the kitchen.' Her face grimaced sweetly, and she tutted. 'Don't pay any attention to her. I'm the movie star!' And without hesitation, she wafted over and gave Gerry a big kiss.

For the rest of his life, Gerry fawned over this moment, telling everyone about the time a movie star had planted one on him. Maureen was a lovely lady. All class. And the fact of the matter was, she was a huge boxing fan as well, and so recognized me instantly. She had recently finished filming a couple of movies with John Candy, and she liked me because she said I reminded her of his character in Uncle Buck.

My time spent in the Motherland is filled with such wickedly quirky moments - unexpected and almost lyrical in their delivery, like notes from a flute. Yet the music in my ears was not always so jaunty. As my personal life began to fray from the constant pull between my two identities, separated by the width of an ocean, I learned that the music could also sound like the saddest song I had ever heard.

*

It was Sean Collins and Des Hanrahan - my early travel guides and drinking companions - that introduced me to a Bunratty Castle musician named Angela Clancy. I fell head over heels and probably would have married her had I not at the time been living such a flighty existence. We stayed together for several years and her brothers, Frank, Christy, and Phil, who had a company called Central Shipping in Mountjoy Square, Baile Atha Cliath (Dublin), were like brothers to me. The Clancy family and I became very close, especially following the death of my father in 1971 and the death of Angela's dad a couple of years later. It was Angela that filled in all the blanks from my grandfather's teachings.

Angela took me to the General Post Office in Dublin where she pointed out the tricolors flying above, to the site of Nelson's Pillar, the Zoological Gardens, Phoenix Park and Croke Park as well. She sang songs of rebellion to me and played them for me on her violin. We traveled the entire country, and she would entertain me with renditions of 'The West's Awake' as we passed through the strange sounding places like Adrahan in Galway. Blown away by the beauty of the country, I was every bit as mesmerized by her ocean-colored eyes as by the endless shades of green now sliding past my vision.

The song, 'Come all you maidens young and fair, all you that are blooming in your prime', to this day reminds me of Angela. The little 'fiddler on the roof', as she was called by my neighbors on her visits to Miami, taught me everything I needed to know about my homeland, and in doing so rekindled the fire first lit by my grandfather. All of this education only intensified my love for Ireland. I had a passion for everything Irish - the people so full of humor, the places so full of charm, the land so full of beauty.

And one morning, I realized that I was smitten with one of its daughters as well; or to be more exact, the daughter of one Mr. Bill McNamara, who appeared like an angel in my life exactly when I needed her most.

I was first introduced to the McNamara family in the late '70s when Dan McNamara, the eldest son of Mr. Bill Mac, helped me put down some fencing on my farm. Dan Mac was interested to hear about my trips to Vietnam. Like so many others, he'd first assumed I was in Vietnam as a member of the United States Army; so, when I told him that I'd over ever entered 'Nam' out of Hong Kong with a CBS news crew (and that, in fact, I had been no fan of that doomed campaign as a matter of conscience), he had seemed relieved and even impressed. A sentiment shared by his father, who subsequently insisted that I break bread with him and his family at their home. This soon enough became an open invitation, and as we sat huddled in deep conversation, roasting to death next to the big old turf-burning stove, everyone enjoyed the bright new sparkle in the eyes of Bill McNamara.

I adored my time with Mr. Mac. As the sweat flowed from my forehead in that smoky ol' enclave, I grinned to myself, wanting to catch every word. I was hearing first-hand stories that fascinated the shit out of me.

Mr. Mac's' best friend was my 'godfather' Paddy Casey of County Clare, who lived in a caravan in the woods. Paddy was a gentleman in his eighties, whittled down to a lean piece of sinew, who could keep me grounded like no other. 'Stay cool, we are all just passing through life,' he would tell me, his eyes shining in the dusky light. 'Some of us make the journey and make a difference in the world we live in, while others just quietly pass through.' These words have never lost their impact.

Paddy was a simple old man who was thrilled by the personally autographed photos I brought to him of Muhammad Ali and Larry Holmes. I wondered how humbling it would have been for two of boxing's greatest heavyweight champions to see their photos hanging on the walls of this little caravan, down a simple muddy road, reeking of the smell of turf, to realize how far reaching their fame truly was.

Paddy Casey had no formal education but, like Don King, must have possessed a genius level I.Q. He was one of the most widely read individuals I ever met in my life, and I often spent cold, damp winter evenings sitting by the turf fire's dim light, listening to (and learning from) a man whose experiences spanned more than 80 years. There was hardly anything he skipped on Irish history. What an education I was getting, better than any national school education Ireland had to offer! My tuition fee with Paddy Casey consisted of a few Hennesey and Cokes, and the stories would go on and on, sounding to me so similar to the words I had listened to as a child with my grandfather.

Paddy and I often made an afternoon tea stop at Christy Farrel's Bar for a few brandies and a couple of pints of Guinness, so that there was a warm glow coming from our bellies as we talked and laughed. I loved that place and the stories he told. So much so that, while he spoke, I resisted getting up even to take a piss! By the time I did eventually make it to the urinal, my dick had usually turtled in so far I couldn't even grab it! But no matter. The romance of Ireland I was experiencing was worth every hardship.

I was also now in love.

Ena McNamara was a nurse in Tipperary and when she came home, we would leave with her brothers to dance and sing and be merry. We fell head over heels. And if it hadn't been for other events in my life, tripping me over as I tried to walk the happy path, the next couple of years might have been close to perfect.

Since 1969, when I finally took an interest in my homeland, my heart had been completely given over to Ireland. Fast-forward to 1978, both my father and mother had passed away, and I was experiencing a severe mental depression.

These were my darkest times.

Still residing in County Clare, I was commuting weekly for boxing shows back in the States - certainly twice monthly - and my mind was fast becoming a hornet's nest. So, when I met Ena, whose moral fiber was beyond reproach, I felt both ecstatic and born anew. She was like a steady hand on my racing chest.

Within only a few weeks, I decided that she would make a good wife.

We married in a wild Las Vegas cowboy-style wedding at the Little Church in the West. For myself, I flew in cowboy bandleader Dusty Drapes and his gang of rogues from Denver. And for Ena, who loved music but who had never been exposed to American pop culture, the Brendan Boyer's band from the Barbary Coast, accompanied by my pals Frankie Carroll, D.J. Curtain, Michael Keane, Paddy Reilly, Jimmy Conway - and all the way from the border in County Monahan, the drummer Mickey O'Neil. These men were among the most famous entertainers back home in Ireland. Ena was blown away. Her family, on the other hand, gave every impression of being flabbergasted.

County Claire to Boston is culture shock enough, but Las Vegas? Their jaws dropped harder than the Titanic on the seabed.

At six o'clock in the morning, the Caesar's house doctor told me I must postpone the wedding. 'You're in great danger,' he said as he pumped his sphygmomanometer. 'Your blood pressure is through the roof!'

I gulped down the remaining sips of my 30th Heineken of the night, and in my alcohol deluded brain came the quip, 'Hey Doc, don't tell me how high it is, how much further can it go?'

The doc just stared dumbly at me. There I was about to have a stroke, and I still can't resist showing off for my pals Stu Tauber, Kevin Dunn, and that Indian Barney from Boston we affectionately call 'the Barnyard', Neil Manning Jr.

I had to pony myself up. A short nap and a swig of mouthwash were the only elixirs at hand. I don't know what difference they made. As I rose from my slumber, my head feeling like an exploding can of Pepsi, I somehow made it to the altar to make my vows - helped down the aisle by the vicar himself!

The rest of the day, quite honestly, is a boozy blur. Sat at the head table in Caesar's Palace, of the eighteen women in our party, only Ena and her sister Nula were not members of the 'world's oldest profession'. Otherwise, the seats were filled by Irish farmers, cowboys, television executives of all sorts, and the Boston boys as well. A preposterous cross-section of characters if ever there was one, which in hindsight - and of course hindsight is always twenty-fucking-twenty - was a recipe for disaster.

This I do remember. We were out of our seats and on the dance floor, enjoying the ambience created by a couple of Colorado cowboys, Doug Day and Pat Brickley. You see, this pair of giant bronc riders had brought in bales of hay and horse nuggets by the ton to add to the atmosphere for the wedding photos. This worked a charm. We all had so much fun pretending that we were in a real-life Western, stamping our spurs and really playing it up for the photographer. That is, until the moment the Boston Irish, after much revelry, attacked Dusty Drapes' country band with the mounds of straw. This of course resulted in a melee worthy of a John Wayne movie. I even got involved a little myself - and had the time of my life for about fifteen minutes! However, Ena's family were far from impressed, and I believe the entire affair foreshadowed the chaos in my life and in our marriage.

I was a horrible husband. Hands to the sky. I was carrying too much mental luggage at the time, too much ego and way too much pain; it's little wonder I screwed up this relationship. She was a great girl, and she deserved much better. It was not her fault or any of her family's fault that I was a man in turmoil. Since my mother's death in 1978, I'd been totally out of control, and it mined our marriage.

For this I have a real and enduring regret.

Thankfully, there was a silver lining to be found. Since we were wedded in Vegas (in a ceremony more reminiscent of a rodeo than a wedding), we both lucked out. In the eyes of the Catholic Church we were never married, so we had peace with the Lord in spite of a bad break up. Still, I owed a lot to the McNamaras of Kilkishen, County

Clare. They kept me inspired when I was truly at my lowest ebb, and to this day, I have nothing but gratitude in my heart for each of them.

I know when I'm wrong. I was wrong to upset a beautiful human being like Ena, who was loyal till the end - even when others tried to poison her against me. The breakdown of our marriage was my failure to own, like a gutted-out sports car left to rust in the corner of some garage, only taking up space. I was back to dating floozies - I didn't deserve any better - and from that point onwards didn't really give a shit about my love life. As far as I was concerned, I'd never marry again. I was all right with the Catholic Church because of the circumstance of the wedding, so I buried myself in my budding rodeo career and the world of championship boxing. As long as I kept moving, I could ignore the heartache. Almost.

CHAPTER VIII

'RODEO DAZE'

I grew up dreaming of being a cowboy,
And lovin' the cowboy way,
Pursuing the life of my high ridin' heroes,
I burned up my childhood days.
I learned all the lessons of a modern-day drifter,
Don't ya hold on to nothin' too long.
Take what you need from the ladies and leave 'em,
With the words of a sad country song.
My heroes have always been cowboys
- Willie Nelson, 'My heroes have always been cowboys'
(Original song by Sharon Vaughn, Universal Music Publishing Group)

Most kids forget about being a cowboy - and the words of a sad country song - when they grow up. The only problem with me is, I never grew up. Marty Corwin (my former producer at Kingvision) and my late wife, Annie, both agreed that I'm 'an immense child in a grown man's body,' and you know what? I like it that way. So, from buying 'Woody', the horse of my childhood dreams, and from my association with agricultural-type folks, I got interested in the Florida Pro Rodeo Circuit.

I knew from the very first moment that I had to ride bulls.

Bull riding is the big event at every rodeo, and I just had to be part of it. So, in the late '60s and into the '70s, I would sneak off to Homestead, Davie, Arcadia and any little town to learn my newfound love of attempting to stay on the back of a wild bull for a full eight seconds. Just like my secret life in Ireland, I kept my cowboy training days to myself. I really didn't think it was a good career move for a young broadcaster to have everyone believe I was totally nuts!

In early May of 1979, however, a new newspaper by the name of The Clare News did a full page spread on me entitled 'Meet the Cowboy from Bunratty'. The following is the text of that article.

Bob Sheridan does some crazy things. He drives a beaten-up Morris Minor, yet uses Trans-Atlantic flights in and out of Shannon like a bus service. He calls it his "Shannon Shuttle." Last year he threw up his £35,000 per year job as a Miami sports commentator to set up a beef farm in Bunratty.

He's an Irish-American from classy Boston who is becoming one of the world's top professional rodeo attractions, and a 16 stone heavyweight who is best known for his television commentaries on world heavyweight championship fights.

He started coming back to the home of his ancestors, who hailed from Donegal, Mayo, and Cavan about 12 years ago, and has bought himself a small farm on the Hill Road, Bunratty, where he has set his dreams on running a pure-bred cattle operation with a prize bull and a few heifers.

A flamboyant larger than life character, Sheridan is straight out of a Harold Robbins best seller. He once bought himself a bar in Miami and turned it into an Irish Pub, just so he'd have a place he could enjoy St. Patrick's Day. On another occasion he paid the bill for every stranger in a restaurant except one ¬because that one person had annoyed him. Sports provided the springboard from a working-class background in Boston where his father was a Most kids forget about being a cowboy - and the words of a sad country song - when they grow up. The only problem with me is, I never grew up. Marty Corwin (my former producer at Kingvision) and my late wife, Annie, both agreed that I'm 'an immense child in a grown man's body,' and you know what? I like it that way. So, from buying 'Woody', the horse of my childhood dreams, and from my association with agricultural-type folks, I got interested in the Florida Pro Rodeo Circuit.

I knew from the very first moment that I had to ride bulls.

Bull riding is the big event at every rodeo, and I just had to be part of it. So, in the late '60s and into the '70s, I would sneak off to Homestead, Davie, Arcadia and any little town to learn my newfound love of attempting to stay on the back of a wild bull for a full eight seconds. Just like my secret life in Ireland, I kept my cowboy training days to myself. I really didn't think it was a good career move for a young broadcaster to have everyone believe he was totally nuts!

In early May of 1979, however, a new newspaper named The Clare News did a full-page spread on me entitled 'Meet the Cowboy from Bunratty'. The following is the text of that article.

"Bob Sheridan does some crazy things. He drives a beaten-up Morris Minor, yet uses Trans-Atlantic flights in and out of Shannon like a bus service. He calls it his "Shannon Shuttle." Last year he threw up his

£35,000 per year job as a Miami sports commentator to set up a beef farm in Bunratty.

He's an Irish-American from classy Boston who is becoming one of the world's top professional rodeo attractions, and a 16 stone heavyweight who is best known for his television commentaries on world heavyweight championship fights.

He started coming back to the home of his ancestors, who hailed from Donegal, Mayo, and Cavan about 12 years ago, and has bought himself a small farm on the Hill Road, Bunratty, where he has set his dreams on running a pure-bred cattle operation with a prize bull and a few heifers.

A flamboyant larger than life character, Sheridan is straight out of a Harold Robbins best seller. He once bought himself a bar in Miami and turned it into an Irish Pub, just so he'd have a place he could enjoy St. Patrick's Day. On another occasion he paid the bill for every stranger in a restaurant except one – because that one person had annoyed him. Sports provided the springboard from a working-class background in Boston where his father was a tinsmith, into international television stardom. His athletic ability got him to the University of Miami where he played the American game of baseball and from there a short stint into the world of professional baseball and then straight into radio.

Radio provided a natural steppingstone into television and Bob joined WCIX TV in Miami and was later signed by Video Techniques in New York, and later by Don King Productions to anchor the worldwide telecasts of championship boxing shows. Bob has done nearly 150 world title fights and is familiar to his new neighbors at Bunratty because they have seen his face introducing each weekly program in RTE's recent sports series on American football.

As a commentator he has been everywhere in the world except the Antarctic and has full plans to put that right as soon as he figures a way to get down to the South Pole.

Five years ago, Bob decided he was getting too soft. 'I was becoming a pussy,' he says. So, at the advanced age of 30 he decided to spend more time being a cowboy. For the past five years he has bruised and crushed his massive frame riding one-ton bulls, when by his own admission he should have been using his own weight in an event called steer wrestling. So why do you do it Bob? 'There is nothing more exciting in the world of sports than sitting down on the back of a wild bull and attempting to conquer your own fear by showing bigger balls than the beast you're attempting to ride.'

Bob has been dropping in on the land of his ancestors for the past 12 years to enjoy the Ireland he heard about from his grandfather. And now he has dropped out.

I have seen too many stars in broadcasting put out to pasture at age 45', he says. 'I wanted to get out before that.'

So now at the ripe old age of 35 he has retired to County Clare. 'I've been going to Goff's Sales for many years and noticed that Americans were buying a lot of pure-bred cattle here,' says Bob. Now he wants to set up his own pure bred cattle export operation and he is also exporting beef pancreas to the United States for the production of insulin.

The brawny Irish American who wears cowboy hats and contact lenses crosses the Atlantic three or four times a month as he is still in demand as a celebrity commentator, and he still loves to participate in rodeos where he is a major attraction."

As my life in Ireland began to deteriorate, gradually and then suddenly, I spent more and more time with the IRA in the States. That's the International Rodeo Association! I had met a rodeo producer by the name of Steve Gander who was on a trip to Ireland with his family. Steve and I spent an entire afternoon at the bar in Jury's Hotel in Dublin and, by day's end, I realized this guy was to rodeo as Don King was to boxing. Steve was very smart and had a plan for indoor rodeo shows that made an awful lot of sense to me, and I wanted to invest in his rodeo business.

I took a trip to the States to visit 'The World's Toughest Rodeo' as Steve Gander named his circuit, and his show was sensational. For the next couple of years, I was hooked, and I spent an awful lot of time with Steve Gander and even began riding bulls at his rodeos. One thing just kind of led on to the next. Here I was in my late 30s, a professional cowboy, and 'learning all the lessons of a modern-day drifter'. Not only was it fun being a child again and 'pursuing the life of my high ridin' heroes', but these guys were some of the very best athletes I'd ever met in my life.

Never mind Muhammad Ali, Nick Buoniconti, or Bob Griese; you had guys like Dan Daily, Tom Walker, Wendal Ratchford, Jimmy Mack, Randy Stephens, 'ol J. W. Wilson, Red Doffin, Jack Weisman and Ronnie Williams - to name just a handful - whose bodies really could handle the kinetic explosion of bull riding as though it was nothing! Night after night I'd compete with these men that no matter how banged up they might be - and they were all banged up to shit - 'You only have to stay on for eight seconds, so 'Cowboy Up!" was the invincible cry.

I've got great memories outside of the arena as well. I'll never forget the night in Minneapolis when the bulls broke out of the farm where we were keeping them. Mike Ladding, his dad Thyrl, Tonch Hertzel, Johnny Brown, Joe Copeland and I saddled up and went to round them up in a residential district. The local cops were scared shitless and were ready to shoot these magnificent beasts. It was like a scene from a movie. You talk about laughing your ass off in minus 15-degree temperatures for about an hour until we had them all back under control.

Then there was the night in Cedar Rapids, Iowa . . . when the cops came up to the top of the Stouffers Four Seasons Hotel to break up a major league pillow fight that had erupted. One of the ropers lassoed and hog-tied one of the cops while his partner laughed hysterically and drank a few beers with us.

The groupies were fantastic too. We had girls in every city and town. Not only were they great for their array of sexual feats, but these cowgirl wannabes were dedicated. I remember one group of ladies that followed us all the way from Dubuque, Iowa to Little Rock, Arkansas in the same weekend. You just don't get groupies like that in professional football, basketball, or baseball!

As I got older riding bulls got tougher, and as hard as world champion bull rider Wendal Ratchford worked with me, the Paul's Valley, Oklahoma cowboy didn't have much success.

I was just too big for riding bulls. I was in peak shape at 225 pounds, but power has nothing to do with staying on the back of a bull. First, you set your rope in position on the bull while he's standing in the chute, then you grasp the loop in the rope that is wrapped around the girth of the beast. All you have is your grip to keep the rope tight and in position. You dig your spurs into his hide and nod for chute boss, John Galiano, to open the gate. Now the idea is to lean forward over your rope, stay in the middle of the big back, and don't hit the bull or touch yourself with your free hand that you use for balance. If you can get a chance to spur the bull at any time, you can get a few extra points; but I never experienced a time when I wasn't in some kind of world of mayhem while attempting to stay on, so needless to say I didn't do too much spurring.

The bull has a lot of weapons to use on you. First and foremost, he knows exactly what his horns are for. So, if he gets a chance while he throws his ass up in the air, he will throw his head back and try to snatch you right out of your seat with his horns. If that isn't enough to scare the shit out of you, the bull will rely on his repertoire which includes amazing power, speed, belly rolls, spins, outside whips, change of direction, big front end drops with an occasional feint, coupled with a high back kick. Along with all of these moves, bulls have very loose skin that tends to slide around with very slight movements. If all this fails, the good hooking bulls will always have one last go at you in an attempt to kill you when you do come off.

Rodeo clowns Jimmy Mack, Ben Eby and Mike Ulmer kept me from an early grave on many occasions. I remember the day of Al Michaels' great call of the 'Do you believe in miracles!' Olympic hockey victory and gold for the United States team. We were at the Pershing Coliseum in Lincoln, Nebraska, and I got the shit stomped out of me when a bull did a tap dance on my body - hitting me in the neck, the ankle, left shoulder, and stepping on my right thigh. To add insult to the numerous injuries

I sustained, all of the time he was circling on top of me he was also pissing on me. Both Jimmy and Mike risked their own welfare to get me out alive. I was one beaten up cowboy, but I still loved it. A week later we were in the Barton Coliseum in Little Rock and a big brindle-colored bull hooked me up into the stands, and I came down on a fixed chair and broke my back. I got some great care at the University of Arkansas Medical Centre, but the first few hours were very tough emotionally.

I thought I had been paralyzed because I had no feeling in my legs.

The next morning a priest came in to have a chat with me. He gave me communion and within ten minutes I had total feeling back. I got cold chills from the experience. One minute I thought I was facing a wheelchair, the next minute after taking communion I was totally healed. You gotta be shittin' me! The Lord just gave me a little warning. 'Time to get back on the straight and narrow,' I thought. What had actually happened was I broke the fourth and fifth lumbar transverse process. I didn't actually hurt the spinal column. In the process the sciatic nerves were pushed together like the pinching of a straw, which limited the blood supply to my legs, causing the lack of feeling. No matter what had happened I was on an emotional high.

The next day my buddy Lonnie, who lost his thumb in the bucking chute, was placed in my room and we had an absolute ball. We'd send out for steak dinners for all the nursing staff to join in with us, and every afternoon - dressed in cowboy hats, scarfs, boots and spurs, and with our hospital johnnies and our I.V. drips in tow - we'd head over to the bar across the street (without permission!) for an afternoon of debauchery before returning to the orthopedic wing absolutely shitfaced.

My rodeo days were great. I loved the friends I met and the times I had. I even loved the hard knocks. I think Linda Montet, writing for a small newspaper in Iowa called The Republican-Standard, captured the role I played as the Bunratty Cowboy/ Irish Cowboy in her column entitled 'Flying Free'.

"The Republic-Standard: January 8, 1980: I used to think interviewing foreigners was boring. It's natural for journalists to be attracted to visiting persons from other countries. After all, they're different, they have a unique perspective on our lives and our society, and they are generally newsworthy.

But my problem has always been finding something different to ask them. After a few years at reporting, and a few hundred rounds of "How do you like America?" and "How do American boys compare with those back home in Tibet?" I have run out of original questions to ask.

A trip to the library will net a few important facts about the interviewee's native home, and might make the questions a bit more professional sounding (i.e. "I understand in Liberia a bush pilot doesn't need a license, is that correct?") but in the long run, who cares?

Like I said, that's the way I used to think. I've changed my mind.

Last spring, upon arriving at the office, sleepy but unruffled, one morning, I was met with a memo of a phone call from a county dairy farmer, instructions on how to get to Frankville via highway 76, and the suggestion that the sooner I started, the better, because there was a visiting Irish cattle rancher waiting for me to arrive for an interview.

"What a way to ruin a perfectly adequate morning! " I groaned, rolling up my pantlegs and stuffing some film in the camera. And to make it worse, there's not even time to go to the library!

I took three wrong turns, backtracked five miles, and pulled up at the farmer's door half an hour late. He greeted me at the door with a pleasant smile, apologizing for being in the middle of breakfast, but adding, "Come right on in and join us."

I rounded the corner from the vestibule into the kitchen, and at exactly that moment a cowboy-booted giant of an Irishman leaped to his feet, spread his arms, hollered, "Shore an' begorra, what a fine lookin' woman!" and planted a huge bacon-and-eggs kiss directly upon my mouth, bending me backwards to the floor in the process.

I might have been totally discombobulated, but at least I was awake. I gathered up my scattered notes, situated my dangling camera, and attempted to begin the interview.

"What part of Ireland are you from? " I uttered — a perfectly innocent question, and one that might give me time to think of a better query.

"Galway!" was his robust response.

"I've heard of that," I offered, pleased that the name was familiar. "We have a song with lyrics about Galway Bay."

That was all he needed. He jumped from his chair again, grabbed the catsup bottle by the neck microphone-style, and belted out, "If you ever go across the sea to Ireland ," kneeling at my feet and clutching my hand to his cheek — pencil and all.

By now the interview was completely out of my control, so I mostly listened to his tales of rodeo riding, Irish style, nodded in the appropriate places, and tried to protect my body as much as possible.

"Would you like to try a bit of snuff?" he asked as we walked toward the cattle lot later, thrusting a round tin can under my nose.

Now it was my turn. "Why not?" I answered, taking a pinch of the stringy tobacco, "but you'll have to show me how. It's my first time."

For a moment he was stunned. Then he laughed heartily, and told me in heavy brogue, "Begorra woman, I've offered the stuff to every woman

I've come across in the last eight years, and you're the first one's ever a' done it." I felt a cheerful slap on my back, and I stuck the crumbly plug between my teeth and lower lip and commenced spitting.

The rest of the morning was spent knee deep in spring-fresh manure, with my left cheek becoming numb and swollen twice its size. I snapped a few shots of the group and the beasts, and then excused myself, scraped my boots and headed for the car.

"You know that stuff will give you the dry heaves," the farmer whispered in my ear as I thanked him for the experience and headed back to town.

He was right."

Linda Montet captured me perfectly . . . 'Take what you need from the ladies and leave 'em with the words of a sad country song.'

Despite my outward attitude, where the world was truly my stage, I knew I'd have to quit the rodeo. I looked in the mirror and realized I was too old, in terrible physical shape, and I had been given one good warning. I made up my mind I'd give it one last shot. In three months 'the World's Toughest Rodeo' was going east and I had to ride in Madison Square Garden.

I worked that summer at a riding stable up in New Hampshire, spent the month of August back in Ireland, and by September I was ready to ride. My neighbors on the Hill Road, John and Catherine Toomey, were coming out to the rodeo on their honeymoon. My brother, Jim, brought down about twenty of his friends from Boston to see me ride for the first time. I had an assortment of television, boxing, and advertising types from New York all there for me. The pressure was on.

I climbed on to this big black crossbred bull with pointed twisting horns. My heart was pounding in rhythm with the bull. As Joe Copeland pulled up my rope and laid it across my hand, I glanced up to see my name on the scoreboard of Madison Square Garden. 'Bob Sheridan, the Irish Cowboy, Shannon, Ireland.' Marty Martins, our announcer, gave me a big build up. I was in a cold sweat, the hair on my neck was at full attention, I was breathing deeply, and nodded to Thyrl Ladding to open the gate. Next thing I knew, I was on my nose in the mud and the shit! The gate wasn't even closed. In a split second, I had been bucked with such violence that I'd slid back on my rope out of the chute, and on the first big jump I was in orbit. My brother Jim's comments were most comforting. 'You fuckin' asshole. I brought 25 people down here for the weekend to watch my brother, the big professional cowboy. Shit, I could have stayed on longer than that!' The fact of the matter is, he probably could have.

But he didn't.

It's just like the thousands of guys I hear every day say in every bar I visit, 'Heck, I'd get into the ring with Mike Tyson for a million dollars.' Yeah, just about anybody would. The only problem is, you have to pay the price to get there before you get the chance to get in there. Before you get the reward.

I had been present for 'the Fight of the Century', as they called it, when Muhammad Ali fought Joe Frazier in Madison Square Garden, and that was definitely a big thrill at the time, but it was nothing in comparison to the last bull I didn't ride in the mecca of boxing. Yes, boxing has been and continues to be great for me. I love the sport and still pinch myself when I realize I'm inducted into the Hall of Fame, but the fact of the matter remains, 'My heroes have always been cowboys.'

CHAPTER IX

'THE KING AND I — DON KING'

I love Don King. I first sat down to write a few words about my dear friend and boss in the late 1990s, and you know what? I've decided to preserve those words. They were from the heart and, I believe, will surprise anyone who thinks they have the measure of the man. Then, in part two of this chapter, I hope to make you smile as I recount a more recent memory, asking you to consider, once and for all, whether King over the past half a century has been fairly portrayed by the media, or whether, in fact, he has been downright vilified. Because, if you're asking me, the man I know could not be any more different.

PART ONE

It is ironic Don King is a boxing promoter. Nothing could be more prophetic. Don is a fighter; moreover, he is a winner. His faith in God and family, along with his desire to be the best, has helped him live the American Dream.

To me, loyalty is his greatest virtue. I've broadcasted every single big fight Don has promoted. Even before the establishment of Don King Productions, he and I worked together for Hank Schwartz and Barry Bernstein at Video Techniques in New York City. Barry told me, 'Don King is the future of boxing. You stick close to him.' Since March of 1974, and the Foreman vs. Norton fight in Caracas, Venezuela, I've remained close to Don King. He has rewarded my loyalty with his absolute loyalty to me. Now, don't get the wrong idea. We are not buddy-buddy. It's a professional relationship. I never approach him, I never socialize with him, and in fact, I rarely even talk to him unless he wants to speak with me. But through mutual respect and appreciation, we both get exactly what we want from each other.

King believes a man's word to be gold, and he will not make a promise unless he can deliver. It is his combination of negotiating style, charisma, and keen business sense that spells worldwide acclaim and recognition.

At an age when most people would be calling it quits and retiring to enjoy the fruits of their labors, the nearly 70-year-old Don King continues to set new records and stage the best fights the sport has to offer. However, few people really know the measure of the man. Don King is often regarded as the 'P. T. Barnum of boxing' for his amazing accomplishments in creating spectacular events. Don has consistently put on more great fights - and more world championships on the same card - than any promoter in history. Several years ago, he embarked on a crusade to make world championship boxing available to people all across America to fulfil a promise he made to bring boxing back to the people. He staged unprecedented cards for previously neglected boxing fans. And when it comes to mega events, nobody comes close to this charismatic genius. Don King was the creator and driving force behind seven of the top ten Pay Per View events of all time, including the top three events ever held. Don's broadcasts are enjoyed in more than 120 countries by over 2 billion viewers.

In the illustrious history of boxing, Don has eclipsed every other promoter in the sport. He has set standards which his 'competitors' can only hope to attain. History tells of great promoters, such as Tex Rickard and Mike Jacobs, but Don King has shattered all marks and is still rewriting history.

It's no wonder Don is renowned as the world's greatest promoter. On June 28, 1997, King promoted the biggest show in the history of the sport. Evander Holyfield retained his WBA heavyweight title after defeating Mike Tyson in three rounds. More than 1.95 million households nationwide and closed-circuit viewers in more than 110 countries watched this tremendous fight, along with 16,331 in attendance at the MGM Grand in Las Vegas. The live gate grossed more than $14 million, making The Sound and the Fury: Holyfield-Tyson II the most successful boxing event ever. For me personally, the MGM was my recovery room following my third heart attack and emergency angioplasty the night before.

There have been many more great nights.

On February 20, 1993, 'the Grand Slam of Boxing' featured four world championships on one card, headlined by Mexican hero Julio Cesar Chavez. Mexico City's Estadio Azteca was the site where 136,274 (132,274 paid) turned out to break the previous paid attendance record set September 23, 1926, for the Jack Dempsey-Gene Tunney bout at Sesquicentennial Park in Philadelphia. For me, it was the most electrifying night as a broadcaster in nearly 30 years, since 'Ali-Boom-Aye-A' in the 20th of May Stadium in Kinshasa, Zaire. During 1994, Don promoted more than 20 world championship fights (WBA, WBC or IBF) for the third time in his legendary career. The grand total for that year was 47 championship bouts, shattering King's world record of 25 bouts promoted during 1986. And people think I'm a bullshit artist when I tell them I've broadcast over 600 world title fights to date and nearly ten thousand in total on radio and TV.

Don King's career as a promoter spans three decades. It all started when King asked Muhammad Ali to do a benefit fight for Forest City Hospital in Cleveland, which was going to be closed for lack of funding. Don went to Ali and asked if he would lend his support to this worthy cause. Ali agreed and Don was on his way.

Following the hospital benefit, Don signed a deal with Ali and George Foreman, which guaranteed each boxer in excess of $5 million, then an unprecedented amount. One of the financial backers King had asked to help in the making of this fight didn't believe King really could pull it off. When he learned that both Ali's and Foreman's signatures were on the contracts that King held, and they were authentic, as proven by experts, the man became enraged and pulled out of the fight. With seemingly nowhere to turn, King was able to get a guarantee from the government of Zaire, Africa. Don King did what nobody thought could be done and, as a result, The Rumble in the Jungle has gone down in history as one of the greatest events in sports history. To this day, my experiences in Zaire are amongst the most memorable of my career.

Ed Schuyler, Pat Putnam, and I have shared many moments together over the years. I truly enjoy the company of these two men for their sense of humor and their ability to hold their drink, but what I admire even more is their fairness in writing about Don King. Eddie can't resist poking fun at Don in his annual column on 'the King's English', where he good-naturedly highlights Don's occasional malapropisms, like 'St. Thomas Aquinine' instead of St. Thomas Aquinas. It's all in good fun, and Don King would be the first to laugh. However, most writers are simply mean-spirited, failing to understand that, in addition to controlling fighters and TV networks, establishing excellent relationships with the heads of rating organizations like the WBC, WBA, IBF, and the WBO is crucial in the business of boxing. Don King simply excels at this, making him the subject of an ongoing media witch hunt that has lasted over twenty years, driven by profit-seeking lies. It's undeniable, especially when you consider that every other boxing promoter plays (or aims to play) the same game.

I should know. Cedric Kushner used me in Germany to call the IBF heavyweight championship the night Francois Botha won the title over Axel Schulz. I'll never forget it, because we needed a police escort to get out of town amidst death threats! I've loved Cedric Kushner ever since the day he caught me coming down the elevator years ago at one of the boxing conventions with two of the sluttiest looking high-heeled, mini-skirted, big haired, huge breasted whores in the world. He echoed in his finest South African accent, 'Colonel, at least they don't look like prostitutes.' How can you not love a guy with this kind of a sense of humor?

Then there is the Duva family. I became close to the Duvas while broadcasting a David Tua fight in Auckland, New Zealand, over Thanksgiving week for Kevin Barry, the Olympic silver medalist who beat Evander Holyfield. I was doing the national telecast for Network 3, my usual spot, and I got to spend a lot of time with them. I felt sorrowful when I learned of the premature death of Dan Duva, who succumbed to brain cancer. His wife Kathy, now playing a key role in steering the company, is a tough businesswoman but a truly lovely person. The silver-haired Lou Duva, a first cousin of wrestling superstar Captain Lou Albano, is a wonderful guy too, and I've always considered him a great boxing trainer. He heads the Duva boxing empire, called Main Events Monitor, but, more importantly, I consider him to be a good friend. Due to Lou's Italian background, he gets linked to ties with organized crime and accused of being a former leg breaker for the Teamsters. But just like most of the rumors on Don King, the stories about Lou Duva's connections with organized crime are nonsense. There is absolutely no connection between organized crime and boxing, and there hasn't been since the early '60s. The media knows this, just as they know that Don is not the cartoon villain that they portray him to be. However, inasmuch as it sparks public interest, both the sport of boxing and its most successful proponent do actually benefit from this unearned infamy.

Today, Don King is one of the most recognizable figures, not only in America, but throughout the world. He is on a first name basis with many presidents, diplomats, celebrities, and civic leaders. His face has graced the covers of Time, Sports Illustrated, Ebony and Jet, as well as countless other magazines and newspapers worldwide. He has appeared in movies and television shows and has been a talk show guest of Johnny Carson, Arsenio Hall, David Letterman, Conan O'Brien, Joan Rivers and Barbara Walters.

Don King's inexhaustible energy has carried him around the world, bringing boxing to new heights. His accomplishments have not gone unnoticed by his peers. In addition to being the only promoter included in the Sports Illustrated list of the forty most influential sports figures of the last forty years, Don King was recently inducted into the Boxing Hall of Fame, an honor bestowed upon him by boxing writers and historians.

It's easy to see why so many great boxers have come to King for promotional guidance. His charisma and style are unmatched; however, it is his unsurpassed work ethic that keeps him on top. Red Barber and Hall of Fame coach Don Shula were a lesson in preparation, but Don King is an absolute slave to his workaholism. How can you beat a man whose mind doesn't even stop when he sleeps?

If ever a man exemplified the definition of the American Dream, it would have to be Don King. Born in the ghetto of Cleveland on August 20, 1931, King is proof that no matter what background a person comes from, anyone who is willing to work hard can achieve and live that dream. Don has become famous for his saying, 'Only in America.' He explains, 'Only in America can a Don King happen. America is the greatest country in the world. I love America. What I've accomplished could not have been done anywhere else.'

Given that they followed a 1968 manslaughter conviction and four years spent in a prison cell, these achievements are all the more impressive. He did not let circumstances defeat him. Instead, he used the time to educate himself and prepare for a life of prosperity beyond the bars of the Marion Correctional Institution, where he turned his life around with intellect and raw determination. What better example could a guy set?

In Don King's new international headquarters, he has assembled his world-renowned team of boxing managers, matchmakers, event coordinators, broadcasting professionals, travel specialists and international sales associates. He has also become the first boxing promoter to build his own in-house television studio and editing facility. His world headquarters in Deerfield Beach, Florida, is an absolute showplace! It's a temple to the success of Don King with the tasteful design of his wife Henrietta. Above his new home it was only fitting that Don installed the largest flagpole in the southeast United States to show people he means what he says, 'Only in America.'

I'll ask this simple question: Is this the same man so unfairly portrayed by Jack Newfield in the 'Frontline' character assassination or in the HBO special? Is this the villain portrayed in the movie 'The Great White Hype?' Not the Don King I've known for 25 years. Sure, Don King has signed a lot of paychecks for me over the years. I'll admit his autograph on a Sun Trust Bank of South Florida check is my favorite celebrity autograph. But I'd do this job for nothing, so when I say, 'I love the man,' I mean it! In one of our few private chats in years, I recently went into his big ass office to ask for a raise in my fight talent fee and before I got the question completely stumbled out, I had my answer. 'Y-E-S! You are my Colonel.' And with one shout to his secretary my income immediately doubled.

Such generosity is the norm for Don.

Away from the cameras, he has always been deeply committed to sharing his good fortune with others. He donates millions of dollars each year to worthwhile causes. Don has been especially supportive of education, launching a campaign to donate school supplies to Title I children in inner city schools. He didn't stop there either. Understanding better than anyone the power contained in knowledge, Don also gave each child a copy of the constitution so that they could learn what he already knows about America. He says it all the time, 'This is the greatest country in the world!'

Don King is like a fine wine; he just gets better with age. The record speaks for itself. Simply put, he IS the world's greatest promoter. The only records left for Don King to break are his own. I can assure you that the Don King you think you know, because of the way the media vilifies the man, is not the same Don King I've grown to know and love over the past quarter of a century.

PART TWO

We were in Paris for an event - the rematch between world cruiserweight champion O'Neil Bell and French challenger Jean Marc Mormeck. After wrapping up the telecast and the post-fight presser, we settled into a charming restaurant with a view over a slice of the city. As I looked out at the softly lit streets of Levallois-Perret, I found myself getting a little buzzed on red wine and more than a little distracted by the sight of so many stunning women. It was our last night in that crazy town, and I was feeling pretty relaxed.

'Colonel, I'm heading to the Vatican to meet the Pope!'

'Oh, yeah?' I raised an eyebrow.

'You betcha. I've got a private audience with him.'

'The Pope?' I couldn't help but chuckle.

'Yep, that's the one. Just got the confirmation. VIP access, just me and a select few.'

Don had a way of making his words strut. Of giving them a rhythm and style, like jazz, that made you sit up and listen. Still, I knew this was bullshit. Pope Benedict didn't grant private audiences, not even to Heads of State. Don King is a big deal, but he's not that big of a deal. Somebody had fed him some faulty info. The work was done, another sold-out championship card in the books. But now, I was feeling on edge. Who the hell had been feeding him this crap?

Knowing that Don was a devoted Catholic, I could sense the excitement rising from his loafers - it seemed kind of a shame to pour sand on his parade.

I tried to explain, 'Don, you're gonna go there on a Wednesday, right?'

'Sure am, how'd you know?'

'I know because that's when he grants his general audience. That's a different thing entirely. Now look, unless you listen to me very carefully, you're not gonna have a private audience with the Pope at all.'

'No no, don't worry about it, Colonel. I've got a priest in Italy helping me out.'

I sighed. 'Don, do you understand that Archbishops and Cardinals, they're all flunkies to the Pope? Your priest in Italy got you into in the VIP section, which is fine, but the problem is - there are about 800 seats in the VIP section!' The smile before me sagged and I felt some darkness creep out. 'I mean, it's great he did that for you,' I continued, 'but let me tell you what I'm gonna do for you. I'm gonna call the Captain of the Swiss Guard, Pino Coco, and Pino will come off duty and he'll take care of you.'

Animated by this opportunity to show off my startling connections within the Catholic Church (something I'll discuss a little later), I instructed him: 'Don't wear your dungaree suit. Don't wear all your jewelry. Don't wear a hat, don't wear anything but a black tie, a black suit, and your cross with all the diamonds on it. That's it - and maybe a couple of rings.' He nodded, but the eyes were vacant. Only half sure that he was taking me seriously, I continued: 'Tomorrow, I'll tell you exactly what to do.'

So, I call Pino, who's a dear friend of mine, and I say, 'Pino, Wednesday Don King is coming to the Vatican.'

'Bob, I know that. That's why I'm taking the day off!'

Damn, these Europeans.

'Pino, you gotta do me a favor. You gotta get about ten Guards on him.'

'I've got four assigned to him already.'

'That's not enough.'

'Are you serious?'

'Pino, you've known me for 30 years, we've been through a lot together. I'm telling you how to avoid a fuckin' scene!'

'Look, tell him how to get to the Porta Sant'Anna (Saint Anne's Gate), which is right next to the Vatican bank, and right next to the Guard's barracks, and have him be there at exactly 10 o'clock. And make sure he understands, it's the Porta Sant'Anna!'

I replied, 'He's gonna have about 30 people with him.'

'If he's got 30 people with him, I can't do much, okay?' Pino was always a straight shooter with me, and he was one hundred percent right.

The next day, I get Don on the phone - with Pino - and I say, 'Mr. King, this is Mr. Coco, Captain of the Swiss Guard at the Vatican; and from there on in they chatted like old pals. See, despite being in the rarefied service of the world's oldest and holiest institution (in what amounted to a blood oath), Coco was actually a huge boxing fan as well, and he couldn't believe he was really on the line with the world-famous Don King! Everything came off great.

Following the call, I told Don, 'Just take your flags, because the Pope isn't going to stand around and have a long chat with you. You're gonna get a picture taken with him and he'll stop by and talk to you for about ten seconds - max.'

So, sure enough, Coco meets Don at the Porta Sant'Anna and escorts him to the front row of the well-attended gathering, where Don, undoubtedly, would catch the attention of Pope Benedict. After all, in my experience, nobody ever missed Don King in a crowded room! While still in Paris together, I had cautioned him as sternly as I could (the man was, after all, still my boss) to forget the entourage, suggesting he might only be able to bring one other person inside, depending on Coco's mood. Don obliged without protest, thrilled at the prospect of having the opportunity just for himself. As a result, not even his priest from Italy, who clearly didn't know a damn thing about Vatican City and its protocols, had made the cut - which caused me to chuckle.

Priest or not, who the fuck did this guy think he was?

Feeling pretty good about myself after hearing from Coco, I was satisfied that my connections at the Vatican had been validated and pleased that Don was getting the VIP treatment he'd been promised. That was, however, until I got the full story of what took place. This next part still pisses me off.

According to my fly on the wall, Don was in there smiling like the Cheshire cat, draped in jewelry, and fidgeting in his chair. Everyone's eyes were fixed on the door at the far end of the chapel inside St. Peter's Basilica, where they expected Pope Benedict to emerge. After a couple of minutes, that same door swings open, and accompanied by the Guard with all their color and pomp, the Holy Father walks into the cloistered area. And guess what? Without skipping a beat, he beelines straight for Don. Incredible! I guess his trademark shock of hair acted as some kind of beacon.

Col. Bob Sheridan with Muhammad Ali.

Col. Bob Sheridan with Mike Tyson.

Col. Bob Sheridan with Don King.

Col. Bob Sheridan with Joseph Parker of New Zealand.

Christmas Card from Don King to Col. Bob Sheridan.

Pre-fight meeting with Muhammad Ali , Dr Freddy Pachecho and Cruiserweight World Champion Bobby Czyz.

Col. Bob Sheridan with Frankie Billy Randall 'The Surgeon' three-time WBA & WBC World Welterweight Champion.

Col. Bob Sheridan with Father Ed McCabe at the Vatican.

Col. Bob Sheridan with Christy Martin comparing Boxing Hall Of Fame rings.

Col. Bob Sheridan with Marty Corwin his producer at Don King Productions for 35 years.

Col. Bob Sheridan with 68th Governor of Massachusetts Bill Weld and Col. James.

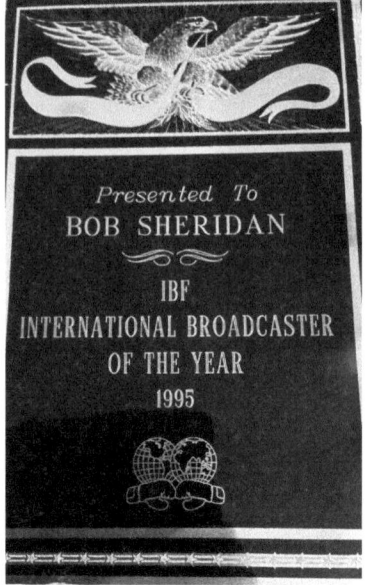

Col. Bob Sheridan with his late wife
Anne Kelly Sheridan and Lucy.

Col. Bob Sheridan IBF award International
Broadcaster Of The Year 1995.

Col. Bob Sheridan meeting & interviewing World Champion Evander Holyfield.

Col. Bob Sheridan with Larry Holmes a/k/a The Eastern Assassin' WBC Heavyweight World Champion (1978-1983)

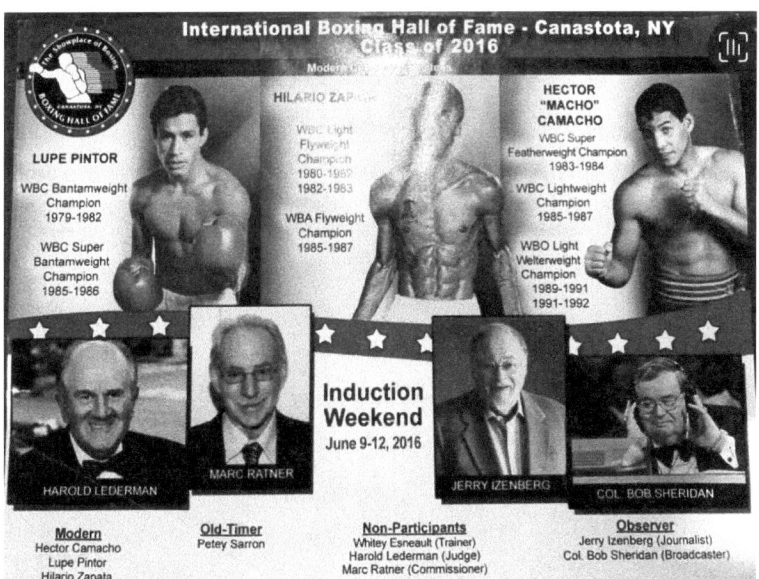

Col. Bob Sheridan with Prince Naseem.

Col. Bob Sheridan with multiple world champion Felix Trinidad and Anne Sheridan.

Col. Bob Sheridan with Rev Colonel Ed McCabe and The Pope of Eastern Right Church (Bartholomew the First) Istanbul, Turkey.

Col. Bob Sheridan with John Horn former manager of Mike Tyson.

Col. Bob Sheridan ringside at work.

Col. Bob Sheridan with Don King and lady friends.

Col. Bob Sheridan with Anne Kelly Sheridan.

Col. Bob Sheridan ringside with Kris Kristofferson.

Dr. Ferdie Pacheco with Muhammed Ali and Luista Pacheco in 1977.

And if that wasn't astounding enough, I then find out that the Pope spends about five minutes chatting with his American guest. What the fuck!

Whenever I go to the Vatican for an audience with the Pope, I get one minute. One! I'd never once had the incredible experience that Don King enjoyed. It was sickening. But I did have one consolation. Don had brought his own photographer, thinking he was going to get a whole bunch of snaps taken with Pope Benedict. Well, in short order, the hands of the ad hoc Jimmy Olsen were nearly shorn off! You see, unauthorized pictures of the Pope are strictly prohibited. Haven't you ever noticed that photographs of the Holy Father are always perfect? How nobody has a picture of the Pope with his finger up his nose or anything like that? The idea is that he must be viewed almost as a deity. Still, Don did manage to get one picture in the bag that morning, taken by the official Vatican photographer - and boy, did he make it count.

For the rest of the day, there was nothing from Don. No thank you. No go screw yourself. Nothing. I hadn't spoken to Pino yet either. Naturally, I was wondering if something had gone wrong. With Don, you never know. And then I see it. Filling my computer screen as I click onto the website, the now-famous photograph of Don standing beside Pope Benedict with the WBC belt front and center of the shot - dedicating his Papal visit to the organization's late, great former President, Jose Sulaiman! I burst out laughing. So much for asking the Pope to pray for world peace! I mean, this guy is just unbelievable. In the holiest place on earth, with the tiniest of windows through which to maneuver, he's still working the angles and making the plays - turning the whole thing into a PR stunt. The man has no off switch.

Weeks passed before I saw him again. Frankly, I was a bit pissed. Then, one random afternoon, as I stood chatting with some of the guys in the office, breaking balls, he bounded over to me with that million-dollar smile, and he said: 'Hey Colonel, my man, you got a lot of juice at the Vatican. Everybody knows you!' I couldn't believe my ears. Radio silence since the visit and that was what he finally comes out with - from the clear blue sky! I had to laugh. It was actually hilarious. 'Don,' I said, with a twinkle in my eye. 'You made me the world's most famous commentator, but if you'd shut the fuck up for a second, I'd be even more famous!

That's mine and Don's relationship in a nutshell.

Now, let me clear up a common misconception. I never worked for Don King Productions; I worked with them. The Colonel was, is, and forever shall be a free agent. I don't even bother with contracts. Nevertheless, to me, Don will always be my boss. After all, I remember well the extreme opposition to our collaboration in the 1970s (and even into the '80s) as racial tensions in America continued to cool following the scorching Civil Rights campaign of the previous decade. Back then, his inner circle made no secret of their belief that a lily-white Mick like me should not have been the face of what they thought of as 'a black company'. But Don stuck with me all the same. All class.

The man simply staged big-time fights. From my side of the ring, I've always aimed to fight back against the trash talk about his character - especially the stuff saying he exploited fighters. Throughout the years, these media-driven claims have stuck to Don like the proverbial tar and feathers. I've even had to square off with Mike Tyson and Larry Holmes, who are both good buddies of mine, over this topic. But we all know deep down, Don made them a boatload of cash. And isn't that what a fight promoter's supposed to do? I sure as hell don't think it's to play babysitter or financial advisor.

At the age of 90, Don King has not yet retired - but he's now very slow in what he does. He still maintains a beautiful office in Oakland Park Boulevard, in Fort Lauderdale, where his daughter Debbie still works for him and is keeping the ship afloat. Sadly, since losing his wife more than ten years ago, Don has lost a lot of his spunk and has gradually faded from public view. An undeniable loss for the sport he once reigned over and a clear indication that the media, who for decades painted him as a man without morals, couldn't have been any more full of shit. In my experience of knowing him, Don has always been above all else a family man, and I believe the loss of Henrietta broke his heart. As will the heart of the boxing world on the day we lose the great man himself.

Knowing Don has been my life's honor. He became one of the most famous people on Earth because his true aim was never to promote boxing, it was always to promote himself. He also understood that every event he staged was only ever an advertisement for the next one. For this reason, I regard myself as one of the luckiest men alive. I don't know too many people who have had the privilege to sit across from an icon like Don, smoke a nice Cuban cigar, and shoot the shit for hours on end. Because take it from me, while an audience with the Pope is a profoundly spiritual experience, an audience with Don King - even as he climbs the very highest branches of old age - is a profoundly entertaining one.

There will never be another.

CHAPTER X

'MUHAMMAD, GEORGE, AND ME — THAT NIGHT IN AFRICA'

I was expecting the call from Barry Bernstein at Video Techniques. I'd been hired by Barry to do the commentary for George Foreman's previous heavyweight title defense against Kenny Norton in Venezuela earlier that year, and with my ego, of course I assumed they'd want me back again for the big one.

I wasn't wrong.

After beating the shit out of Kenny in a couple of rounds, the most anticipated showdown in boxing was set. Foreman was going to meet former champion Muhammad Ali in Zaire, Africa, in a blockbuster event. This was no secret, as Ali himself had announced the fight to the world while sitting next to me at the El Poliedro, in Caracas, moments before Big George mauled poor Kenny in a matter of minutes.

'George Foreman and I have just been offered five million dollars apiece by the Government of Zaire,' he said live on the air, moments after getting into it with another heavyweight rival, Oscar Bonavena of Argentina, who was in the ring for the introductions along with the great Joe Louis. 'So, if he can win this fight tonight, which I don't think he will, he'll have to defend his belt in the Congo!'

Ali was doing color commentary with me that night, and he was hyped - a ball of bristling energy. We knew each other well from the 5th Street Gym, where he trained and I loitered, getting my education in the art of prizefighting. In fact, earlier in the broadcast, he had even referred to Miami Beach as our shared stomping ground, to which I quickly replied, 'We've certainly done some stomping around Miami, Ali.' So, I felt comfortable around Muhammad and confident in my interactions with him - unlike so many others in the media who were overwhelmed by the tidal wave of his personality. But in the aftermath of Big George's destruction of Norton - a man against whom Ali had not only split two fights the previous year but had also suffered a broken jaw - even I struggled a bit to control him.

I had to grasp his shoulder and hold the microphone firm, to contain the excitement fizzing from his body. He was damn near hysterical, as he yelled, 'I admit he hits *hard* but if a man can stay out of the way for five rounds, stick him, move, stay out of range, be in good shape, he'll retire George Foreman!'

Eyes blazing, he continued: 'I'm gonna whoop him, of all places, in Africa, in the Congo, where the La Moomba boys are!'

He was full of adrenaline. Hyping up the audience at home and himself too. Then I said something that really got his blood hot.

'Fighting in your home territory, you couldn't be any happier about…'

Ali cut me off. 'Why would you call Africa my home territory?' he demanded to know.

'You've been telling me that for ten years!' I came back with, not sure whether he was clowning or whether I had really caused offence.

'That's right,' he answered. 'And if you come over there talking like that, we'll *cook* you!'

Then he stormed off, leaving me mostly amused, but also a bit rattled. Surely he would not let them barbeque me!

In any case, I was sold. Whether or not this was to be his last hurrah, Ali remained the top attraction in boxing and figured to be fresh enough to at least pose a respectable challenge to the young champion - though, like most everyone else, I couldn't see him holding off Big George for the duration. Too big, too strong, too goddamn vicious. As a fight fan, I couldn't wait for the official announcement of the fight; but as a friend, in spite of the bravado being displayed by Muhammad, I couldn't help but feel a little scared.

Back in Miami, I simply carried on with the grind of my packed-out schedule. I was a workhorse who thrived on being kept busy, on having someplace to be at a specific hour for a specific length of time - doing what I did best. Funny as it sounds, working back-to-back 18-hour days - between the travel and the prep and actually being on the air - was for me like being tapped into a surging energy supply. I guess I had something to prove; I sure as hell had big ambitions. It was this mindset that allowed me to visualize my success and really go after what I wanted. If I was going to call fights for a living, I told myself, then I *had* to call the big fights. Otherwise, what the hell was the point? A number of weeks had passed when I finally got the phone call … telling me what I already knew.

The job was mine.

Based on my performances in the Buchanan-Otero fight and the Foreman-Norton massacre, which had particularly impressed Bernstein and his business partner, Hank Schwartz, I was going to be the lead commentator for the Ali-Foreman mega-fight in Zaire, now signed and sealed and about four months away.

I planned the trip with military precision. At that time, in Miami, I was covering an array of sports on both radio and television - daily shows with daily commitments. The truth of the matter was, despite the size of the carrot dangled in front of me, leaving the country at that particular moment was far from ideal. In fact, it was damn near impossible! I had a decision to make. Should I be content with the steady, well-paid work I was currently doing which had already garnered me huge regional acclaim. Or should I instead go all in on my ambition to be the best and most recognized boxing commentator in the world? Well, I spent about six minutes making up my mind. Ultimately, it was a no-brainer. While football had been taking up most of my time and seemed to guarantee an illustrious (and lucrative) career, I just couldn't resist the allure of big-time boxing. The pull was always at my back, tugging at my collar. I was great at calling fights, and I knew it. Now, at last, was my time to shine.

The fight was scheduled to take place on September 24, and my dance card was fully booked right up until a couple of Sundays before, when I was slated to fly out with the rest of the media boys from New York. As luck would have it, I was in The Big Apple that weekend anyway, covering the Dolphins against the Jets. I therefore had no logistical issues on the day and actually arrived with energy to spare! I was going to need this energy. It was a long journey with two stopovers, flying first to Iceland, then from Iceland to Germany, then from Germany down to Zaire and the Presidential Palace!

Well, we got two-thirds of the way there.

Hearing the news was like hearing a death-knell. Big George was cut, the result of an errant elbow in sparring, requiring eleven stitches. The fight was likely going to be postponed - perhaps even cancelled.

Instantly, the atmosphere of the room plummeted. The real problem was that nobody knew how long George would need to heal. Four to six weeks was the norm; however, if you knew the sport, then you also knew that with injuries (and in particular cuts) there could be no guarantees. To me then, the situation was crystal clear. Either the fight would take place within the next six weeks, or else it would be cancelled. Why? Because the rainy season in Zaire was coming, and once the rain arrived, any hope of staging the outdoor event would be flushed down the toilet.

Either way, I wasn't prepared to stick around. I was too goddamn busy.

While most of the other media guys were more than happy to continue down to Zaire and await further news, I didn't have four to six weeks to spare. Nor for that matter did I particularly want to sit on my ass for that length of time in the equatorial climate of deepest Africa! So, while still in Germany, I waved goodbye to the boys and did a 180 back to the States, only half expecting to be recalled.

To tell the truth, I chose to put the job completely out of my mind. Television is a fickle business, and I had no iron-clad reason to think I would be rehired should the whole thing fall apart. Don King had performed a minor miracle by coaxing all that cash out of the pocket of Mobutu; who knew if he would ever be able to repeat this magic? To me, the odds of him doing so seemed long. So, as a way to mitigate my disappointment perhaps, I decided it was best to focus on what I had rather than what I *almost* had.

Thankfully, five weeks turned out to be just enough time for Big George's cut to heal, and I could let out a monumental sigh of relief. I'll be honest, I would've been devastated if the fight got scrapped, even though I was trying to keep my cool. But hey, the big man upstairs was on my side this time - just like he was for everyone else. The fight was reset for October 30, 1974. Once again, I prepared to set off for Zaire.

The whole experience was nothing short of incredible.

Originally, I was going to be staying at Nsele, the ritzy northeast part of the city where all the big shots, including Ali, were holed up. But I had access to Muhammad whenever I wanted. I wasn't desperate like the rest of the press corps to be close to him. Instead, I wanted the real Zaire experience, so I decided to hang out with my buddies from the British media at the Memling Hotel in downtown Kinshasa. I have to admit - I briefly questioned the wisdom of my decision. It was kind of hilarious, really. You see, after landing in the afternoon and stepping foot into the country, I found out that the road from the airport to Nsele was a four-lane highway, all smooth and shiny. It almost felt like I was still back in the States. But the road into Kinshasa, well, let's just say it was nothing more than a dirt track.

I checked into the hotel with ITV's Reg Gutteridge and the rest of the British press boys. Keep in mind, I don't have one ounce of animosity towards the Brits. Most of the press men are great pals. It's the British government's policies in Northern Ireland I can't live with. The man on the street, fine by me. For example, I love Ron Land, Frank Warren, and Prince Naseem, and I'm extremely fond of former heavyweight champion Frank Bruno and former lightweight champ Jimmy Watt.

Then of course there's John Duffy. John was the hotel manager on the Queen Elizabeth II, who treated me like royalty for years. One occasion in particular sticks out in my mind. On board with my twelve pals, including Joe Maxse of the Cleveland Plain Dealer, Ed Schuyler of the Associated Press, and Pat Putnam of Sports Illustrated, he pulled out all the stops for his Colonel. We got on the ship the night before the Tyson-Douglas fight in Tokyo at 1700 hours and ate and drank like we were going to the electric chair until 5 bells. John picked up the entire twelve-hour tab. Now unless I'm completely nuts, I can't hate Brits in general. In fact, even the soldiers in the North were only soldiers doing their job and I respect that. It's the politicians who fuck everything up - just as I was witnessing now in Zaire. It was clear Mobutu had absolute power in the country; however, I was there for a sporting event - a pretty damn big one! And while I could of course sense the authoritarian climate (and the consequent fear), I couldn't dwell on a situation over which I had absolutely no control.

There was so much else going on.

Open workouts, pressers, meetings. I was there for all of it. But I'll admit, I spent most of my time drinking. Here's what you need to understand: in Zaire at that time, there was a shortage of glass. So, drinking 'Timbo' and 'Shimba' beer out of quart bottles (for about 10 cents each) made us all big spenders in the hotels.

One of my favorite beer stories occurred over at the International Hotel where an underage-drinking Carl King was signing for all the beer his little belly could handle. The only problem was that he was signing his tabs 'Gerald Ford'. Then the page came, 'Telephone call for Gerald Ford, Mr. Gerald Ford.' When the pool boy brought the phone over to Gerald Ford, the young Carl King almost shit himself under the watchful eye of his mom, Henrietta. Even then Carl was a chip off the ol' block. Thinking quick on his feet came natural. 'I didn't know Dad brought President Ford over here, Mum.' Then, before the pool boy got any closer, he dove into the pool and completely dispelled all of Jimmy 'the Greek' Snyder's theories on black swimmers. Carl hauled ass across the pool in a performance that would have made six-time Olympic gold medalist Mark Spits jealous!

Then there was the lovely dark-skinned girl I danced with and rubbed up against all night. I was really a horny bastard that night. I was about to experience my first local piece of ass. The anticipation would give a dog a bone. That is until my lovely ebony beauty lifted up her skirt and whipped out her porno star John Holmes-sized licorice stick to take a piss on the side of the street. I was in shock that my date had a bigger dick than mine, but I didn't panic. After all, they don't put erasers on microphones, so I'm pretty quick on my feet as well. I immediately fixed her/him up with good ol' Sid Hulls of the British Press Corps. I understand from the British boxing writer, Colin Hart, that this story is still legendary on the sporting banquet circuit in jolly ol' England - for good reason!

I've got to tell this story as well. It's not as funny as fixing up a Brit writer with a horny looking transvestite, but it still needs to be told. It happened at the Saturday night weigh-in held in the Stade du 20 Mai (the 20th of May Stadium) in the very ring where history would be made in a couple of nights. This weigh-in was critical to the promotion because it was being carried live around the world, and especially on ABC's Wide World of Sports in the United States. This was the final big promotion that would put asses in seats on Monday night, so this translates into millions of dollars at stake.

Something was wrong. Howard Cosell was handling it for ABC, Harry Carpenter was fronting for BBC in the United Kingdom, and I was hosting the world feed. There were five minutes to airtime and through the screams of horror coming from the production truck into my earpiece, I understood we had problems with the audio. But that wasn't the half of it. We also had no video in New York, which meant something wasn't squared away - the studio producers at ABC back in the States, in blind panic, immediately wanted to scratch the feed. Besides the chaos in the production truck, there were 25 thousand people in the stadium for the free weigh-in just to catch a glimpse of Ali. The noise was deafening. While George Foreman was bedecked in native garb walking like a huge animal, Ali still had the locals' believing Foreman was a white man with no black roots. The shouts of Ali-Boom-Aye-A were in full force. My personal excitement had the hairs on the back of my neck at full attention. In the sweltering heat I had the chills, and we were inside of two minutes with no video in New York.

The language coming out of the truck sounded like the finals of a cursing and swearing contest between the Association of Retired Sailors and the International Brotherhood of Dockworkers. There was a minute to air. 'Scratch the weigh-in,' comes a voice from New York. 'Hang on, you fuckin' idiot,' returns Jack Murphy directing from Zaire. All of a sudden, with about 15 seconds, I figured we must be in the eye of the storm. Bracing myself, I hear Jack Murphy's Assistant Director Mary Vee say, '12 seconds.' Jack with a relaxed, 'Inside of 10 seconds. You look like shit, Bobby! You're going to billions of people, so don't fuck up. Three, two, one.' And Gaylord, my stage manager, cues me.

There was nowhere to hide.

With the Jack Murphy-induced smile on my face, the words began to roll off my tongue like we'd rehearsed it for days. 'From Kinshasa, Zaire, in the deepest and darkest part of Africa — Hello again, everybody. I'm Bob Sheridan…'

While the confusion in the ring made for a great TV show, technically we were sound, and I was good, and I knew it. For me it was great prep for the real show on Monday. I was full of confidence and after working fights with the likes of Redd Foxx and James Brown, before he was the Godfather of Soul, and an array of other celebrity and Hollywood types, it would be great working with a real pro like David Frost, who was used to doing live telecasts. Little did I know at the time that David had never been this close to a world heavyweight championship fight in his life, and that he was such an Ali groupie, because of his love for Ali, that he totally lost it during the live action of the fight. Still, David did a great interview before and after the fight, and I had NFL Hall of Famer Jim Brown and former champs Joe Frazier and Jimmy Ellis to play off during the fight. The telecast went super - with one exception. My miscall of the knockout created a cry for 'a quick call' on the 10 count.

I actually blew the call. When you're a sportscaster, you can only call what you see. Anybody can analyze with 'slo mo' replay in an after the fact discussion with several experts. But to be accurate and call action while it's actually happening is a very special skill that takes thousands of hours of work to perfect. Anyway, what I saw was George circling in the center of the ring, ready to fall like a bull following the final sword plunge through the heart. Ali pulled the final right hand; he knew George was totally exhausted and finished. So, Ali never threw what would have been the most devastating punch of the fight. He didn't need to hurt the big warrior anymore. For the first time in my career I was seated back, off the apron, so they could get better 'on camera' shots of us at ringside. At the time I thought this was great because being a hopeless showoff, I loved mugging for the camera, and this was a mega mug for sure. Don't forget, this was a television landmark at the time. It was the first occasion that all four communication satellites were being used simultaneously. We were going to one billion people live and I loved the fact I was the anchorman on the largest live TV show in the history of the medium. What I didn't realize at the time was that a simple five feet off the ring position would have a profound influence on my call of the knockout.

With the huge crowd, and with the thundering stadium noise, and David Frost going absolutely bonkers sitting next to me at the moment of truth, I couldn't hear the official counting for the knockdown, a situation I never faced in all the years of calling fights and the hundreds of knockdowns and knockouts I had described over the years. On top of that the referee, Zack Clayton, was a bit indecisive. He reminded me of most of those British refs that do about five feints before they will do something as simple as breaking up a clinch. So let me take you through what I saw, what I said, and how simple it has been to correct the mistake I made and will never make again.

It all happened in an instant. With big George's collapse to the canvas at the center of the ring, I started to call exactly what I saw. Not a bad thing for a play-by-play announcer to do. I should have said, 'He's down, the count is up to 2,' then a brief description of what a billion people could see was happening, then complete the count with Zack Clayton, 'eight, nine, ten,' and 'Muhammad Ali has done it, he's regained the title, and the world has a brand-new heavyweight champion.' Everything would have been fine, the watcher wouldn't be looking for a 'quick count' on the replays, and I wouldn't have been vilified by some Sports Illustrated writer who did his evaluation from a closed-circuit location back in the States. I was brutally criticized, and it really bothered me, because I felt in my heart I was absolutely the best boxing commentator in the world. But I made a mistake, and I knew it, although as an athlete I'd seen the great Ted Williams strike out, Sandy Koufax give up home runs, and world champion all-around cowboy Dan Daily get bucked off. So, in spite of the fact that there are no erasers on microphones, I wasn't contemplating the death plunge with a samurai sword.

But here's where I made my error. With the officials counting for the knockdown, Zack Clayton turned his back to the fallen Foreman, while ordering the jubilant Ali back to the neutral corner. He was sort of indecisive in his moves but very precise when he picked up the count at 4. Since I couldn't hear the man counting for the knockdown, I saw Clayton's arm come down and, following the description of Ali being sent to his neutral corner, I say, 'one, two' when the count was actually four and five. I scream, 'Foreman's not going to make it,' and I then see Zack waving his arms just after I had said, 'the count is up to 8.' When I saw his arms wave, I went into the celebration of the moment, 'It's all over! It's all over! Muhammad Ali has done it…'

What I should've done - and what I always do now under similar circumstances - is say, 'nine and ten and the fight is over.' But, once again, things always seem a heck of a lot easier after the fact.

With the exception of this one night, as emotional and rowdy as any in boxing history, nobody has ever questioned my call of the end of a world title fight in some fifty years and a thousand championship endings. What really got to me was the fact that the guy doing the Sports Illustrated article never bothered to call me to get my side of the story. Within two days, I had sparked a worldwide uproar over what many people believed was a quick count orchestrated by that 'villain Don King'. While reporters are always quick to jump at any chance to bury Don, they never let accuracy get in the way of a good cheap shot. The only problem is, I happen to believe that the truth of what actually happened would've made a much better story than another attempt to vilify my soon-to-be boss. But not one writer bothered to question me.

You see, in those days, when writers began jumping on every opportunity to get on radio or TV, there was a jealousy factor. Broadcasters were making more money than even the best columnist of the day. 'The knights of the keyboard' were no longer the center of attraction. The broadcasters were the new breed of journalist and by the time their stories were getting back home, television and radio had made all of their hard work practically obsolete, except for the gifted boxing writers like Dave Anderson of the New York Times, Ron Hobson of the Quincy Patriot Ledger, Tom Archdeacon of the Dayton News, the late Jim Murray of the Los Angeles Times, and the late Bob Waters who could write better with a bottle of Scotch in him than most men could sober with a three-man research team.

I remember Bob Waters so well when he first arrived at the Memling Hotel in Kinshasa. Bobby Goodman, public relations man turned matchmaker, had sent up a bottle of Chivas with a great looking hooker to his room. Now Waters had a wonderful sense of humor and called down to the bar where Bobby Goodman was entertaining the troops with pails of 'Timbo' and 'Shimba'. In the middle of this press 'piss up' came the call from Bob Waters to Goodman. 'Bobby, thank you for the beautiful bottle of scotch, and even more for the absolutely ravishing whore. But I have one more request.' Bobby Goodman, 'Anything, Bob.' Bob Waters, 'Could you send me up a hard on?' Needless to say, after a 24-hour trip to equatorial Africa on a routing that took us to Iceland and to Germany, Bob Waters was not able for the thoughtful gift arranged by Bobby Goodman. As Bobby related this hilarious conversation just completed with Waters to the 8 or 10 media types in the bar, the laughter had hardly subsided when stepping smartly into the bar came Waters. A Cheshire cat would have been envious of the shit-eating grin beaming on the rather large face of one of the great old boxing writers of all time as he proclaimed, 'Now I'm ready to drink!'

There were of course other memorable moments. Like the time Ed Schuyler of the Associated Press and I were in a drunken stupor and thought we were going to be eaten by Mobutu's lions at Nsele!

It's funny how easily you can forget that you are in a jungle.

Ed and I had traveled up to Nsele to show our faces. It was my second or third night in Zaire, and after thirty or so beers, I had decided it was essential that we track down Muhammad in order to say hello. To see and to be seen, as it were. Muhammad had a villa out in the presidential grounds and was known to be highly social. Stepping out of our taxi, therefore, we believed it would be no trouble at all to find him and that, by doing so, we would in fact be making his night! So with this thought in our frontal lobes, we picked a direction and found ourselves enveloped by the warm, musical night, like two wandering zebras.

The roar came out from behind the shadowy vegetation, dreadfully hidden and sending birds fluttering in all directions.

HOLY FUCK!

We shit ourselves and bolted in the direction of a nearby building. I remember turning to Eddie and saying, through the ice of my sweat, 'I don't know about you, but I'm getting inside. I don't wanna get eaten by a fuckin' lion!'

Suffice it to say, we didn't find Muhammad that night. It was at an open workout the next day that I found a moment to chat with the great man, a hive of sweaty bodies and recording equipment swarming around him. Of course, he was in scintillating form. I expected nothing less. Whenever the attention of a room flowed in his direction, he would always be switched on. This was something that really impressed me about him, as I could be sitting alone with him, and he would be quiet as a mouse - distant, almost vacant. Then I would notice his eyes roving about the room, searchingly, until they locked onto somebody else's. Ali, you see, as a devout Muslim, had no vices in life *except* his weakness for beautiful women. They cast a spell over him. But when that camera lens was pointed his way, boy oh boy, did he come alive. In my experience, the only other person capable of turning it on like Muhammad - when it was showtime - has been Don King. They both had that ability in spades; though even Don paled against that version of Muhammad, in the days and weeks leading up to the fight.

He shone like a supernova.

'Hey, remember those Miami beach days, Bob?' he liked to ask me. The Champ and I went way back. I think he genuinely was fond of me; I was crazy about him. As he left the ring after shocking the world in Zaire, a few nights later, with the monsoon rains driving down with apocalyptic timing, I knew for sure I was witnessing greatness. I also knew that I had to haul ass to get back to my day job!

Here's one more story.

The kid running the casino in Kinshasa was from Miami of all places, and a University of Miami graduate like myself. He was a sports fan, and I realized a Bob Sheridan groupie when he moved me to a lead seat at a specific blackjack table and told me, 'Be sure to play with black $100 chips.' That was a lot of money for me but as a military man, I know when to follow orders. I proceeded to win chip after chip and Bob Waters was borrowing and blowing them on the roulette wheel faster than

I could win them. To this day, I have no idea how many thousands of dollars Waters borrowed from me, but I eventually grabbed two grand for myself and avoided Bob Waters like the plague for the rest of the night. Now Bob Waters was a guy I adored, and it was fitting at the end when Pat Putnam and Ed Schuyler proclaimed amidst nearly 500 floral arrangements at his wake, 'Waters looks great. He looks like he just won the Kentucky Derby.' Eddie should've known, as this crotchety old journalist was not only a fine boxing writer but a superb turf writer, who in the end preferred writing about the ponies to covering prize fights. But like everybody else who was there, I don't believe he would've swapped his experience in Zaire for any other event in the world.

CHAPTER XI

'THE HEAVYWEIGHTS'

Back in the late 1960s, I found out what a true heavyweight punch feels like.

The network I worked for in South Florida wanted to film a short feature during which I would spar, one minute apiece, with three of the best heavyweights in the world. 'Sure,' I said, without a drop of hesitation. 'Sign me up!' I was always game to do something out of the ordinary, something a little crazy, and everyone agreed it would be great television to see the guy with the microphone going at it with (and of course, taking a few licks from) the actual pros. However, it was only when I arrived that morning, carrying with me my sports bag and a filthy hangover, that I realized that those sons of bitches - for the sake of entertainment - were actually throwing me to the wolves!

My opponents, at the 5th Street Gym in Miami Beach, in this order, would be Muhammad Ali, Joe Frazier and Jimmy Ellis.

'Oh, you in trouble now Bob!' Ali yelled from across the suddenly shrinking gym. Aware that he was only clowning, I nevertheless shit myself.

You see, Ali, the former champ, was still in exile for refusing the draft - a stand for which I had the utmost respect - while Frazier and Ellis were each staking their claim as the new top dog in the division. So, whether for laughs or not, I was actually about to 'throwdown' with three of toughest SOBs on the planet!

At six feet and weighing around 220 pounds, I didn't feel overmatched physically. The real problem was, without having had so much as a single amateur fight, I was completely outgunned technically. I might as well have been trying to dunk on Wilt Chamberlain on a basketball court. Only my pedigree as a brawler from the streets of South Boston would give me a fighting chance. Or so I naively thought.

First up is Ali. The camera is rolling and he's doing his usual 'Ali Shuffle' - a sight far less pleasing to the eye than discombobulating to the senses when you're actually in the ring with the man. I want to land one blow - just one! With the determination of a warthog, I follow and chase and stumble after his long torso, trying my best to get those slippery legs of his to stay in one place. As the seconds slip by, my teeth are clenched and my fists are balled, and I'm giving it everything I have. But hitting Ali - or even coming close - was like trying to swat a shadow. And a dancing one at that! It wasn't happening. Ali, for his part, took great pleasure in dislodging my headgear with a series of light yet stinging lefts.

'That all you got, Bob?' he kept saying in a gleeful voice.

Yeah, pretty much, I thought.

Next up is Joe. Joe kind of muscles me around the ring, touching me to the head and body continuously. As lightly thrown hooks alternately rattle my skull and punish my midsection - softer than I'd taken it to be - he motions for me to throw back, smiling through his gumshield. So that's what I do. Two lefts and a gutsy right hand bounce off the forehead of Joe, whose smile stretches even wider. Nuzzling at my chest, moving me this way and that, he motions again for some return fire - only this time I'm a little more hesitant. You see, even with Joe holding back eighty percent of his power, I could still feel the force of his vaunted left hook. The message was loud and clear: anytime he wanted to, he could take my head off.

Finally, I squared off with Jimmy. Jimmy and I used to play basketball together, and I considered him a friend. This perhaps gave me a false sense of security. Jimmy was a small heavyweight who, in fact, had come all the way up from middleweight to compete in boxing's glamour division. Compared to Frazier, it was like being in the ring with a house cat. So, when Jimmy says to me, 'Try to hit me Bob,' tapping a glove on his chin, I really fuckin' go for it. I throw a hefty right hook behind a flurry of jabs, which sinks deep into his ribcage. What a shot! I think - suspecting I may have even winded the heavyweight stud.

Next thing I know I'm on the deck.

You see, Jimmy had this ability to roll his shoulders to the right and hide a punch. It landed squarely on my chin and dropped me like a sack of shit - my head and body numbed by the impact. 'You want to keep going?' Jimmy kindly asks, as I stare up at him from the canvas. The famous cartoon stars are bright in my vision, but I manage to say, 'Well, we're not finishing with me on my ass!' Tapping my gloves together and giving a snort, I then get to my feet and attempt to see out the rest of the round, my legs feeling shaky as hell. Mercifully, Jimmy only flicks me with a couple more jabs and when the minute is finally up, my opponent gives me a charitable hug and says, 'Why Bob, you should've ducked!'

Thus my respect for the power of the big boys was forever cemented.

Since I've been the lead broadcaster on most every major heavyweight championship fight since the late '60s, right up to and including Lennox Lewis, Wladimir Klitschko and Tyson Fury, I have a slightly different perspective to a lot of the so-called boxing experts. I've known every heavyweight champion since Floyd Patterson. Some have been good friends; others just casual acquaintances. Yet my respect for these men has never been influenced by anything other than their ability and their accomplishments. As far as I'm concerned, whomever is in possession of the greatest title in sport can do no wrong.

The most exciting fights for me were The Rumble in the Jungle and The Thrilla in Manilla. However, the absolute best heavyweight championship fight I ever called was the Larry Holmes vs. Ken Norton WBC heavyweight title fight at Caesars Palace in Las Vegas - a fight that truly went down to the wire. Unfortunately, Holmes and Norton - though respected - never became icons on the level of Muhammad and Joe. Therefore, the Ali-Frazier fight in Manilla was voted the top fight of the century by Ring Magazine at its 75th Anniversary Celebration, followed by Ali's upset win over George Foreman the year before.

Personally, I disagree with that order. I believe the fight in Zaire stole the show for its setting in the former Belgian Congo and for the shockwaves sent out by its iconic 'rope-a-dope' ending. Honestly, being in Manilla wasn't quite as exciting for me as a broadcaster. In fact, at times, it was even hard to watch.

By 1975, both fighters had noticeably slowed down, and the bout was more a brutal clash of wills than a boxing match. With one victory apiece in their rivalry, Ali and Frazier had become bitter enemies by this point, and the lead-up to the trilogy fight was as hostile as any in recent memory. Muhammad, especially, was merciless in his taunting of Joe, who never forgave him for his words. Over the ensuing fourteen brutal rounds, both men suffered so much damage in the ring that they ended up in the hospital - battered, bruised, and forever changed.

'It was the closest to death I have ever been,' said Ali years later. Being seated so close to the ring myself, I could easily believe him. You see, to accommodate the American viewers, the fight was scheduled to take place at 10 AM local time in the Philippines - in a climate that was indeed hotter than Hell. Inside the Araneta Coliseum, the ring temperature is estimated to have been more than 120 degrees Fahrenheit, with the overnight moisture inside the stadium - come fight time - still sizzling up into the atmosphere. It was so goddamn hot at ringside that I remember taking off my jacket to discover that my shirt had been completely soaked through - and I was barely even moving!

God only knows what it was like to fight in that heat, much less to have absorbed all that punishment. Of course, money and ego lured both Ali and Frazier back into the ring many more times after this night, but Manilla undoubtedly should have been the last hurrah for both men - as subsequent tough losses would sadly demonstrate. For Muhammad, the effects of the later beatings he took were obvious; for Joe, they were a little more under the hood. However, for a young broadcaster who loved the sport, it was still a tremendous honor to have called The Thrilla in Manilla, despite the price paid by its protagonists. Just as it was to call Holmes' breakout performance against Norton, three years later.

Holmes engaged Norton in a battle every bit as savage. The difference was - both were at the peak of their respective careers, able to keep their shape a little better and protect their craniums more effectively. Nevertheless, wicked power shots were exchanged throughout and, entering the fifteenth round, the scores were dead even. Nobody had a clue whose hand was going to be raised at the final bell. I went berserk calling those final minutes, bellowing: 'Two finely tuned machines, in magnificent shape, battling for the most coveted trophy in all of sport, the Heavyweight Championship of the World!'

Holmes, of course, eked out a win on the judges' scorecards with his performance in that final round - and a superhuman desire to win. Norton never again fought up to that level, but Holmes went on to become what I still say is arguably the greatest heavyweight champion of all time. His defense, his ring prowess, his power jab, his quick hands, his deceptive foot movement, his knowledge of how to beat an array of opponents - his skills were unparalleled. And as he defended his title 20 times, all were on show. But nobody possessed more of the immeasurable quality that all great champions must possess.

'The Heart of a Champion'.

I remember Larry going down on June 22nd in the Garden against Mike Weaver. I remember it so well because June 22nd is my birthday. When Larry went down, the fight was over - but it wasn't! Glassy-eyed, jelly-legged, he got up to win. IMPOSSIBLE! And Earnie Shavers, who may have been the hardest hitting heavyweight puncher of all time, caught Larry, and sent him down like that cartoon character carrying an anvil off a cliff. Once again, Larry scooped himself off the canvas, got through the rest of the round, and somehow won the fight. Again, IMPOSSIBLE!

Then there was the night in the igloo in Pittsburgh. My feet were frozen to the ice under the ring, but the action in the ring was red hot, and for five seconds I thought Renaldo Snipes was going to become the new heavyweight champion of the world. Why five seconds? Because Snipes had knocked Larry down right in front of me and with the referee's count at four, Larry's eyes were glazed and rolled back in his head and his foot was quivering. From my vantage point on the apron, I could stand up and look into his face. 'The count is 5. I don't think he can make it!' I screamed at the worldwide audience. Well, not only did he make it to his feet by 10, but he actually won the rest of the round and went on to knock out Renaldo Snipes and retain his title. Since that night, I've been a Larry Holmes super fan, and he will always be the greatest heavyweight I've ever seen, including Rocky Marciano, Sonny Liston, Muhammad Ali, Joe Frazier, Mike Tyson and Evander Holyfield.

Here's my reasoning. While the measure of success in our society is mostly based on the almighty dollar, in boxing it's slightly different. Here, I say it is to be found in the overall picture of one's life - meaning, in addition to his accomplishments, the fighter's health and wealth. On both fronts, Larry is a winner. I think it's hard to argue with my logic here, especially when you compare Holmes to the majority of his fellow greats. Only Gene Tunney and Rocky Marciano before him, and Lewis and Klitschko after him, can claim to have ended their careers so unscathed physically and so well off financially. And they were all great fighters. But greater than the 'Easton Assassin?' I say absolutely not.

But hey, ranking fighters is subjective, and even after my near 50 years of working in the sport, I defer to the knowledge of other experts all the time. I get a lot of information from trainers as I prepare to do my world telecasts. Angelo Dundee, Hank Kaplan, Lou Duva, Moe Sims, Duke Durden, Bobby Goodman, Vonzel Johnson, Jim Martin, Murray Goodman and Payton Sher are just some of the men I've depended on over the years to help me. When it comes to the heavyweights, all of these men had impact over the years. Recently, however, I've worked with Don Turner.

Don is a good, decent and honest man. He's a great teacher and without question one of the premier trainers. He engineered the Holyfield fight plans for Mike Tyson and has worked with over twenty world champs. If I had a young fighter coming into boxing, the man I'd want to train my boy is Don Turner. So, when I want to discuss heavyweights for an alternative opinion from a man whose boxing knowledge is second to none, I go to Don.

We started to talk about Rocky Marciano. 'Rocky was truly one of the all-time greats,' he told me. 'The reason I say that is because he always had to fight an uphill battle. He was a small guy, but he had the best leverage of any fighter. On a given night he could have beaten any heavyweight. A lot of people say Marciano was a small heavyweight, but Evander Holyfield is a small heavyweight, and he is certainly one of the all-time greats because he is one of the smartest heavyweights.

'It is very hard to say, on a given night, who'd win,' Don went on to say, 'but I've known them all from Joe Louis up. At any one of their peaks, it's tough to determine the absolute best. Joe Louis and Sonny Liston would be in there. Ezzard Charles was one of the greatest. Charles had 122 professional fights. After he was stopped by Jersey Joe Walcott, he was never the same, but look at the guys he beat. Charlie Burley, Archie Moore, Gus Lassrich, Pat Valentino. At one time Ezzard was the busiest heavyweight around. Can you just imagine if he trained high tech like Evander Holyfield?'

Now, Don could explain why each fighter in history should technically be included with the top heavyweights, but I asked him for his top five all time heavyweights in ALL categories. So here we go - from the most knowledgeable man in the sport today with boxing experience spanning six decades.

#1: Evander Holyfield, because he was the smartest and best trained;

#2: Larry Holmes, a very close second, with his ability, intelligence and unparalleled heart;

#3: Muhammad Ali, with his speed and reflexes and charisma like no other athlete in history;

#4: Joe Louis, for his vaunted power, and patience and technique! and

#5: Mike Tyson, Ezzard Charles, Rocky Marciano and Joe Frazier, all the same type of fighter who could beat anyone on a given night.

I ask Don Turner if he really believes Evander Holyfield is the greatest heavyweight of all time - and to tell me more about him.

He answers without hesitation: 'Evander's faith in God is a big edge. It makes him strive to be the best. His ability to transfer his intelligence into the ring is unbelievable. It seems like there is a light switch, from the nice guy outside the ring to the bad guy inside the ring. At the Tyson fights he was totally convinced he could beat him. He knew all Tyson could do was throw hooks and a few uppercuts, then he'd have to rest each time. A half step left or right, Tyson was squared up and wide open to be hit, while he was off balance, and Evander had the leverage with his power shots. His drills in the gym with different sparring partners made all of his moves automatic, with each mistake Tyson would make.'

Most people think the problems with Mike Tyson were numerous and self-inflicted. Sure, we have his association with Don King, the 'yes men' in his corner, poor trainers, no Kevin Rooney or Teddy Atlas to train him, his three year layoff while he was in prison, his wealth, bad women, fast cars, too much money, too much fame, bad lifestyle, poor character, an abused childhood, social ignorance, poor diet, lack of concentration on boxing, poor competition at the beginning of his career, taking the championship at too young of an age against poor opponents that held the titles he won, Gus D'Amato's death, Jimmy Jacobs' death, and a series of frightened opponents when he got out of jail.

Still - and much to my surprise - Don Turner says, 'It's none of those problems. It's plain and simple. Evander Holyfield was smarter in the ring than Mike Tyson. In the early part of Tyson's career, when victory after victory came easy, he stopped learning to be a smart fighter. Mike is very, very easy to beat. All you have to do is stand up to him and take those half steps and half circles around him and when he stops to rest, you bang him. You see, in Evander's case it doesn't come down to brute strength. It's drill, drill, drill on the weakness of his opponents. Any big heavyweight who is willing to work, to take pride in his body and his craft, and who is a good athlete to begin with can become a champion. Staying champion is another story. That's where the money and the lifestyle can ruin the best of men.'

We talk about Riddick Bowe since he was able to beat Evander. Of course, we all know Evander was not well when he lost the title, but I'm more interested in his thinking of what happened to Bowe's career. Don is candid on Bowe. 'He's a good guy. His enemy is food, and he doesn't like to train. Once he got a pocketful of money, it was a matter of time before he would self-destruct.'

I asked about a few other heavyweights who once (albeit briefly) held the 'Greatest Title on Earth', and in particular Michael Moorer. Don Turner says, 'Michael could have been a real force in boxing, but somehow he always seems to get tied up with the wrong guy teaching him. Every fighter is a head case in a matter of speaking, but Moorer has to be handled in a certain way because he is very sensitive. Teddy Atlas is a great coach, a fine teacher, but I think he was wrong for Michael Moorer because the Vince Lombardi slave-driving approach is just the wrong way to handle him. Freddie

Roach was the same, but it's the fighters who make trainers. A lot of people think it's the trainer who makes the fighter.'

I can't resist asking Don Turner, 'If that's the case, is it true that Evander Holyfield made Don Turner a great trainer?'

'Listen, Colonel, Holyfield already knew how to fight. All I had to do was remind him of what he is really capable of doing. The rest is drill, drill, drill, and his desire to be the best he can possibly be.

'Mike Tyson? I just don't think Tyson could ever beat Evander Holyfield. Mike could beat everybody else around because he had the punch and the aggressive intimidating nature to handle everyone else.

'George Foreman? He was a great fighter, a powerful fighter, but a bully who was very sensitive and got conned out of the title by Ali. Losing to Jimmy Young and quitting the ring, and then coming back to win the title at age 44 by knocking out Michael Moorer was a phenomenal feat.

'Jersey Joe Walcott? A great fighter. His left hook could knock out the best of them, including Joe Louis. Walcott had Louis' number but simply got himself caught. Louis had better hand speed, but Walcott had more savvy. Jersey Joe was cunning, and he confused Joe Louis like Billy Conn did.

'Joe Louis? One of the all-time greats. Power, power, power. But like Tyson he had trouble with movers. That is why Ezzard Charles, Billy Conn, and Walcott all gave him problems.

'Floyd Patterson? Quick hands and fast, fast, fast. About the same size as Evander, but I think Holyfield would win if they fought in the prime of their careers, because the Peek-A-Boo style is tailor-made for Evander's half step to the side for the angle. Evander would eliminate that style as well as the wide punches that Patterson threw just like Mike Tyson!

'Larry Holmes? Larry Holmes in my opinion is absolutely the smartest heavyweight that ever lived. He didn't gamble early, he always used the jab to break down his opponents, and his heart is every bit as big as Evander Holyfield's.'

One of the great rumors in boxing is that the last of the heavyweight fights to be fixed were the Ali vs. Liston fights. Don Turner knew all the individuals involved, so I have to get his opinion. After all, if those fights were indeed fixed, then the logical question is, 'Is Ali really the greatest of all time?' Don Turner says, 'Well, I don't believe they were fixed. However, I do believe that possibly the Muslims could have been involved in intimidating opponents. I really believe that Ali won. I think Liston was outclassed by Ali, and if there were any intimidations going on at the time, Ali's skill had the ability to outclass Liston at that stage of both of their careers. Liston had real trouble with guys who could move. He couldn't stop Eddie Machen, who could move, and I think Liston just 'dogged it' in the Ali fights.'

And Don Turner's final comments to me: 'Evander and Michael Grant were my fighters, but I love Ali. I love Ali the person, but I still think Larry Holmes and Evander Holyfield are better fighters.'

I agreed wholeheartedly with Don's analysis. While I loved Ali and felt privileged to have watched his career unfold, I still feel Holmes was a better fighter for a longer period of time. Ali should have retired after The Rumble in the Jungle and certainly after the beating he took in Manilla. Subsequently, he had no true speed and his reflexes were off. Holmes, on the other hand, even in his forties, was good enough to give a fellow great like Holyfield all he could handle in their championship fight.

But hey, that's just my take. It doesn't make me right, nor does it make you wrong. Although, when you're in seven boxing Halls of Fame, and you've been broadcasting for fifty years, and you've covered over 1000 world championship fights, I think you're entitled to *at least* have an opinion. Sound fair?

CHAPTER XII

'ANTARCTICA'

Most people I speak with about Antarctica think I'm crazy. When I tell them I'd love to go back to one of the most beautiful, wild, dangerous, and yet peaceful places I've ever been, usually I'm given that look. You know the one I'm talking about. Brow slightly furrowed, nodding along while thinking about just how in the hell they can escape. Well, all I can say is, until you've tried something for yourself, don't knock it! Prior to my trip in the late summer - which is early spring down there - in the year of 1989, I'd been to just about every place else in the world. Travel is my life-long passion and the only real education a person needs. So, when my stage manager, Casey Seipes, began telling me about an Antarctic expedition he was planning, with a view to making a documentary for television, I just *had* to tag along.

Casey was more than just a stage manager for me at the big fights. He was a brilliantly talented television producer, director, and writer who *chose* to work with me on the big fights, just because he and I were such a good friends. Sadly, Casey passed away some years back. It was a shock and one hell of a blow. But being that I much prefer to celebrate a life than to mourn it, I wanted to tell this truly amazing story. I think he would have agreed, trekking down to the South Pole to film a documentary is almost as great an adventure as being at ringside for a championship fight.

Since Casey was such a good writer, I thought I'd let him tell the Antarctic adventure in his own partly fictionalized (though highly entertaining) account.

'I Only Have Ice For You'
By Casey Seipes

It was late in the summer of 1989 when another cold flight from Los Angeles touched me down in the humorless humidity of Minneapolis. It felt good to be leaving L.A. for a lot of reasons, not the least of which my 15-year career as a film cameraman was going stale. Too many car spots and toy commercials were taking their toll. But that was just an excuse. I was trapped in a marriage hell rejected as too bitter and that didn't leave me a lot of options. Instead of chewing off a limb like a deranged coyote, I put off the inevitable and agreed instead to join an expedition that would take me to Antarctica, the world's most desolate and breath-taking continent. As we taxied to the jetway, I was feeling more than a little anxious. Not just because this would be my first trip to the South Pole, but because I would once again be working with the legendary raconteur, Colonel Bob Sheridan.

I had spoken to the Colonel the week before. He was calling from Gorbachev's dacha in the Balkans. Seems he was finalizing our travel arrangement with the Russians who would be providing air transport out of the U.S. and into Antarctica. In an effort to show just how big their balls were, the Soviets were placing an Illushin 76, the largest aircraft in the world, at our disposal.

"Wait'll you see this bugger, Case. It's bigger than Jimmy Swaggert's whorehouse tab. We're filling her up with 23,000 cases of Stoli and Matrushka dolls to trade for lumber with the Canadians. But first we're going to need horses. And beef. Lots of beef. You speak Spanish. Maybe you can go to work on the Argentines."

Nothing the Colonel ever did surprised me.

The following week, I was met at the gate by Gordon Mauser, a sales rep for a notorious clothing company who was designing the extreme gear for the expedition and hoping to ride along on the massive marketing wave.

"I've got a surprise for you," he said after making cursory introductions.

I was whisked off in a private town car to the University of Minnesota where his company had set up a huge manufacturing assembly line for our gear. Many of the support staff were already there. We were asked to strip to our skivvies and were measured meticulously, right down to finger size and toe spread on each of our feet.

The next morning at the hotel, there was a pounding on my door. Grumbling, I threw open the door and there stood Colonel Bob Sheridan. Now, I have many memories of my Colonel: ringside at arguably the biggest championship fights in boxing history; bungee jumping off bridges in New Zealand; calling a herd of cattle for a face-off on a desolate roadside in Ireland; surrounded by 20 of the most beautiful and dangerous women in Las Vegas, poolside at the Mirage Hotel. But nothing prepared me for the sight that morning.

The Colonel was swaddled in custom expedition gear from head to toe. He wore custom wolverine mushers' boots and a gale-force storm parka so thick, his arms could not reach his sides as he spun furious circles in the hall like a misfit model. He wore a balaclava covering his face and a turban on his head. He waddled like a massive killer Arabic penguin. All I could envision was a huge balloon at Macy's Thanksgiving Day parade. He threw his arms wide. "Casey, lad. I've been shopping. We've got all we need. Look at me. I move like a cat."

I stared in disbelief and focused on the custom embroidery.

"You know the best part? Underneath all this, I'm wearing women's panties!" He never misses an opportunity to cash in on his sense of humour!

Two nights later, after a short hop out of Minneapolis, all seemed to be going well as we taxied to a halt in the middle of runway 27 Right at Miami International Airport for a routine fueling stop. Three tankers sped out to meet us in the middle of the tarmac. Watching comfortably from my bivouac in the rear cargo hold, I wondered how a Russian flight crew arranges for fuel at a major U.S. airport, especially for a craft with five 16,000-gallon fuel tanks. Do you just pull up and say "Dosva danya, please to be filling up now?"

As I mused on this question, I looked out my starboard portal and saw the Colonel directing the fueling operation with command parade precision. The men in the tankers never once questioned his authority as he barked orders.

"Put yer backs into it, lads. This bird's got a mission from the lips of God and we've got a schedule to keep."

Stepping back on board, the Colonel gave me a short salute and headed up the circular stairs to the bridge. Moments later, the four mammoth engines fired up and we taxied back out into position. I marveled at the massive size of our craft. The 747 first class cabin compartment we dropped in the forward cargo hold took up only half the width of the plane. The ceiling height at the centre of the plane was well over 17 feet. Before we loaded the plane in Minneapolis, we had a full football scrimmage with the Russian flight crew. (They kicked our butts and the network weenies cried like babies.) From stem to stern, the Illushin 76 was 212 feet long, 38 feet wide and weighed over 200 tons. This bugger came into town like T-Rex on tour.

There were 53 of us and 48 sled dogs aboard our massive bird as she thundered down runway 207 Left. The fuselage shuddered and the starboard wing seemed to groan into lift-off. Suddenly, quick as a cat, the Colonel was down the stairway eyeballing the wing.

"What's up?" I queried as I sidled up to the big guy.

"Number two starboard flamed out. We're going to have to set her down." "Miami?" I managed.

His eyes glimmered as a sly, leprechaun grin crept across his face.

"Havana," he said with a little shimmy.

And once again, he disappeared up the stairs.

JULY 23: HAVANA, CUBA

As much as I've always wanted to visit Havana, arriving in late July in the midst of a massive heat wave with 48 dogs was not my idea of a good time. I'm pretty sure the dogs just back from Greenland in their thick winter coats felt the same way.

"Seminiov says it'll take four or five days to get the parts. They've got to fly them in from Moscow." We were sitting poolside sipping Mojitos and smoking Romeo y Julietta cigars the size of Fiats as the Colonel ran down the latest.

"What'll we do until then?" I asked.

"Call the network and see if we can swing a nightly feed. Tell them we'll offer hourly updates on the state of the U.S. Embargo. In the meantime, sit back and soak up some of this local colour."

Just then two beautiful young Cubanitas walked by wearing dental floss the color of sunset. In a flash, the Colonel was up and on the trail.

"Can you gorgeous Senoritas help me? I'm wondering. Who is your dentist? He does beautiful work." Their giggles echoed all the way back to Boston.

The next eight hours were spent in frustrating attempts to get in touch with the network. Phone calls to the mainland from the La Libertad Hotel were running about $20 per minute and once I finally got through, it took another 40 minutes to convince the news director we had anything newsworthy to offer. Of course I had nothing, until the Colonel arrived.

"We're having dinner with the President," he announced without a trace of irony. "Bush is here in Havana?" It was all I could think of.

"Wrong President." He smiled benevolently. "Castro. El Jefe himself. Defender of the poor and oppressed. I called Gorbachev. He said raid the humidor."

He looked around my spartan room. I had a cheap little TRS-80 Radio Shack computer set up on the table.

"What's this?" he said as he picked it up and looked underneath.

"It's a cheap laptop computer from a cheap American company."

"Perfect. We'll give it to Castro. He'll love it."

DINNER WITH THE PRESIDENT

Sometimes it feels like Cuba is stuck in a time warp, with a bad paint job. If you ignore all the neo-classical sculpture of dead Communist heroes, it's pretty much 1955 all day long. Every street corner of Havana is a classic car show with some of the hottest music this side of New Orleans. Petr Holvquist, the photographer from National Geographic, and I emerged from the hotel and immediately spotted the Colonel playing congas with an impromptu taxi band. They finished with a flourish of horns and drums and began to laugh.

"Boys, meet some friends. This is Tito, Saco, Jesus and Manny. They play at the Tropicana. The real Tropicana."

Suddenly I realized I was seeing the Colonel in his full-dress uniform for the first time. His collar was trimmed in gold braid. The brim of his hat was covered in scrambled egg and his chest was a mosaic quilt of ribbons and bars.

"Nice suit," Petr said.

"We're headed into military country boys. Two things Latin America understands, guns and uniforms."

The three of us piled into Saco's vintage Havana taxi, a purple 1953 Plymouth coupe, and headed to the Soviet Embassy. The back seat was bigger than my hotel room.

We were greeted formally in the massive ballroom and ushered into a receiving line. I watched Castro shake hands with his guests as he was introduced to the explorers and the Soviet hosts. He looked like every picture I had ever seen of him while I was growing up. He was wearing pressed guerrilla fatigues and he smiled thinly without much enthusiasm. He looked like he was punching a time clock.

When the Colonel stepped up, Castro's face broke into a broad smile like a kid on Christmas morning.

"Colonel Sherideen. We meet at last." He embraced him with a huge bear hug.

"Senor Presidente. The pleasure is mine." The Colonel offered a crisp salute.

Just as I was about to meet the President, Castro threw his arm around the Colonel and led him off like a long-lost comrade. I didn't see them for the next two hours.

As we were about to leave, I saw the Colonel and Castro standing next to a massive statue of Lenin in the foyer. They were laughing like old college buddies.

"Casey, come meet El Jefe."

I guess I shouldn't have been shocked by the Colonel's informality. I should have expected it.

"Mister President, this is the lad I was telling you about."

"Senor Seepez. You are lucky to be traveling with such a great teacher."

"Yes, Mister President. I am." I had no idea what he was talking about.

"See that you take care of him." He shot me a menacing look that chilled me.

"Yes, sir," I stammered.

"Colonel?" Castro continued, "I will see you on your return voyage. I wish you a safe journey. Your goods will be waiting at the airport."

"I'll look forward to it, Senor Presidente."

With that we were ushered out the door. Saco was waiting for us.

"What in the hell was that about?" I said as we climbed into the cab.

"Commerce, Case. Good old fashioned American capitalism!"

The Colonel and Castro hit if off really well. In fact I'm pretty sure Castro said to Bob, -"You know, Colonel ... I'm tired. How would you like to be the boss for a while." The Colonel grinned like a catbird and settled back into the plush seats. We drove into the Havana night in silence.

JULY 30: LIMA, PERU

The next two days were a blur. I was sick with dysentery from the Embassy food. I had a fever and spent most of my time in the bathroom. I vaguely remember boarding the plane and flying to Lima. Yves, the French expedition leader, gave me something from the medical kit and I crawled into bed at the hotel. Sometime during the night I was awakened by automatic weapons fire. There was a tremendous firefight right below my hotel window. At least I think there was. Suddenly, a huge explosion rocked the building. Moments later, a military victory march began to play from tinny speakers on the street. As the smoke cleared, I swear I saw the Colonel riding in an armed military transport along the boulevard. When I asked him about it the next morning as we boarded the plane, he looked at me with steely eyes.

"Nothing happened last night. Nothing at all. And all of Peru will sleep better because of it." He then offered a short tight-lipped nod and took the hand of Genevieve, the reporter from Paris Match.

BUENOS AIRES: (Quite possibly our last night on earth).

We have a lovely dinner with three very hot and very young Argentine girls. On our way out, the Colonel disarms a man with a gun, saving the life of the owner of the hottest disco in Buenos Aires. Meister Briehagen is impressed. We spend until dawn at the disco.

AUGUST 1: PUNTA ARENAS, CHILE

Punta Arenas is a scabby, crusty little town stuck like a cigarette butt at the tip of South America. It's at the end of the world and it was our last stop before Antarctica. We arrived early Sunday morning exhausted after a long turbulent flight from Buenos Aires. There was no one to meet us at the airport, not even a customs officer. The Colonel hustled our rag-tag group into some trucks he commandeered from a couple of teenagers with AK-47's from the Chilean Air Force.

"This uniform thing is really working out for you, Colonel," Petr cracked. "When in Rome, lad."

As we drove through town, the streets were eerily quiet. Our trucks were the only vehicles on the road at 7 AM on that Sunday morning. Suddenly we turned a corner and found hundreds of people lining the main avenida. Our driver balked at the Colonel's suggestion to move on.

"What's up," he fired to me.

"Que Hay?" I ask.

"El desfile, de los banderas," he replied as if it were self-evident.

"It's a parade, Colonel. Some kind of flag ceremony. Probably homage to Pinochet."

Sure enough, a ratty military band was headed our way. They were playing what sounded like the theme from "The Godfather." Everyone in the crowd hung their heads almost in shame. The sanctity was overwhelming.

"Cover me, boys."

The Colonel leapt out of the truck and started pumping hands with the stunned crowd. He marched along smiling and shaking hands like a polished pol. After too many years of totalitarian rule from a vile hate monger like Pinochet, who led the league in human rights abuses for 17 straight seasons, the crowd really didn't know what to make of our Colonel. They weren't used to warm and affectionate military men.

His energy was infectious. Suddenly everyone was smiling, cheering even as he marched through the streets raising his fists and shouting "Viva Chile!" The band struck up a rousing number that sounded like something out of "Music Man" and the crowd went wild. The Colonel stole kisses and slapped backs and led the band back to our truck, where he hopped in the passenger seat. With police lights flashing and the crowd screaming, we got a full military colour guard escort to our hotel. Welcome to Chile.

That evening, the mood had changed dramatically. We were summoned to a meeting by the Russians. The entire expeditionary force, including the press, crammed into a tiny hall adjacent to the lobby of the only hotel in Punta Arenas. Seminiov, the de facto Soviet ringleader, stood in front of us looking like the Nazis were just outside of Moscow.

"We have a situation." The Russians loved to talk like that, especially Seminiov who was obviously some heavy party apartchik back home.

"Don't talk to him. He is KGB," one of the Russian flight crew told me at the departure banquet before we left Minneapolis.   He nodded gravely, almost conspiratorially, as if we shared some valid common experience. "Sure," I thought. "I know what you mean. I live next door to one." I figured they were all KGB.

"You will listen very carefully and follow instruction," Seminiov hammered with his thick accent. "We leave tonight. Or tomorrow. Maybe two days. Maybe more. We wait for weather. You must be ready."

The meeting was dismissed, leaving most of us wondering what was really going on. The Russians were stonewalling, refusing to go into detail. We were supposed to be ready to leave on a moment's notice. We'd have 30 minutes to board the plane or be left behind. Most of the expedition leaders demanded more information. I left when the shouting began.

Two hours later, I was hunkered in the bar with some of the press corps and a few network hacks. Stu Shandon, a Pulitzer Prize winning writer from New York was the first to speak up. He'd spent two years in Laos and Cambodia. "We're not getting the whole story. There's something going on with the plane."

"Maybe it's time to call in the Marines," I said.

"Regular Army will have to do." It was the Colonel, who slipped in next to me and ordered a beer. "It's not the plane guys. It's the runway."

"What?"

"The Captain is, shall we say, concerned? Seems the bagmen dropped a bit of intelligence along the route."

"Civilian speak, Colonel?"

"Simple physics. The Illushin 76 is the second largest aircraft in the world. A few feet shy of a C-5. Built to ferry tons of fully loaded extruded aluminum. Trouble is, she needs a 4700-foot runway to land in one piece. The runway at March Air Force Base on King George Island is 4200 feet of ice."

The collective jaws of our little group hit the floor with a decisive thud. Sedgewick and Hardaway, the reporter and photographer from Outside Magazine were the first to speak.

"My God, man. That's suicide."

"I thought Everest with the Chinese was crazy. This is nuts. With the Russians driving that bucket?"

It was true. While the Illushin was an amazing craft, amazing in the sense it flew considering its size, it was a bit disheartening flying on the beast. Besides the first-class cabin box, the plane was pretty well stripped bare. It was, after all, a military transport. Little things gnawed on our nerves. Maybe it was because the latrines kept backing up, or the way the flight crew would suddenly start scrambling in-flight for no apparent reason.

One look around the cockpit did little to instill confidence either. Exposed wires and harnesses hung from above and below the bridge. And all those gauges and dials labelled in Cyrillic characters somehow made it even more disturbing.

"Look," the Colonel offered, "these guys fly these things in and out of Siberia for God's sake. They never crash. Well, almost never. And our pilot Skatchkov is an ace. He's practically a celebrity over there. He's got more medals than me."

"What's with the weather?" Petr asked.

"We apparently have a four-hour window. Things can get pretty nasty out on the peninsula. The weather moves fast. They want us ready to move at a moment's notice. I suggest we all turn in and get a good night's rest. Tomorrow's gonna be great." He raised his glass.

I took his advice and turned in early. Just to be safe, I packed up my camera gear and settled in. I didn't have to wait long. At 3 AM the building began to shake, or I thought it did: Consciousness came slowly, and I realized someone was pounding, really pounding on my door. I shot out of bed ready to head for the airport. I threw open the door to find Nikoli Boyarsky, one of the Soviet flight engineers. He looked worried.

"Gasey, comrade. You must come." He was struggling with the language. "You must spinnish."

"I must spinach?" I couldn't wrap my head around the words.

"Spinnish. Talk to crew."

"Spanish?"

"Da. Colonel says come." He smiled. I realized he was drunk.

"The Colonel needs me to speak Spanish? What time is it?"

"Da."

I threw on my clothes and jumped into the cab Nikoli had waiting downstairs. We tore through the town for ten minutes or more and pulled up to a squat warehouse lit with a single bare red bulb over the door.

"Come, today." Nikoli yanked me out of the cab. As we moved inside, I was swallowed by the ambiance. The room was bathed in pink light. Etta James "At Last" was playing on a cheap phonograph. I was led through a doorway hung with red plastic beads to the bar where the Colonel sat in his underwear holding court. He was surrounded by several young women and most of the Soviet flight crew.

"Casey. Welcome. Nice place, huh?" He grinned and held up a beer. "Sit down. I'd like you to meet someone."

"My first whorehouse, Colonel. Congratulations."

"Casey, this is Maria Teresa. The patron saint of Punta Arenas."

A small, squat woman of fifty flashed a toothless smile and extended her hand. It held a business card. The card read, "Palacio Mustang, Pta. Arenas." There was a prominent black Playboy bunny splashed across the card.

"Con mucho gusto," I said.

"Punta Arenas, what's that mean? Whore's Arena?"

"Point Grit. Named for the sand scattered by these foul winds. What on earth are you up to Colonel? We're supposed to be ready to leave any time."

"Not without a flight crew, lad. Besides, the boys were a bit nervous, and I thought a trip out here would help take the edge off. I was hoping you could negotiate a package deal with Maria here."

I just smiled and shook my head. Even in his knickers, with his ample belly grazing the table's edge, I knew I was in the presence of greatness.

A few hours later, we had a disturbing conversation.

"You know, there's something you should know."

"What's that?" I really didn't want to know.

"I was talking to Julian."

"Of course. He showed me the charts for KGI. It's pretty hairy."

"Great." I had a feeling it wasn't.

"Here's the runway." He cleared away the bottles and an ashtray from the table.

"It's got an 18-meter ice cliff face on approach, here." He indicated the edge of the table. "And the runway's 4200 feet. Actually 4257, but who's counting? What that putz Seminiov didn't tell us is over here at the far end of the runway," he held his beer off the far edge of the table for emphasis, "is a cliff that drops 700 feet into the ocean." He smiled.

"Shit."

"Skatchkov's got balls of steel. We'll be fine. You might want to be in the cockpit with your camera through. Should be some great footage."

AUGUST 3: SOMEWHERE ABOVE THE DRAKE PASSAGE

We'd been in the air a little over two hours when I made my way up the circular stairs to the bridge. Looking out the windscreen, I was suddenly shocked. We were surrounded by nothing but white. We were wrapped in clouds and being buffeted by some serious winds. In was unnerving. The Colonel was camped out just behind the co-pilot at the navigator's station.

"Rough going, Case. We're still three hours out and bucking headwinds the whole way. "

"What's the forecast?" I was hoping for good news.

"Could get dicey. Storm's brewin' off the peninsula and moving west. South Orkney's taking it in the shorts. Sustained winds to 60 knots."

"No problem is here. Plane is strong," Captain Skatchkov said as he slapped the Colonel on the back. He looked over his shoulder and winked at me. I hated that. If he'd raised a vodka glass in toast, I don't think I would have been surprised. The Colonel's booming laugh echoed all the way down the stairs as I made my way to the cargo hold.

For the next couple of hours I tried to stay busy with my gear. I cleaned the lenses over and over. I desperately wanted to avoid thinking about the obvious. I must have fallen asleep because the next thing I knew, Petr was violently shaking me.

"Wake up! The Colonel says you better get your ass to the bridge. We're going in."

I could feel the whine of the engines throttling down on approach. I scrambled from my berth and barely had enough time to grab my camera. I took the stairs two at a time and as I reached the cockpit, I could see King George Island stretched out some two miles ahead of us and closing fast.

The air in the cockpit was tense. Skatchkov grunted terse commands in Russian as I shouldered the camera and struggled to brace myself between the pilot and co-pilot. The runway looked like a postage stamp stuck to an ice cube as we screamed in low. The runway began at the crest of a 50-foot ice cliff that hurtled towards us. There were two sets of landing lights that looked as if they had been stapled into the sheer ice face. I could see plumes of drifting snow billow off the edge of the runway.

"Here we go boys. Hang 'em high and hard. We're goin' in." The Colonel seemed perfectly at ease.

Through the tiny viewfinder, I could see the lip of the runway looming larger and larger. Skatchkov was determined to use every inch of the runway. But he was coming in too low. For an instant, I pulled my eye away from the eyepiece and all I could see was ice stretching before us. Just as the nose of our massive craft slipped past the edge, there was a sickening crack and the nose slammed down toward the ice. I was thrown forward across the control bridge and into the co-pilot.

The leading edge of my lens caught the co-pilot just above the left eye and he pitched forward with a groan. For an instant, there was pandemonium in the cockpit as the engines screamed. In slow motion, I could feel the plant drift to the starboard side. We were starting to slide. The rear end of the plane started to come forward. Skatchkov was yelling in Russian. I tried to get up but it was no use. My face was buried in the instruments.

Suddenly I was grabbed by the scruff of my parka and hurled backward. All I could see was the roof of the plane. I managed to grab the camera and I saw the co-pilot still slumped in his seat. The Colonel suddenly reached past me, his hands flying across the throttles. With one hand he grabbed the stick and with the other he pulled back on the right throttle.

"Goose the port engines," yelled the Colonel. "Full flaps."

Skatchkov pushed the left throttle forward and the plane started to straighten out. The massive thrust reversers kicked in and the plane shuddered as the ice runway hurdled below us. On my knees, I watched as we blazed past the tower. A squadron of soldiers in emergency trucks stared with their mouths gaping. Up ahead I could see the end of the runway and the ocean beyond.

We stopped just 60 feet shy of the end of the runway. Skatchkov let out a whoop and slapped the Colonel on the back. The co-pilot smiled sheepishly through the handkerchief he held to his eye. I muttered my apologies, wiped a spot of blood from my lens and made my way to the door.

From the runway, I kept my camera focused on the doorway. After most of the passengers were off the plane, I zoomed in as Skatchkov and Colonel Bob Sheridan appeared in the doorway arm in arm. They were both beaming. At the base of the stairs, The Chilean Commandant stepped forward and saluted both men. A cheer arose from the crowd of soldiers below. As the two men made their way to the ice, the Commandant pulled two huge runway lights off the back of a truck. In a display as formal as any medals ceremony I'd ever seen, he presented them both to Skatchkov and the Colonel.

AUGUST 31: THE SOUTH POLE, ANTARCTICA

With the pale pink sun just about to become a memory on the ice-glazed horizon, I watched the C-130 sent to pick up the support team dip its wings as it passed. I knew the Colonel was offering his final salute to our team. He was on his way to hook up with the Russians and the Illushin 76 for his long trip back home.

Later that night as the camera team huddled in our tents, while the mercury flirted with -60 below, I found a frozen 3-pound Cojalajote steak wrapped in a magazine ad for Amana microwave ovens. And a bottle of Stoli nested inside a Matrushka doll.

CHAPTER XIII

'THE COLONEL'

How the hell did I become a Colonel in the United States Army? Well, to set the record straight, I'm not a Colonel in the United States Army. I was commissioned through politics. My brother, Jim, was a rather heavy contributor to whatever political power at any given time was in Boston, the Commonwealth of Massachusetts, or the United States. My dad taught Jim to 'romance' the 'pols' of Massachusetts, mostly because it could be real beneficial to business. But what my brother learned, and ultimately what I have learned, is that politics in Boston is also a whole lot of fun!

It is where all the real action takes place. From the days of James Michael Curley - who got elected Mayor of Boston while he was in jail - to those of 'Tip' O'Neill - who was a real close friend of my dad's (and later became the Speaker of the House in Washington, D.C.). Of course, if you're on the inside, you have to know the Kennedys of Boston. Yes, my dad was a friend of J.F.K. when the young senator became a member of the Ancient and Honorable Artillery Company of Massachusetts and later President of the United States. With this kind of political juice, it was not difficult for me to get into the most prestigious historical military organization in the United States.

After all, I was a legacy. Not that I had shown much interest in becoming a member for most of my youth. The truth was, I had no interest, not even when my brother Jim followed in my father's footsteps and joined the ranks back in the '70s. That is, until I bumped into the son of my father's best friend, Brigadier General Robert L. Man, one afternoon, on the off chance.

Rob was a Past Commander of the Ancients and, in 1981, when I moved back to Boston from Ireland, I thought it would be a good time for me to hook up with the oldest chartered military organization in the western hemisphere - dating back to 1638. In many respects, this was one of the best moves I ever made in my life.

Here's some history.

In the early part of the 1600s, the wealthy landowners and leaders of the new colony formed a militia unit for the protection of the early governors. It was kind of an offshoot of the Honorable Artillery Company of London that was formed about 100 years earlier. The only older chartered military force that is still active is the Swiss Guard in the Vatican. Let that sink in for a second.

The history of the Ancient and Honorable Artillery Company is extraordinary, although it is often portrayed by local Boston writers as a bunch of old beer-swilling alcoholics. The reason for this is simple - to this day, some of the most influential men of Boston are members of this organization, with kind of an elitist attitude towards membership. Where you have an organization filled with hardworking, hard partying men, you'll often have enemies. Dimes are regularly dropped to the local political writers, who often write critical columns, usually based on a disgruntled wife's report of one thing or another involving the Ancients. It's always great sport to quote former Boston mayor James Michael Curley who, at a roast one night, described the Ancients as 'Invisible in war and invincible at the bar.' Well, the fact of the matter is, the Ancients have actually distinguished themselves in every skirmish during the pre-revolutionary days, and in every war from the Revolution to those in Afghanistan and Iraq.

Four presidents of the United States, including James Monroe, Chester Alan Arthur, Calvin Coolidge, and John Fitzgerald Kennedy, have been members of the Company. In this day and age, the mission of this grand old Company is largely ambassadorial and ceremonial with a goal of promoting pride in the American flag. However, because of their total ignorance on the subject, the local jerks who love to write negatively about the Ancients know nothing of this. Furthermore, they are too lazy even to try to understand the purpose of what we do.

It's easy to poke fun at a bunch of mostly retired military men (and an increasingly larger number of civilian men who have joined the Ancients) simply because they think promoting pride in the United States of America and her flag is still important. Especially in the period when writers like Boston Herald columnist Howie Can and his like chose to disrespect everything. It's no wonder we got a generation of disrespectful kids who don't even know how to stand at attention or take their ball caps off at the playing of the National Anthem at Fenway Park.

While Can and other cynics knock everything for the purpose of entertainment, the United States Department of Defense and the U. S. Department of State still happen to believe that the Ancient and Honorable Artillery Company of Massachusetts is a distinguished and equally important organization. The Department of State is directly involved with each Fall Tour organized by the Company Captain Commander. The fact that seven Ancients have been recipients of our nation's highest decoration for valor, namely the Medal of Honor, often goes unmentioned by the local Boston 'rags', and that is a disgrace. Three of these brave war heroes are presently active in the Ancients. Lt. Commander George Street, Captain Tom Hudner, and Sergeant Charles A. MacGillivary have all distinguished themselves with heroic actions in Korea, and in Charlie's case in France during World War II. Every time I read some bullshit one of these asshole Boston so-called journalists write through stupidity about the Ancients, it really bothers me.

Actually, it drives me nuts.

Every year since my induction in the spring of 1982, I've participated in the Fall Tour of Duty with the Ancients. I take pride in doing my part to promote American patriotism, and, furthermore, it's the perfect opportunity to meet and get to know some of the most powerful military men in the world - something I always cherish. When we're overseas, it's as guests of the State, usually coordinated by the United States Embassy in whatever country we visit. With the Ancients, I've paraded inside the gates at Buckingham Palace; in uniform in the former Soviet Union; and through Checkpoint Charlie before the Wall came down in Berlin. We've been received by the President of the United States and royalty of every stripe, from the Queen of England to the King of Thailand. I've participated in ceremonies from the Bridge on the River Kwai to the graveyards of the Brazilian troops who fought with our Eighth Mountain Division in Italy, to shaking hands with His Holiness Pope John Paul II in a private audience at the Vatican.

In my early years as an Ancient, I learned military history from my best friend, the federally recognized Colonel Stuart P. Tauber. As a member of the Massachusetts Army National Guard, and a true military historian, his help in training me to become a convincing Sergeant, a Colonel and Finance Officer, was invaluable. I was elected First Sergeant of Artillery and later elected Finance Officer, which carries the rank of Lieutenant. But the proudest day of my life was when I attained the rank of Colonel as an *aide de camp* to the then governor of Massachusetts, Edward King. The order was signed by Major General (MA) Vahan Vartanian on 3 December 1982. Nobody in the history of 'Coloneldom' ever got more out of his rank than me. It's become a nickname, a pet name, and it's more than a name, it's my created character.

To celebrate my new rank, General Bob Marr threw a 'wet down' for me on our Fall Tour of 1983 in Hong Kong, and at the same time made me his chief of Staff. The celebration went on for about three days. The party was fantastic and the honor of being Chief of Staff for such a distinguished Past Commander of the Ancient and Honorable Artillery Company of Massachusetts was an honor I cherish to this day.

Now, being Chief of Staff in a company whose primary purpose is ceremony, was of course right up my alley. Generals like a lot of pomp and circumstance and General Marr is no exception. My manner of constantly paying tribute to the General and ensuring that every person in our company pays the proper homage to him is actually legendary amongst our troops.

I remember the Fall Tour of 1985 when we were in Brazil for a military ceremony. We were there to decorate the graves of the Brazilian troops who gave their lives fighting with the American forces while liberating Italy. The leaders of the European economic community were in a conference at the Rio Palace Hotel, which also happened to be the abode of our men and officers. I went over to Fort Copacabana where the Brazilian army, under the command of General Mora, was headquartered. There, I met with Captain Silva, my counterpart on General Mora's staff, who immediately recognized my rank and stood up to give me a formal salute. Thereupon, I assured Captain Silva - who appeared a little flustered by my unannounced arrival - that I was there on an informal visit just to see the old World War II gun emplacements on their base. His shoulders relaxed and he nodded, appearing to buy my little story and to be genuinely pleased to greet me. Then, after schmoozing the young captain for about twenty minutes, I was ready to make my move on behalf of General Marr.

You see, I had arrived that day with a singular goal in mind: to extract as many resources as I possibly could from this unit. So, as brazen as the sun, every time Captain Silva said, 'No problem,' I'd just carefully ask for one more thing.

Our conversation went something like this:

'I've got a bit of a problem with General Marr. I need to get him a staff car.'

'Oh, that's no problem at all,' says Silva. 'What time?'

'Well, it is a bit of a problem because you know these generals, you never know when they'll move out, so I'll actually need two drivers to cover the 24-hour shifts.'

'Of course,' says Silva.

Pushing my luck, 'You wouldn't have an English-speaking interpreter I could use as a bodyguard?'

Siva's immediate reply, 'The driver will speak English and will be armed.'

Now, I won't lie - I'm slightly taken aback. Should I go for it, I'm thinking to myself? Oh, what the fuck. All he can say is no to a bird Colonel speaking on behalf of an American General, so I went for it.

'I'll need a motorcycle escort for the car.' And when Captain Silva replies, 'One or two?' I say, 'Well, he *is* a general.'

And Silva comes right back with, 'So it will be two.'

I had all I could do to hold back the smile. I knew the general would love this treatment, and when Silva said, 'Colonel Sheridan, is there anything else I can do to accommodate you and the general?' I nearly asked him for a helicopter, but I didn't have the balls. I stood up, thanked Silva for his assistance, and told him to have the car there at 19:00 hours. He gave me a fine salute and expressed his gratitude. Then I skipped down the stairs like a kid leaving a candy store. It was a job well done, and, swelling with pride, I could barely wait for 7 PM to roll around to escort General Marr down to the front door of the hotel - just to see the look on his face!

When the hour came, I met the driver and the two men on motorcycles on the street, and I immediately gave each of them about a pound and half of Brazilian cruseros. This was entirely necessary on my part. You see, the inflation was so bad you needed to tip with handfuls of cash because anything less was worthless. It took two shopping bags to carry just $200 in the local currency.

Once I had these men fully on my side, I had a bit of a problem moving another big fancy car away from the front door. I needed to have the General's car in the perfect spot, or my show would be ruined. When I questioned the front door attendants, I was informed that the vehicle in question belonged to Herr Willie Brandt, the Chancellor of West Germany. Well, in my mind, that settled the matter. With a stern look on my face, and a wad of cash in my hand, I snapped in my most military voice, 'Would you rather be at war with Germany or the United States of America?'

Not surprisingly, it was no problem at all for them to move Chancellor Brandt's car in one big circle while the General's car, complete with flags and motorcycle escorts, slithered up to the front door. I couldn't have timed the thing any fuckin' better. As if on cue, General Marr appeared on the road, and the staff and I then straightened our spines and gave a resounding formal salute. Responding with a sly grin, the General then ducked into the backseat, and we disappeared into the warm Brazilian night, ready for some fun.

Now, I could tell you how we spent the rest of that evening, but then I'd have to kill you . . .!!! Suffice it to say - it was a night to remember!

Stu Tauber, who is a regular Army double G.I. and a federally recognized Colonel, is truly a military historian. Stuart is my best friend, and he is very quick to point out that on rare occasions, when anybody questions my rank, that I am indeed a 'real Colonel.' I'm just not a Colonel in the United States Army. Stuie has taught me everything I need to know about the military. Even though I've played this little General Marr story for laughs, the fact of the matter is, I take my title very seriously. On the very formal military occasions when we have to show respect to, or pay tribute to, any of the brave heroes of forgotten wars, I carry out my duties on foreign soil and back home in the United States with the absolute dignity the uniform I wear deserves. Furthermore, because of my zeal to play the proper role as 'the Colonel' when it is necessary, I've taken it upon myself to learn everything I possibly can concerning our military forces deployed around the world.

Many of the influences that are leading to a weaker military force really concern me. When I see the United States forces getting weaker because of politics, it really frightens me. From reading extensively about the world of international arms, I can tell you the stockpile and availability of atomic, nuclear, and biological weapons for purchase is really alarming. We tend to think the Communist problem with the fall of the Soviet Union is no longer a threat. This is, without question, wrong! Are you at all familiar with 'The Communist Rules For Revolution' captured by the Allied Forces in Dusseldorf, Germany, way back in May of 1919? Just see if any of these Communist 'rules for revolution' strike any chord of concern for you:

A. Corrupt the young, get them away from religion. Get them interested in sex. Make them superficial, destroy their ruggedness. Feminize the men and masculinize the women.

B. Get control of all means of publicity and thereby:

1. Get people's minds off their government by focusing their attention on athletics, sexy books and plays, and other trivialities.
2. Divide the people into hostile groups by constantly harping on controversial matters of no importance.
3. Destroy the people's faith in their natural leaders by holding the latter up to contempt and ridicule.
4. Always preach true democracy but seize power as fast and as ruthlessly as possible.
5. By encouraging government extravagance, destroy its credit. Produce fear of inflation with rising prices and general discontent.
6. Foment unnecessary strikes in vital industries. Encourage civil disorders and foster a lenient and soft attitude on the part of the government toward such disorders.
7. By specious argument cause the breakdown of the old moral virtues: honesty, sobriety, continence, faith in the pledge word and ruggedness.

C. Cause the registration of all firearms on some pretext, with a view to confiscating them and leaving the population helpless.

Now remember, these are not my words, but those of a captured Communist document from the early part of this century. On top of this 'the Colonel' has learned other disturbing facts. Our biggest threat to this nation is the Communist Chinese. The fact that the Red Chinese People's Liberation Army owns companies that are being allowed by our government to set up business in a former U.S. naval station in California, as well as crucial airfields near the Panama Canal, is in the works as I write this book. Hopefully, by the time this work is published, enough Americans will become aware of some of these activities in order to stop the progress of Communism that is knocking on the very shores of the United States of America.

And hopefully, too, some of the cynics that waste their time knocking groups like the Ancient and Honorable Artillery Company of Massachusetts will begin to realize some of their own shortcomings. We need a strong press that does its job, doesn't allow politics to suck them in, and will take note of the warnings inherent within 'Communist Rules For Revolution'. It's not too late.

CHAPTER XIV

'THUNDER DOWN UNDER'

It always amazes me how far reaching the hatred for British politics can be. The tentacles of disdain reach all the way to the South Pacific into Vandemans land or that penal colony better known as Australia. The New Zealanders are not great fans of the crown either. It's no wonder the 1984 Olympic silver medalist in Los Angeles - who beat Evander Holyfield to become a national hero - is a Kiwi from Christchurch named Kevin Barry, the very name of an Irish patriot. Well, my fight telecasts have been carried 'Down Under' for some 40 years, and I can say without qualm that I love the folks in both great countries. If for no other reason than I have an Irish name and so do most of them!

The feeling appears to be mutual. New Zealand Airlines upgrades me to first class almost every time I travel from the States to Auckland, no questions asked. I love my job but sometimes I'm still left giddy by the special treatment I get. As you know, since I'm rarely seen on local TV in the United States, I'm a relative unknown in my native Boston. However, one night at the end of a fight telecast for Network 3 in Auckland, some 14 thousand miles from Boston, I mentioned I'd be at A. J. Hackett's Bungi Bridge to jump at 3 PM the next day in Queenstown in the South Island. Much to my surprise when I arrived at a quarter to four at the bridge, there were nearly 300 people there to see my jump. I almost shit!

You see, I have acrophobia; that means in layman's terms, 'scared shitless of heights!' The conversation went like this: 'You know, I weigh over 300 pounds.'

'No bother mate, we've thrown people off here in jeeps.'

'You know, I had a heart attack two years ago.'

'Ya, Colonel, ya big girl's blawse.' (That's New Zealand slang for being a pussy.)

Next thing I know, Georgie Calvert's wife, Janet, informs me she has always wanted to try this jump. I don't even like walking out on the bridge. In fact, hearing the news Jan was going to jump, I felt a sudden trickle of piss roll down my leg. Within a minute, Jan had made the leap and the chants of 'Colonel, Colonel, Colonel, Colonel' began to sink in. This giant of a man who thrives on being bigger than life is really a coward when it comes to heights. I once worked with my brother's roofing construction company in Boston, and to this day I'm the only V.P. of a roofing company that was never on a roof in his life!

There was no way out. I had to jump. My biggest fear now wasn't the height, or even pissing in my pants - heck, I'd already done that! I was actually more concerned that I'd shit in my pants in front of all my fans.

'Holy Shit!' I screamed, as for an instant I conquered all fears and was upside down, heading for the bottom of the gorge.

It wasn't over. I was snapped back up like a rag doll and almost hit that fucking bridge on the way up! Everything now was as if in slow motion, and with all of those people there, I could swear I heard my mate Georgie laughing his ass off, as down I went again! For me, it was one of the few times in my life I was totally silent. My dick was so far up inside of me I was beginning to believe I was a 'big girl's blawse'.

When it was over, I was experiencing a sort of euphoria, kind of like the time I was trampled by the bull in the Pershing Auditorium in Lincoln, Nebraska. 'Let's do it again!' Now I'm back on stage. The ultimate show off had conquered his biggest fear and I felt good about myself. I said I felt good, but far from well. There were nearly 700 steps from the bottom of the gorge to get back up to my waiting public. I pushed myself, and with the aid of two nitroglycerin pills, I finally made it. Indeed, the climb up was worse for me than the jump itself. When I got back to Boston and told my cardiologist, Dr. Schulman, what happened, he accused me of needing a psychiatrist, not a cardiologist. On subsequent trips to the South Island of New Zealand, I've avoided the 'Bungi Bridge' in Queenstown like the SAS was standing by 300 strong with orders in hand to shoot the Colonel on sight.

All in all, I love my mates in New Zealand. They love me and we all love Ireland. That's not to say we don't play a bit rough when we get together - all of us children still, stuck in the bodies of grown men! Poor John Lamb ended up with three broken ribs when I bounced him off a wall in a bar, after he nearly broke my leg fucking around with me. One St. Patrick's night Kevin Barry came into our suite in Las Vegas sporting a pretty good package from the day's festivities. Jokingly, he rips me out of bed, restrains me from behind and yells at the top of his lungs how he's always wanted to butt fuck me. Bottom line, my asshole was never in any real serious danger, but this big bastard who I love like a brother and is a whole lot younger and stronger than me ended up with two broken hands.

Now, Kevin Barry is a major league TV and sporting celebrity in his native New Zealand, so naturally I took the opportunity of George Calvert's Christmas party, about 200 strong, as the main speaker, to announce to all in attendance that 'Kevin Barry is a Queer.' For his Christmas present I was going to butt fuck him right then. The crowd went crazy in the alcohol drenched state everybody was already experiencing while celebrating Christmas. I had already arranged with my bodyguards Pancho Limon and Bob Daily - along with Kevin's bodyguard Glenn Moore - to stay out of it. I got about 6 or 8 of George Calvert's sons and mates to help out. These kids are some pretty rough lads, a couple of whom are professional boxers. I plotted with them to hold Kevin Barry down. My intention was to mount him from behind and mock shag him in front of the jeering crowd. The only problem was, all participants were laughing so hard that Kevin, being the powerful bastard that he is, wiggled free. He head butted me between the eyes and playfully beat the living shit out of me!

We made a truce after that, drank numerous more pints, and joined forces to make proper assholes out of ourselves, and terrorized the little South Island summer holiday community until 6 AM. So, business as usual!

I had first met Barry at the '84 Olympics when I was covering the Games for Canadian television. As a professional boxing commentator who worked for Don King - calling the biggest, glitziest fights in the sport - I was naturally regarded by the network as an expert of the highest caliber. As such, I was given carte blanche over my schedule by the producers, who trusted that I would situate myself according to the best talent on display. In reality, I didn't follow amateur boxing at all and couldn't have cared less which fighters I covered. Therefore, I essentially picked them out of a hat - all except for one.

The exercise took less than five minutes. While in my day job I prided myself on being prepared as humanly possible (even overprepared), here I was content just to show up and have a good time. To enjoy the Olympic experience. This was a vacation for me, and I'd be damned if I wasted any of it studying. So, knowing diddlysquat about him, or whether the guy even knew a right hand from a left hook, I assigned myself to Kevin's opening bout purely on the basis of his name. That's the honest truth. Of course, by the time the final had come around with Kevin going for Gold, I looked like a regular Nostradamus!

The network gushed over my prescience and really thought I had done my homework. Obviously, I was only too pleased to accept the plaudits, basking in them like some know-it-all emperor. However, silently, I marveled at how goddamn lucky I had gotten, and how swell things in life can go when you actually don't give a shit. Kevin could have been knocked out in that first round, and I might never have seen or heard from him again. Instead, he made it all the way to the final, beat a legend of the sport in the semis, and went on to have a stellar career in professional boxing both as a fighter and as a trainer.

We also became great friends. Sadly, to this day, people claim that Kevin Barry didn't deserve his silver medal. That his disqualification victory over Holyfield was at best dubious and at worst bogus. Well, that's all bullshit as far as I'm concerned. A foul is a foul and when it ends a fight, there is no other choice to be made. Sure, it's not how anyone wants to win, and it does strip the achievement of some of its shine, but in hitting Kevin with a punch off the break and knocking him out, Evander forfeited his place in the final. Bottom line. Unfortunately, the brawling Kiwi himself could never quite manage to see it that way, throwing away the silver medal as soon as he arrived home. In his mind, despite what anyone told him, he didn't deserve the prize. I've damn near lost my voice over the years trying to convince him otherwise.

You see, Kevin and I really did hit it off after the Games - brought together by simple coincidence but turning out to be genuine birds of a feather. We've had some hellraising times, particularly on St. Patrick's Day when all bets are off. As a pair of youngsters in the '80s, we drank, whored and gambled until our livers were groaning, our dicks sore and our pockets empty. And still we refused to call it a night! It was Kevin who introduced me to the promoter Dean Lonergan of Duco Boxing, an instrumental figure in my career. Dean was a former professional Rugby League player doing big things in boxing, and it was through my connection with him that I began to broadcast fights in New Zealand and Australia in the first place. So you might say that I owe Mr. Barry a slice of my fame in the Southern Hemisphere.

Although … fuck him!

The people down-under immediately embraced me. And for my part, I've always loved making the trip - the culture in both countries reminding me so much of my days in Ireland. Just fun, friendly people everywhere who love to drink, who love to fuck, and who don't take anything too seriously. The locals especially, whom I hunt out like ferrets, have given me endless pleasure. I don't know if anyone's seen Crocodile Dundee or Walkabout Creek, but those are the kind of characters you reliably find. In my case, they're almost always at the bar, given that I'm a boozehound who spends most of his time on the road dwelling in pubs. But the fact of the matter is, I love a good piss up, and I love a good brawl. So I suppose there's more than a bit of Crocodile Dundee in me, too!

My best friend of all is Georgie Calvert from Christchurch. A tough old coal miner who became a very wealthy promoter and entrepreneur, I've spent more nights getting shitfaced with Georgie than I have calling world championship fights. They used to hang guys for what we did for play. Whenever he would come to Las Vegas to blow fifty or a hundred grand, I'd teach him how to gamble (meaning how to manipulate the casinos), and whenever I'd be in his neck of the woods, we'd drink, sing and be merry for days on end - owning to the fact that Georgie owns a chain of pubs. Basically, when we're together, we're just like two kids. We love each other's company and never fail to have one hell of a hoot.

I remember one year in particular, when my late-wife Annie was still alive, we'd been spending Christmas with him and his lovely wife at their home in New Zealand. Georgie had a beautiful estate with a swimming pool, and his pool, I noticed, was a foot longer than mine. Well, you guessed it - at the first opportunity, I knocked out the end of my pool and commissioned a three-foot extension. So, the next time he was sipping a cocktail on my lawn, and he said to me, 'Hey mate, shame that my pool is bigger than yours.' I took great delight in saying, 'Not anymore Georgie. I added three more feet!' It had cost me about fifty thousand dollars in total - but fuck him. He wasn't going to have a bigger pool than me, even though he's a multi-millionaire and I'm a struggling actor.

That's our relationship in nutshell.

Covid has kept me away from those distant shores for longer than I would have liked, but I'm making plans for my return. To catch up with Georgie and with all my other mates as well. In the boxing world, you see, I've become very close with a couple of Samoan heavyweights from different eras, David Tua and Joseph Parker. Both were trained by Kevin Barry, and both are among the nicest people I've ever met.

On my first ever visit to New Zealand, I was actually met at the airport by David and his family. Forged in the image of a bull, the young contender (whom I'd never formally met) instantly recognized me and offered to take my luggage with an easy, welcoming smile. I was a bone fide celebrity in his part of the world, capable of causing a bit of a stir, but I was in safe hands with my new friends. They took me straight to their parish church where I listened to the pure spiritual music of the Samoan culture, which actually gave me chills, and joined them in prayer. It was a Protestant Church and I'm a Roman Catholic, but I didn't give a shit. To me, it's all just about believing in a superior power.

I was then invited to their home where his mother, Noella, cooked me a wonderful, traditional meal, and where the whole family just took unbelievable care of me. Something which I've always remembered.

David should have been the champ. He hit like a mule, that signature left hook! He flattened so many guys with that punch, particularly in his early career. When he did finally get his chance at the title, against the undisputed champion Lennox Lewis, he just came up short. With *short*, of course, being the key word in David's case! At 5'10", his diminutive stature for the division was always his biggest obstacle. To be effective he needed to be in tremendous shape, to throw sixty or seventy punches a round. Unfortunately, he enjoyed the buffet a little too much for that, and he basically ate himself out of title contention.

Joseph, on the other hand, as a former WBO titleholder, still can be champion. Fast, strong, athletic, relatively young. He can go all the way - once again - no question. Hell, had it not been for the excessive interference of the referee when he fought Anthony Joshua in England, we might already be talking about him as a great heavyweight.

More than anything, though, he's just a lovely, lovely man. After Annie passed away, he would call me multiple times a week, just to make sure that I was keeping my chin up. These calls gave me an unbelievable lift and did as much as anything else to help me overcome my grief. Joseph loves my stories, and he also loves hearing about my guns. Well, I've got a battalion of them both, so we talk for hours. Him, asking me questions, and me, educating him on the life of an Airborne Ranger!

I have wonderful friends in Australia, too. Filled with so many genuine crazies, I fit in down there like a didgeridoo at a music festival. But the guy I really love in Aussie Land is the former three-weight world champion, Jeff Fenech.

A popular fighter in his time (and a damn good one too), Jeff was a street thug like me, and we always had a great time together. He's married to a famous singer with superb 'feet' and has done extremely well financially. Jeff is also unbelievably generous. I remember the night that I was inducted into the World Boxing Hall of Fame in Los Angeles. I had about twenty of my buddies with me from Boston, and as we toasted my induction in a swanky, high-priced bar, I started to feel really good. It was Jeff, though, who really put the cherry on the cake. Firstly by sitting down with us, which thrilled my little group to no end. And secondly, by picking up the bar tab not only for my preternaturally thirsty table but also for everyone else in the place! He absolutely insisted on it. And Jeff wouldn't just buy you one drink; he'd buy you a bottle of whatever you were drinking. I mean, he must've spent thousands! That really shows what a great guy he was and how much fun you could have with him.

I've had many former fighters do color-commentary with me. Out of everyone, though, Jeff has been the funniest by far, because he doesn't give two fucks. I remember once on the air he kept calling me 'Colonel Sanders', really tickling himself and smiling like a ten-year-old at the back of the classroom. So, during a commercial, I turned to him and said, 'Hey. If you call me Colonel Sanders once more, you son of a bitch, I'll slit your throat!' And he just laughed even harder. But that's the kind of relationship he and I share. And afterwards, of course, we went out and got well and truly shitfaced together!

Speaking of getting shitfaced. A few years back I was with the great Joe Frazier for a whistlestop 'Speaking Tour' of the South Pacific. This was a great thrill for me and a good earner for us both. Sponsored by a trucking company and organized by the Aussie promoter Mick Gatto (along with a guy named Bernie Balmer, known affectionately to all as 'Bernie the Attorney'), we toured around all the automobile dealerships - accompanied by former pro boxer Alex Vella, who was a pretty damn interesting character in his own right. Alex, you see, earned infamy as the head man of the four-thousand-member biking gang known as The Rebels, and - let me put it like this - as I write, he is currently on hiatus in Malta!

But back to the point. Joe was an absolute sweetheart of a guy - when he was sober. When he was drinking, it was another story altogether. He would get kind of mean and surly and even at the age he was then - in his seventies - I wouldn't have dared fuck with him. But hey, I'm Irish, I'm a bad drunk too! So me and Joe had got along fine as drinking buddies. And as for the events themselves, Joe seemed to really enjoy these because (for someone as famous as him) he had been such a down-to earth guy. And they paid us a LOT of money! All fantastic, of course. But for the cash, they also worked us half to death.

This I will never forget. Having been whisked from the airport straight to a venue with about 1000 people in attendance, I asked Joe a question, just to get the ball rolling. We'd done a few of these things by now and we both knew the drill. However, for a full seven seconds, as the spotlight shone on our little panel, no answer came back. Complete silence. Then I looked over and realized instantly what was going on. Joe, who had been struggling a little physically that day, was fast asleep. I mean, literally drooling!

Straight away, I covered for him. 'Well, I know I might be kinda boring, but you gotta understand, Joe's getting up there in age too. He's a little tired now and he's a little impaired but remember - he was one HELL of a fighter!'

We only had one small issue after that. Joe wasn't too pleased that the promo cut to introduce our Q&A sessions had included highlights of his match against George Foreman in 1973, when he lost the title. He was bounced off the canvas six times in that fight and considered it an embarrassment. I had to try to convince him otherwise. 'Joe,' I said. 'We have to leave that in to show everybody just how goddamn brave you were. Who else could have gotten up all those fuckin' times? That took character!' And finally Joe acquiesced, partly through my powers of persuasion, but mostly because he was so tired.

He just wanted to go back to sleep.

CHAPTER XV

'THE DIRTIEST BUSINESS'

In 1991, I was appointed Chairman of the Massachusetts State Racing Commission by Governor William Weld, a man who would probably have run for president of the United States had he himself not been royally fucked by politics. Just as Governor Weld was a great governor, I was probably the best racing commissioner the state has ever seen. I don't say that because of ego. I say that because, I'll readily admit, that as good of a commissioner as I was, I was just that bad as a politician.

Governor Weld resigned to become the United States Ambassador to Mexico, a move engineered by the national Democrats to clear the way for Congressman Joe Kennedy to become the governor of Massachusetts. President Clinton believed that Kennedy could easily win the Democratic nomination for governor of Massachusetts and then go on to beat Republican Governor Paul Cellucci. So, he dangled this carrot in front of Weld, knowing that it would be damn near impossible for the aspirational governor to pass up. However, Weld had no idea that once he resigned his post, that old fart Jesse Helms then had the power to block his nomination for ambassador. It was a complete set-up.

Helms came up with some bullshit about Weld being light on crime, suggesting that with all of the drug problems in Mexico, he would be a bad fit for this job. Well, Bill Weld was a federal prosecutor before being governor. Anyone who knows anything about politics knows that Weld would have made an excellent U.S. Ambassador to Mexico - not to mention an ideal presidential candidate. Incensed, Weld went down to Washington to attempt to fight for his job, but, just like when I tried to keep my position as racing commissioner, when the powers that be want you out, 'You're fuckin' out!' Despite the political sophistication and survival instinct of Weld, when he stepped up to the big leagues in Washington, they ate him alive. So, for the time being, another good man was out of politics.

In my own case, when I took over as Commissioner of Racing in Massachusetts, horse racing was dead and dog racing was on its way down. In four short months, I was instrumental in getting legislation passed to open two horse racing tracks and get 2 million dollars appropriated for the Department of Agriculture to promote thoroughbred racing in the state. I had done all of the groundwork for Don King to promote a 7-million-dollar race at Suffolk Downs in East Boston. We were going to pay 3 million dollars for first place, 2 million for second place, a million dollars for the show horse and a million to the field. We had plans to run the race between the Breeders Cup and the Arlington Million when most of the world's top horses would already be in the United States.

Don King wanted to have a racing field made up of the United States Triple Crown winners, plus horses from Australia, New Zealand, Hong Kong, India, the Arabian Peninsula, three or four European horses, and a couple from Latin America. The purse offered would attract the world's best, along with one Massachusetts bred horse. We were going to beam this race around the world to every track that had betting, as well as on Kingvision worldwide. The race was more than an idea. The race was in the works. Suffolk Downs was under renovation, and I had completed the preliminary work with Don King's number one legal man, Charles Lomax. At the same time, I was also working on improving greyhound racing with the track owners and dog men - an endeavor in which I really believed.

Dr. Andelman and I were on a program to improve track safety for dogs. I was on top of the Adopt-A-Greyhound Program and working with our own judges and chemists to improve track and racing security. Honestly, I felt that I was getting really good at this job. My background as a State Commission judge for eight years had given me a good feel for politics, plus I had been a banker - so I was adept at the financial end of the business as well. All the pieces were in place for me to succeed. I was the first commissioner that could actually sit down with each of the track owners and digest their exact personal agendas. This was important because each of the track owners had his own political juice. The Jockey's Guild, the horsemen and dogmen, and the lobbyists from harness racing to Gamblers Anonymous were all on the front burner with me. For the first time in Massachusetts racing history, the Commonwealth had a high profile guy who could promote racing and not just police it.

Unfortunately for my political career, high profile newcomers to Massachusetts politics don't last too long. That seemed to be the trend anyway. Captain Chad Foreman, whose brother was Minority Leader Peter Foreman, Speaker of the House Charlie Flaherty, Public Safety Commissioner Jimmy Roach, State Police Commissioner McCabe, and the Lieutenant Governor himself, had all attempted to warn me. But by the time I paid any attention, it was already too late; my fate in the position was sealed.

My political tutors were the Governor's aide Steve Tocco, General Joe Milano and my immediate boss, Secretary of Consumer Affairs Gloria Larson. They were all great champions of 'the Colonel'. When I started meddling in 'off track betting', the shit started to hit the fan. I had the power to get the legislation, and this must have pissed somebody off. Everybody on the Hill has his own agenda and my right-hand man, Mike Callahan, a career political figure in the State House, tried to slow me down, but I didn't get the message. After all, I was working 18-20 hours a day and I was on the move.

After returning from a trip to the Vatican in March, I took the job as commissioner. This was only June and while, as I mentioned, I was high profile in the newspapers or television almost daily, I thought it was a great way to put racing on the map. Up until this point everything that came out in the press was very positive - effusive even. After all, I was doing a great job, so I was not surprised at the glowing praise. Then, suddenly, as my push for 'off-track betting' began to heat up, the media turned on me. I knew that the writers were being spoon-fed bullshit. However, since not a shred of truth was contained in any of the 'hit pieces' that began to flow, I initially didn't really care. But then it started to get dirty.

The writers - who must have been on somebody's pad - turned vicious. Making me look like an asshole was great sport. If I wasn't drunk at the Governor's Inaugural with two black prostitutes, I was getting my military title embroidered on the cuffs of my shirts. I was accused of selling drugs at an Ancient's Change of Command Ceremony, and of frequenting well-known brothels deep into the night. The day after I turned my financial records over to the Ethics Commission, there was a big story on how 'the Racing Czar' may be forced to resign because of financial problems. If you took time to read the story, it actually pointed out how I owed $2300 on a 33-thousand-dollar Mercedes Benz automobile. Politics is not a business about truth; it's a business about perception.

With all the flak I was getting in the media, the Governor's legal eagles, Marc Robinson and Bob Cordy, called me to the Governor's office to 'good cop, bad cop' me into issuing an apology for my actions. Basically, I told the two former prosecutors to go fuck themselves. 'I refuse to apologize, and I won't resign.' But the wind had changed direction. Soon after, my attorney Colonel Al Johnson, a former partner of F. Lee Bailey, advised me that 'the cards are stacked against you,' and that I should think about resigning. When I found out my car was bugged and the telephones in my office and home were tampered with as well, and then that my apartment had been broken into, I had already made up my mind that I was going to step down.

As much as I loved the job, it had become a hassle. I had become 'a liability' to the Governor and the Lieutenant Governor. But I wouldn't go easy. There were some problems in Ireland, so I decided to take a two-week vacation on the state's tab. I had put in enough hours to take a year's vacation, but the two weeks were fine. I came back to Boston to resign quietly. Al Johnson, the lawyer who successfully defended Patty Hearst years ago, and was handling the high-profile case involving Pam Smart, the schoolteacher in New Hampshire who had her students kill her husband, was looking all sad in his big office when I went in. Al was upset knowing I was about to resign a position I loved. I opened up with an equally sad face saying, 'Al, well I guess I have to resign, but before I do, you've got to tell me one thing.' I was, of course, joking, and asked Al with a very serious face, 'Are you fucking Pam Smart?' Al Johnson almost shit himself laughing, and as bad as it was for me, I laughed for ten minutes with him.

Thank God for humor.

Following my resignation, Speaker of the House Charlie Flaherty, Secretary of Consumer Affairs Gloria Larson, and Director of Public Safety Jimmy Roach all had to resign. Within the space of a year, Marc Robinson, Bob Cordy, and Steve Tocco were all gone from the Governor's office. The next three commissioners of racing all fell flat on their faces. Peter Foreman was replaced as the Minority Leader. The President of the Senate, whose brother was Whitey Bulger - the convicted organized crime boss - disappeared from the Hill. And, additionally, FBI special agents trying to investigate the Lieutenant Governor came to my home to attempt to get some dirt on Governor Paul Cellucci!

The halls of power, it seems, are filled with dominos.

I hate to admit it, but as I get older, I'm getting more cynical. However, I choose to believe I'm getting smarter as well, and there is something to be said for the wisdom you gain with age and experience. Why should a novice politician like me feel bad for his failure? What happened to Governor Bill Weld is worse, and what's happening right now to President Donald Trump is even worse still.

My brain can accept that the political landscape is a fucked-up place. The thing that bothers me is that politics do not end with governments. There is politics in everything. Every business, every sport, every army, and every religion. Human beings have been lacking in morality and ethics since time immemorial, from Commodus to Putin - and that's not about to change now. I just keep going back to the words of my old godfather, Paddy Casey. 'We are just passing through. The idea is to have more good times than bad, and more good acquaintances than bad, and one or two real friends in your entire life make it all worth living.' Those are pretty profound words from an 80 plus year old man who had no formal education and lived in a little 15-foot caravan with no toilet or running water for most of his life.

CHAPTER XVI

'ME AND THE HOLY SEE — THE VATICAN'

Traveling to the Vatican with the Ancient and Honorable Artillery Company of Massachusetts, my heart was pounding all the way. On the plane, I couldn't seem to get comfortable, and in the car, I fidgeted so damn much that my ass was making music on the leather! Never in my life had I felt this nervy, this on edge, but I suppose it was natural. After all, I was there for a specific reason - to have a private audience with my one true hero, Pope John Paul II.

It was the fall of 1987. I was at the Tomb of Saint Peter himself, celebrating Mass with Father McCabe and a Swiss Guard named Tino Coffee. Just to be there with the opportunity to shake hands with the Holy Father filled me with so much excitement that I could hardly stand myself.

I had become a Vatican groupie. As I learned more about the Church, I became a better Catholic, and the priests and I would travel to the Vatican for any excuse. Our connections inside the Vatican soon gave us free rein. Swiss Guards were assigned to escort us any place we wanted to go within its parameters, and we never failed to take full advantage of their hospitality. I remember one day spotting Cardinal Casaroli sitting in the garden behind St. Peters. I motioned for the Swiss Guard to pull the car up and stop. 'I want to speak with the Cardinal.'

Tino immediately said, 'No, do you know who that is?'

'Yes Tino, he's Cardinal Agostino Casaroli, Secretary of State, number two in command, and probably the single most powerful man in the Catholic Church, and he just happens to be a friend of mine.'

I told a little white lie in the Sunday afternoon shade of the rock on which Saint Peter himself once stood.

I got out of the car and walked over to the Cardinal, stuck out my hand and said, 'Colonel Bob Sheridan from Boston, over here for the installation of the new Swiss Guard. I don't mean to bother you, but I wanted to take this opportunity to bring you the best wishes of Cardinal Law.'

He motioned for me to sit down, which I did immediately. All I could think of was that Tino, the Swiss Guard, must think me and Casaroli are 'budsos'.

The Cardinal was actually delighted that anybody would speak with him. Too busy to ever see formally, and too powerful to ever engage informally, he lived what must have been a very solitary life. My impromptu greeting, then, as he sat alone in contemplative silence, must have been a real novelty! However, as I had learned years ago in my many meetings with Miami Dolphins head coach Don Shula, you don't linger too long. So, after about a minute, I wished the Cardinal well, he returned greetings to Cardinal Law of Boston, and would you believe it, he embraced me and motioned a blessing as I departed for the car, a shit-eating grin on my face.

Getting into the car I said, 'Good guy.' Father McCabe, who was fully aware of my scam, had a bigger grin on his face than I did, but Tino was in shock.

In my many travels with Father McCabe - who was the Chaplain for the Headquarters Company of the Massachusetts Army National Guard of the Yankee Division (and was also Chaplain of the Ancients, the ceremonial unit I was attached to) - I met the Papal Nuncios in Japan, Thailand, and Chile. In fact, I entertained the Cardinal of Thailand and was his driver in Boston for a day during his visit with Father McCabe. He sent me a beautiful painting of 'The Seven Blessed Martyrs of Thailand'. Little did I realize that, with the proper introduction, these powerful men in the Catholic Church are just regular guys. This was never more evident than the night the Papal Nuncio in Japan came outside the palace to hail a taxi for me, Father McCabe, and Father Bob Durkee. Talk about VIP treatment! I was both gob smacked and flattered.

Thereafter, I was the military escort to Cardinal Vlk of Prague in the Czech Republic, getting to know him real well. And of course, when Father John Allen and I had drinks in the Papal Nuncio's palace in Chile, I never could have dreamed that Cardinal Angelo Sodano (who was only a Bishop at the time) would replace Cardinal Casaroli when he retired as the Vatican Secretary of State in 1990!

Our influence in ceremonies at the Vatican has expanded over the years, primarily because of the close connection of the Swiss Guard and the Ancient and Honorable Artillery Company of Massachusetts. Recently, Father McCabe and I took it upon ourselves to entertain the young Swiss Guards when they came to Boston for intensive English studies at Harvard University. Major General Jimmy Lynch, my sponsor into this historic unit of military status, is a close personal friend of Colonel Buchs, the Colonel Commander of the Swiss Guard. Colonel Buchs always gives Father McCabe and me the best seats during ceremonies involving the Holy Father and the Swiss Guard.

At a recent installation of the new Swiss Guards, where they actually take their oath to protect the Holy Father, I sat between the Admiral of the 6th Fleet in the Mediterranean and a Marine Corps Lieutenant General. And you guessed it. By the time the ceremony reached its conclusion, just a few short hours later, the Admiral, the 'Three Star,' and I were like old buddies! They had really taken a shine to me. So when the Colonel commanding the Vatican Guard went to introduce me to these two distinguished military officers, I took great pride when simultaneously they said,

'Oh! We know Colonel Sheridan.' I loved it. It sounded like the three of us were long-time buddies. Colonel Buchs had no idea that we had just met that day. I am equally sure that fact didn't hinder my status in the eyes of the Pope's number one bodyguard.

Then things just kept getting better.

You see that same day, when I was introduced to the Holy Father himself, John Paul II actually uttered, 'Hello Colonel.' My jaw landed on the floor, and I could have died that very second, a happy man! Since then, I have taken great pride in saying to anybody who thinks I'm famous for being a sportscaster that that really is nothing. 'You know how big I am?' I say to them. 'You know what the Pope calls me?' And, of course, they think I'm completely full of it. But hey, that's what happens when you live as crazy a life as mine. Most people can't fathom your experiences.

However, without a doubt, my greatest moment in the Vatican was when Father McCabe brought his mother and father over to Rome for their 50th wedding anniversary. It was March 15, 1991. Father McCabe arranged for us to actually get into the Holy Father's private apartment for a picture with the Pope and his parents together. Despite all the mega events I had covered in the world of sports and all the other crazy stuff I'd otherwise done in my life, still nothing could top this. My thoughts were, 'I just can't believe where I'm standing.' Now we only had about 30 seconds to be alone with Pope John Paul II, and I was so excited I actually forgot to get a picture alone with the Holy Father. But I do have a beautiful picture of Father McCabe and the Holy Father displayed in my living room in Boston, offering me some consolation!

So yes, I have had some incredible experiences over the years on my many visits to that famed city-state. Some of the best of my life - without question. But inevitably, there have also been some sad moments involving the Vatican and the Swiss Guard. On one of our trips, Father McCabe and I had the pleasure of dining in the apartment of Deputy Commander Alois Estermann and his wife. Estermann was a crucial figure in the Vatican, responsible for the day-to-day 'hands-on' operation of the Swiss Guard. He would eventually become the commanding officer of the elite military unit, the world's oldest military organization. Instead, in the spring of 1998, on the eve of the Deputy Commander's installation as the new commanding officer of the Swiss Guard, Alois Estermann and his wife were both gunned down and killed in that same apartment below the Pope's residence. The killer was a disgruntled young Swiss Guard who Estermann had disciplined earlier in the week. Shortly before, Estermann's parents had arrived in Rome, expecting to attend a ceremony in the Vatican. Instead, the ceremony they attended turned out to be their son's funeral.

That was a somber day inside the borders of the Vatican, just as it had been when Albino Luciano - who took the name of Pope John Paul - died in his sleep on

September 28, 1978, of a suspected heart attack. Mystery still surrounds the death of the 'Smiling Pope', as he was known. Nevertheless, I believe it was by divine guidance that Cardinal Karol Wojtyla of Poland, as his successor, became Pope John Paul II.

Boston's Cardinal Humberto Medieros is credited with saying, 'It was as if the Holy Spirit had touched us that we elected Cardinal Wojtyla.' All of the cardinals had gone into seclusion to meditate and pray following several unsuccessful ballots to elect a new Pope. Suddenly the Polish cardinal comes out of nowhere and is elected Pope. Time has since shown John Paul II to be a great man. I loved him. I prayed to him and for him, and I feared for the Catholic Church when he died.

I've learned over the years to have great faith in God, and I credit this to the leadership of Pope John Paul II. The glow that surrounded him was unparalleled. I saw him in Boston, Miami, and in Ireland, where thousands of people gathered to catch a glimpse of this most holy of men, and where they prostrated themselves at his feet. To think that I've been practically alone with him in his own apartment in the Apostolic Palace in the Vatican City State, where he called me 'Colonel' and looked me straight in the eye, always blows my mind to smithereens.

You see, I really am a Pope groupie.

You don't have to be a practicing Catholic to appreciate the works of Pope John Paul II. My military, banking and boxing travels have provided me with the experiences very few people in the world can claim. I don't have any real answers for the future of the Catholic Church, but if you're still reading this book, you already know I certainly have my opinions on everything, including the Catholic church.

The future of the Church will depend on the Vatican's attitude toward the modern world. I foresee significant growth in the Catholic Church coming from African nations. Generally speaking, Africans have no tolerance for Canon Law, a celibate clergy, or the doctrine developed by European theologians over the centuries. The Catholic Church appeals to the downtrodden and the poor, so third-world countries will play an ever-increasing role in the Church. However, several issues still need to be addressed and corrected. The most pressing problems will continue to be birth control, abortion, the ordination of women priests, marriage for priests, and the Vatican's position on divorce and remarriage following a divorce. Ultimately, though, it's the quality of the men and women at the helm of power that will decide the fate of this institution.

One thing I've learned is that political corruption is rampant everywhere. Whether it is in Boston politics, the Commonwealth of Massachusetts, the United States of America, the United Kingdom or the world of sports, 'greed' is the driving force of political corruption. To find out that the legal profession as well as the medical profession are by no means unscathed is not surprising. And history tells us that political corruption even takes place in the politics of the Catholic Church.

For two thousand years the Roman Catholic Church has survived. Whether it was in the times of the Holy Roman Empire, the corruption of the renaissance Papacy, or the more recent Vatican Bank scandal, somehow, and I truly believe it is with divine guidance, good prevails over evil.

In my lifetime, Pope Pius XII and Paul VI internationalized the Curia and the College of Cardinals; Pope John XXIII called the Ecumenical Council that began big changes in the Church while I was growing up; Pope Paul VI brought the Council to its conclusion by instituting changes and reforms; Pope John Paul began the reforms that eventually exposed and dealt with corruption in the Vatican political structure; and Pope John Paul II, while perhaps guilty of reversing - or at least slowing down - any radical reform in the Church, straightened out the Vatican's finances and brought the Church to the millions of Catholics around the world with his extensive travels.

His use of the media was not only influential in the fall of Communism behind the Iron Curtain but also led to a brand-new interest in the Catholic Church and the Papacy worldwide. Changes, however, will be slow to come. After all, the Church has a 2000-year history, and there are very few institutions that have survived for that length of time. With that being said, it's worth questioning the arrogance of intellectuals who think the Church is in any real trouble. The Vatican is fully aware of the public opinion polls and all other forms of negative feedback as well. As Father Thomas J. Reese wrote in his book on The Vatican and its Politics, 'Church history teaches that there are periods of progress when the Church responds with intelligence, reason and responsibility to new situations.' If the Catholic Church is going to continue to grow in the 21st century, reasonable change is the key.

I pray that will happen. After all, my own faith has brought me back from the brink many times over.

The clergyman I would turn to most for help, guidance, morality issues, or a simple boost to my faith was a ruddy-cheeked Protestant minister named Reverend Durkee. Father Durkee was a truly holy man, and I showed him respect with a kiss on the cheek each and every time we met. His wife Diane, too, was like Mother Teresa to me. Even on her death bed, she inspired me. She knew I was a bit of a rake, but just like Jesus Christ himself, she would never turn her back on me. I mention this now because I truly believe I am guided by the Holy Spirit. Do you think it's just coincidence that while I had great disdain for Ian Paisley and his band of Protestant hoodlums, with hate clouding my vision like steam on glass, the good Lord put me in the path of the most holy and respected family I know? The Durkees are Protestants to be sure, but I loved them as much as I loved anyone. Remember, my grandfather was an Orangeman until he became a Catholic when he married my grandmother, Annie Graham. In spite of my grandfather's Orange blood, it was his inspiration so many years ago that turned a red-blooded American boy into a green-blooded child with a romantic love for the 'old country'.

My grandfather couldn't help his soft-heart yearning for Ireland. Somehow, whenever I get in trouble, I feel he's watching over me from his lofty perch on one of those series of tri-colored clouds.

When you're close to the Church, you learn to be a man of great faith. Otherwise, it would be absolutely impossible to be a practicing Roman Catholic. It's all based on tremendous faith - and it's with this inner faith that you tend to believe in your own convictions and are not at all afraid to put your faith in others.

It was the Sacred Heart of Jesus that graced the home of every Catholic in Ireland and I'd often get the shivers when I thought the eyes of Jesus were following me across the kitchen to the bathroom. Was he really keeping an eye on me? I don't know, but I believe Jesus Christ is personally with me at all times. This faith was taught to me by my father, encouraged by the Benedictine monks at St. Anselm's Monastery at college in Manchester, New Hampshire, and presently in the hands of the several priests that advise me on a nearly daily basis.

With the help of God, I live and travel better than all the millionaires I know. This lifestyle prompted Colonel Dick Civiterese to echo one of my favorite quotes concerning me. Dick first says of himself, 'I am a millionaire. But all I want to do is live like the Colonel!'

This always brings a smile to my face.

CHAPTER XVII

'IT'S A WONDERFUL LIFE'

Whenever I'm asked, I always tell people The Rumble in the Jungle was my most memorable fight; however, the fact is, my most memorable fight was the John Conteh fight in Uganda that never took place.

'Can you leave tonight? John Conteh is fighting in Kampala for the light heavyweight championship of the world, and Jack wants you to call the fight.'

'Sure,' I say, 'but where in the hell is Uganda?'

Mary said, 'Fly to Nairobi, then we'll have a flight pick you up and fly you to Entebbe. I'll ring back in two hours and have your flight arrangements, so we can have you met. You can't get in without a visa, so the government officials will meet you!'

The next day I was on the road. Traveling to New York, and then to Paris, and then to Rome, and then finally to Kenya.

As I flew first class from New York to Paris, I met a real sophisticated lady flying to meet her husband in Paris. This lady, who as it turned out was actually the wife of a 32-year-old president of an airline - this beautifully preserved 50-something lady with huge melons, dripping with sexuality - really turned me on. It took three bottles of some fine French wine, a little port, and some Irish cognac, but I got her all heated up by little kisses on the neck, her ear, and the tops of her heaving breasts, and then some real deep wet kissing. Her hand went under the blanket and grabbed my cock. I almost came right then, but this heavy petting and kissing went on for over three hours in the dark of the Atlantic crossing. It must have been something about the romance of Air France, only I don't think so! I was just a young horny guy, and she oozed sexuality. I wish I could tell you I nailed her, but I didn't. It would have made a better ending, but if I did her, it would have lasted all night. To this day, I hardly ever fly the Atlantic when I don't think of this woman, her looks, her make up, her body, her smell, her soft voice, her softer hands, her puddle in the seat, and my stiff dick!

What a start to an amazing adventure to come (no pun intended).

In Paris, I transferred to Alitalia Airlines and the farthest thing from my mind was the John Conteh light heavyweight championship fight. That wasn't about to change. You see, once I got my mind clear of Mr. Airline President's wife, my thoughts swiftly turned to my upcoming destination - about which I precisely knew zip!

Moments after landing in Kenya, dabbing at my neck with a handkerchief and stretching out my legs, I realized that I might as well have been on another planet.

Feeling my balls begin to slow-roast, I was met by my escort, Patrick Odeumbo, and flown to Entebbe where I was escorted by a military convoy to the Holiday Inn in Kampala. I had learned from my trip to Zaire that autographed pictures of Muhammad Ali were better than cash (even if Angelo Dundee signed Ali's pictures for me). Once I gave Odeumbo the picture of Ali, he thought I was the greatest guy he ever met, and I knew I owned him. There was nothing he wouldn't do for me, including setting up a meeting with Idi Amin himself.

To my surprise, Amin, President for Life, was anxious to meet the American sportscaster. I had just settled in my digs at the Holiday Inn when I learned Conteh broke his hand, and the fight was in question. I had to work fast because I knew the fight would be postponed and the likelihood of me ever getting to Uganda again was very limited.

Amin's troops threw everyone out of the hotel except for our TV crew, the fighters and sparring partners. I thought the power they had was great as long as I was on the inside. My new pal, Patrick, hung around me like a bitch in heat, but he turned out to be a most valuable friend. He actually arranged for me to meet this fat fuck in shorts who wanted to play basketball with me. The guy couldn't move but he could shoot pretty good. And the game that we played - at his insistence - was called 'outs'. 'Why the fuck not?' I thought, by then just pleased to be out of the hotel for a few hours. I think I had him O-U to nothing before I realized I was actually beating 'the President for Life', Idi Amin Da Da himself! I almost peed my pants when I saw Odeumbo and the bodyguards and other soldiers concealing laughter at the way I was trash talking and shitting all over this brutal dictator. I admit my decorum changed drastically when I knew for sure it was Amin who, by now, was leading O-U to O-U-T. I went with my left-handed sky hook, and it was all tied up at O-U-T to O-U-T. Should I beat his ass? After all, he had executed thousands for saying a whole lot less than I already had said.

'Fuck him,' I said to myself. 'If he hasn't got a sense of humor, I'd be dead already.' Besides, he thought from the Ali-Foreman telecast last fall that I was a whole lot more famous and important than I really was.

With that I elected to go with a short jumper about three feet from the hoop! S-W-I-S-H! The pressure of the Celtics-Lakers finals at Boston Garden was on him with this simple shot. His troops were silent, Patrick was holding his breath, Amin was shaking, and it was just before he started his move to the bucket when I came out with, 'It's so quiet you could hear a mouse fart!' He stumbled in laughter. I thought he was felled by an assassin's bullet, but somehow he got the shot off. The ball hit the rim and shot straight up. As he collapsed to the deck, the ball miraculously went through the hoop, and the crowd of about 15 cheered and began firing off the AK-47's. I almost pissed myself between the laughter and the terror of the distinct possibility of being executed. I had a lot of balls, but I didn't care to be separated from them, so I immediately declared him the winner!

I was really in his favor now. He had a broad smile in spite of the fact that he was beat to shit from his fall. Although I only saw him one more time from a distance, I'll never forget this experience. It was bizarre to the extreme and yet, in my crazy life, not all that surprising. Hell, half the shit I've seen and done over the years, even I have trouble believing actually took place. I remember that Dick Descutner, my boss at WCIX-TV, the South Florida-based TV station, thought I was full of shit when I returned from Uganda - bursting with tales about my encounter with Idi Amin Da Da! As was so often the case in my life, reality smacked a little too much of fiction. But hey, what could I do?

Here's another little episode that sticks out.

Back in the '90s, I was working over in England, calling the contest between world featherweight champion Tom 'Boom Boom' Johnson and British sensation, Prince Naseem Hamed. I couldn't have been more hyped for this one. Not only was 'Boom Boom' a dear friend, but I considered the Brits - with their soccer-style chants - to be absolutely the best fans in the world. And of course, I loved the hooligans as well!

Following Hamed's eighth round stoppage of Johnson, which had left me a little depressed, flanked by the troupe of Don King Productions, I returned to my shithole of a hotel on the London Docks about a mile from The London Arena. The quality of the hotel is key to the story; as is the fact that some of my dearest friends in boxing also happened to handle Johnson, whose record indicates he's one of the greatest featherweights in the history of boxing. Tom Johnson was a great kid and a super champion - and so were his handlers. Debbie King took over the management reigns from Jackie Kallen, but while Don King was grooming Debbie and Carl King to run his empire in the future, for the present Duke Durden, former Las Vegas boxing commissioner, great matchmaker and a very experienced boxing man for over sixty years, was the camp coordinator. I love Duke because he uses a K 55 Mickey Mantle bat to hit and he once told the owner of a restaurant on the French Riviera that if 'the Colonel' can't eat there, then the champ and his 11-man entourage will leave the premises. Needless to say, I ate.

Anyway, I knew there would be a huge crowd back from the London Arena following the fight. And seeing how small the bar was in my pokey hotel, I gave the night barman a £100 tip to ensure instant service when I returned. After all, my brothers-in-law Mick Kelly, Shaggy O'Shea, Jer Cahill, and a buddy of theirs from Waterford, had made the trip over from Ireland. Buying for Tom Johnson's corner was automatic, but now I was under extreme pressure to entertain the boys from home as well.

As I walked away with two tray loads of pints amid a sea of thirsty Brits, one lad made this dumb comment: 'Have a look at that n***** lover buying all the drinks.' He lobbed these words in my direction like rocks at a store window.

Being a true Irishman, I delivered the drinks to the table without spilling a drop. I then quietly told Vonzel Johnson, by now a huge heavyweight, and that little peanut

Virgil McClendon that I might need some back up. Now, while Virgil is small, he was a tough street kid from Columbus, Ohio, who had recently survived a good stretch in state prison; in other words, this active little professional fighter is one tough motherfucker and, on top of that, one of my best friends.

I loved Vonzel so much that I often passed us off as cousins, explaining that my mother and his mother were sisters, and his mum married a black guy. Hence the difference in the pigmentation of our cousinly epidermis. You get the idea. I loved these two men and nobody, especially this dirtbag Brit, was going to insult them in my company.

As we strode towards the bar, Duke Durden said in his country ass New Orleans drawl, 'Hey, Colonel, you need any help?' I was pretty fired up and answered, 'Let me see, there are eight of them and three of us. You sit your tired ol' country ass down. This won't take long.' When the three of us arrived at the crowded bar, the big mouth said to me, 'Oh! You're really a tough guy with your friends!' Vonzel: 'What did you call us, British asshole!' 'I called you all n*****!!!' came the reply. Well, that really got everyone's attention. You almost had to respect the balls on this fuckin' guy. However, in the next 60 seconds, the idiot in question - along with his group of flunkies - was to experience more violence than he had dreamed possible in his life. Suffice it to say, Duke wasn't needed.

We all avoided the cops by going up to 'Boom Boom's' room for pizza and beer. I had to laugh out loud. One stupid moment of bigotry and we had turned this place into a scene reminiscent of 'The Bridge at To-Ko-Rhi'! We all agreed it was the most fun any of us had had since high school - at least outside of a boxing venue. Besides being tabbed 'his hooligan announcer' by my boss and producer Marty Corwin, I felt pretty good about the whole episode. Sometimes in life you run out of cheeks to turn. And being that I was at least a hundred-and-fifty pounds overweight, and prone to coronaries, my stamina in the heat of battle (although certainly challenged) was incredibly up to par! Though there was a sad aside: Tom 'Boom Boom' Johnson was no longer the featherweight champion of the world.

That was another one of those nights - of which I've had too many to count in my lifetime - that took a truly crazy turn. But when you do what I do for a living, you find that craziness somehow becomes the norm. Top-level boxing - more so than any other theater of entertainment - has a way of spinning hurricanes around itself, and for much of my career I've sat happily in the eye of the storm. From the infamous 'Fan Man' flying into the ring to delay the Evander Holyfield vs. Riddick Bowe rematch, to champagne bottles and various other missiles showering the ring in Germany when Francois Botha defeated Axel Schulz, I've lived through so many 'holy shit' moments that I can barely separate them. These days, my brain feels more overcrowded than Calcutta. It's no easy task, therefore, to recount fifty years of memories - especially when the events that make up those memories come so thick and fast that they actually begin to feel normal. So, before Alzheimer's *really* sets in, I'd like to share some of my reflections from ringside, spanning the past five decades.

They say I've called over 10,000 fights. Well, they've been saying that for years - a dozen at least. So, maybe I've done 12,000 fights, or 13,000 fights, I really don't know. What I do know is that I've been recognized for my work. After all, I'm now in seven boxing Halls of Fame while Muhammad Ali - 'The Greatest' himself - is only in three! But of course, the fact is, I've been doing this for longer than most people have been alive.

Remember, the first world heavyweight title fight I covered was all the way back in 1968, when Jimmy Ellis and Jerry Quarry ducked it out in Oakland, California, for the vacant WBA championship. I turned up with a blonde on each arm and settled immediately into my 'bigshot' persona, knowing intuitively that it was all just a show. Ever since that night, parked within range of the blood and the sweat (the reason for my perennial red tie) and thrilled beyond measure each time I arrive at ringside, I've had the privilege of calling for some of the very best fighters in history. The great heavyweights of the '70s. Ali, Frazier, and Foreman. The great middleweights of the '80s. Hagler, Leonard, and Hearns. And the great lighter fighters of the '90s and '00s. Julio Cesar Chavez, Pernell Whitaker, and Floyd Mayweather. And these are to mention but a few that I've covered.

You name them, I've probably called for them.

Here's what I've learned: a champion fighter, much like a champion racehorse, in the best possible sense, is a complete freak! After all, so many ingredients go into the making of a great prize fighter. First, there's the speed. I've had the pleasure of watching in live action some of the speediest fighters in history, from Hector Camacho to Manny Pacquiao. But the fastest fighter I ever witnessed in the flesh, bar none, was Roy Jones Jr. In his pomp, Roy's feet barely touched the canvas and his hands created optical illusions. Knocking down Reggie Johnson in a title defense, television couldn't even pick up the fast one-two that dropped his opponent. It was less a combination of punches than a blur of colors. A few years later, I was at the commentary desk alongside the great Lennox Lewis the night that Roy - a former middleweight who stood under six feet - captured the WBA heavyweight title from Johnny Ruiz, who incidentally had just caught his wife in bed with another man a day or so earlier. So his head was all fucked up. But nevertheless, even at age thirty-five and laden with excess muscle, the punches of Jones from first round to last popped like artillery fire.

Then, power. No contest here. Nobody I saw ever hit harder than Earnie Shavers. They selected me to induct Earnie into the Nevada Boxing Hall of Fame because I'd been there for most (if not all) of his big nights. So, believe me, outside of the guys he cracked, no-one understands the true extent of his power like me. Watching him hit the heavy bag made my ears ring; watching him clobber his opponents - with either his right or his left - made my entire body shake! Ali said of Shaver's power that 'It shook my kinfolk back in Africa!' Holmes claimed upon being nailed by Earnie that he thought he'd been electrocuted. And Ken Norton, well, poor Kenny couldn't say much of anything.

Defense. A bit trickier to call. Ali with his footspeed had great defense, as he could float around the ring for the full fifteen rounds and effortlessly dictate the terms of engagement. Opponents such as Sonny Liston, Cleveland Williams and Zara Foley were given fits by his movement - the swiftness of which I can personally attest to. Remember, I once shared a ring with Ali - albeit briefly - and while I am no pro boxer, I can tell you firsthand that he was damn near impossible to pin down. Further to that, I was privy to thousands of rounds of sparring in which the only blows that touched him were the gusts of wind that followed a missed swing - and even *those* weren't solid enough to mess up his hair.

Larry Holmes also had great defense. Unlike Ali, whose defense was based on footspeed, Larry's was spearheaded by the left jab. Guys would try to smother him, to walk him backwards and attempt to drain his power. But very rarely could they pull this off. His left hand was so good that either defensively or offensively, he could knock you out. With Larry, everything worked off that punch.

I also have to mention Pernell 'Sweet Pea' Whitaker. The man was a ghost inside the ring. Even as a shot fighter, against the likes of a young Oscar de la Hoya who was already a three-weight world champion, he was damn near impossible to hit flush. Of course, I was at the Alamodome in San Antonio, Texas, the night he boxed circles around Julio Cesar Chavez to scrape a draw on the judges' scorecards. 'Sweet Pea', who barely got touched in twelve rounds, really got the raw end of the deal that night. I even told Don King, my boss, to cut the shit when he mischievously tried to sugarcoat the result. There was just no denying that Whitaker had bested his foe. The way that he dipped, dodged, spun and swiveled, to uncannily avoid punches - whilst always remaining in the pocket - was unparalleled.

Chin. Mike Tyson absolutely could take a great shot; his head being firmly fixed to that slab of beef he called a neck. Remember, Mike was only ever stopped in the late rounds, and Buster Douglas could dent iron with his right uppercut - as he proved when he felled the undefeated champ. To me, though, nobody could absorb punishment like Ali. Look at the murderers' row of punchers he faced. Frazier, Foreman, Shavers, I could go on. This undoubtedly led to his Parkinson's Syndrome, because while Ali was never knocked out, his cranium in those fights (and especially in sparring) nevertheless absorbed frightening amounts of punishment. You see, whether you have on headgear or not, when you get hit on the chin, your brain still crashes up against the side of your skull and explodes into a concussion. It doesn't make any difference whether a guy goes down or not. That's still what happens. Microscopic arteries in your brain rupture and bleed, and it causes brain damage later in life.

Sadly, that's the bitter reality of our sport … all we, as spectators, can do is respect the fighters for the incredible risks they take and celebrate their achievements.

Intelligence. Sugar Ray Leonard without question was the smartest fighter I ever saw. He stole so many rounds with the 'Ali Shuffle' in the last ten seconds before the bell that it was a sight to behold. Throwing flurries, biting down on the gum shield and looking again like the Sugar Ray of old, he would leave people on their feet and screaming in delight. Of course the judges were swayed! They were only human beings. If I hadn't spent so much time with him, I would have been swayed too. Remember, he was trained by Angelo Dundee and had shared the gym with Ali himself. He had learned from the best.

Technique. Julio Cesar Chavez in his prime was nearly perfect: his footwork, his punches, his defense, as crisp as any ever seen in a boxing ring. Later in his career, he got involved with cocaine and that really diminished him. You could already see the decline setting in against Meldrick Taylor in their classic first fight. Still, he caught up with the little Philly badass in the end as Taylor must have swallowed a quart of blood. Richard Steele gets criticized for the stoppage, but one more punch and Taylor was a dead man. I don't care if he's out in front on the scorecards, this is a prize fight, and it ends when the referee says it ends or the bell rings. And Richard Steele, the referee, made the right call.

Talking of making calls - here's my biggest call of the chapter. The greatest fighter I ever saw in my life, in the flesh - without question, Ricardo 'Finito' Lopez!

Lopez could do everything.

Number one, he was strong enough to hold the title, making 21 title defenses. Number two, he never got knocked down. Number three, he retired undefeated. Number four, he'd fight anybody, anywhere, anytime. Number five, he could throw punches with knockout power, despite being only 112 pounds. And number six, he could combine offense with defense better than anyone. Which is of course the hardest thing to do in boxing.

If not for his diminutive size, the guy would have been a global superstar. His legs were just as good as Ali's and his jab was equal to that of Holmes. But it was in the blaze of an exchange, whether in the first round or the last, that 'Finito' could move his hands more artfully than a violinist - and create the same sweet, sweet music.

I'm extremely friendly with Ricardo. Every time I see him, he comes over and gives me a big hug, which is always a great thrill - especially considering that the Mexican media follows him everywhere he goes. I remember getting a text from WBC President Mauricio Sulaiman, thanking me for being so kind to Mexican fighters. I believe this was prompted by my constant gushing appreciation of Lopez.

They're all my pals, the fighters. I have a blast with all of 'em.

Mike Tyson once told me that I was his favorite commentator and that a fight without me wasn't a fight at all. Larry Holmes, Sugar Ray Leonard, Joseph Parker, they all call me at least once a month. And Stevie Collins, 'The Celtic Warrior', remains one of my very best mates in the business. Stevie always had the ability to surprise me. Calling a fight together up in Bonnie Scotland, the former super-middleweight champ disappeared moments after a power cut had torpedoed our broadcast. 'Where the fuck did he go?' I was thinking, left alone at the desk. Well, the power returned and so did my color commentator. He looked pleased as punch as he said, 'Didn't I tell you that I was a master electrician?'

I am also great friends with Naseem Hamed. I remember one day Naz was walking down the street, drowning in a sea of fans, and I yelled over, 'Hey Hamed, what the fuck are you doing, smoking Marijuana?' This was in New York prior to the Kelley fight. Those ears of his wiggled a bit and he flashed a wide, mischievous grin. 'The fight's official,' he yelled back. 'The Colonel is here!' He then crossed over and paid his respects. I loved my interactions with Naz. Sure, Ali may have been the greatest showman I ever saw, but it's hard to think of too many other fighters that entertained more than the 'Prince'.

Another great character was Roberto Duran. To this day, he's a really fun guy to be around, as 'loco' as ever. More famous than the Lord himself in Panama, Duran (who has no money) is looked after by the millionaires over there. Like so many of his contemporaries, he fought well into his forties because he needed the scratch. I called the contest between him and Hector Camacho (who, incidentally, is in the same Hall of Fame class as me), and it was a horrible fight. It was just two old men waltzing around. I'll never forget, Al Bernstein, sitting next to me, summed it up when he said, 'Colonel, not even you can make this a good fight!' Which was both a joke and a compliment.

However, my closest pal of all was Jimmy Ellis. Jimmy and I played basketball together back in the Miami Beach days; he was humble, funny, and always quick to flash a toothy smile. Decades later, I remember attending the WBHOF in Los Angeles, excited as hell because I found out Jimmy was going to be there. It was heartbreaking when my old friend didn't even recognize me, his son telling me, 'Colonel, my dad knows who you are, but he can't remember anything.' Jimmy died a short time later.

Fighters, when they climb through those ropes, put everything on the line. My respect for their bravery is colossal. Bobby Chacon, the two-weight world champion, prior to his passing, couldn't walk through a door jamb without hitting both sides. Terry Norris, the great 154-pounder who sent Sugar Ray into retirement, by all accounts isn't much better off. It's heartbreaking to say, but fighters suffering from CTE (or with punch drunkenness, as it used to be known) are more numerous than anyone would care to admit. A career in pro boxing - and I cannot emphasize this enough - is a perilous way to make a living, especially when you consider that ninety percent of fighters leave the game flat broke. Spend as much time around fighters as I do, and you come to understand that, while the money is a bonus for them, the vast majority of these guys fight because they were born to do so.

Which brings me to the most brutal fight I ever called not involving a death. Nigel Benn against Gerald McClellan was a feverishly exciting (though ultimately tragic) ring war. For all practical purposes, Gerald had Nigel knocked out in the first round, coming out like a steam train and nearly flattening his foe. Then, somehow, after being put through the ropes in the opening minutes and beaten senseless for nearly ten rounds, Nigel came roaring back to virtually kill McClellan. I still feel a twinge of guilt for assuming that McClellan, remaining on a knee while being counted out, blinking rapidly and pawing at his eyes, had quit. We all learned later that he was having a stroke, but as I watched him rise from the canvas and walk unassisted back to his corner moments after the referee had waved his arms, my reflex assumption (shared by nearly everyone else watching I'd wager) was that the fight had simply been knocked out of McClellan. However, I'll say it once more: as a sportscaster, you can only call what you see. Gerald was a warrior who lived and died by the sword, and his near-fatal brain injury (likely caused by one of the many violent headbutts that occurred during the fight) cast a cloud not only over the event in London, but it also cast one over the sport itself. Solemn doesn't even begin to describe the mood among the staff of Don King Productions as we absorbed what had taken place and readied ourselves for the flight back home.

Looking back at that fateful trip, the only good memories I can muster are of spending time with my mates in the British media. I've always been very fond of these chaps. Firstly, because their expense accounts were usually better than mine, and secondly, because they have always loved a good knees-up!

Unlike many of the U.S. journos who can be self-important assholes, the UK guys know how to let their hair down. Reg Gutteridge, Harry Carpenter, and Colin Hart (just to mention a few) were all fantastic guys to share a jar with. Then there was the great sportswriter for The Observer newspaper, Hugh McIlvanney. Hughie was old school, a Scottish literary genius who was always looking for the nearest bar. We would seek each other out, like a couple of ol' thirsty scoundrels, and shoot the shit for hours with Glenfiddich warming our breath. And finally, to my other great pals (or should I say brothers-in-arms) Ian Darke and John Rawling, who both have a special place in my heart, I must also pay tribute. They were cubs when I met them, wide-eyed and bushy-tailed, but always willing to get into as much trouble as I could find for them. We all knew that this job of ours was pretty unique - and ultimately just a blast. We'd go on the road to an exotic place, a week before a fight, we'd eat, drink, and whore, and at the end of it all, we'd watch a few fights. That's when it became serious, but the rest … easy money.

These gents feature prominently in some of my best (and blurriest) memories of the big fights. However, my absolute best friends - and this will come as no surprise - were Pat Putnam from Sports Illustrated and Eddy Schuyler from the Associated

Press. Older than me but never acting like it, both were hardened drinkers in the mold of Oliver Reed, and both were fantastic guys to be on the road with. They were also great at their job, and I followed their example unfailingly. Work hard, play harder. Why bother doing it otherwise? For me, the social side of the job was always its main attraction - the reason I love being around the fight-game. I also just plain love the sport itself. I've given my life to it, after all. And guess what? Despite the rumors of its demise, boxing is as healthy as ever.

The numbers don't lie. Eight, ten, twelve times a year, in Las Vegas, we have monumental fights taking place, all of which generate extraordinary sums of money. Especially around the holiday weekends, when you have your Pacquiao's and your Canelo's and your other PPV attractions appearing on the Strip. This has never changed and will never change. Why? Because of human nature. People clamor to attend the 'big fight' because they want to be with the beautiful people, *and* they want to mingle with the dregs. It's always been that way. Folks are attracted to both the glamour and the danger - the honey and the bee's nest. That's the appeal. So, in spite of what gets said, boxing still reigns as the number one combat sport. Because it makes ten times what the others do!

Everybody now is saying that MMA does it this way and that way, but our guys are making tens of millions for big fights, while their top fighters are lucky to make one or two. That's the difference. Still, the world loves to shit on boxing. Never mind how well it's *actually* doing. The big criticism is that it suffers from not having a centralized power. That the multiplicity of promoters, managers and commissions are too fragmented and profit-driven to give the fans the best available fights. Well, they can say what they want, and they can write what they want - but it will never change. There will never be one organization with one promoter, because there's too much money to be made. Across the board.

Forget the major promotional outfits; you have in existence guys like Artie Pellulo, Lou DiBella, Kathy Duva, Dean Lonergan, Kevin Barry and Georgie Calvert putting on events around the world and making good money. Never in a month of Sundays would they give up their own promotions to join a single organization. Nor would the sport's governing bodies - namely the WBA, WBC, IBF and WBO - choose to consolidate themselves, either. After all, they are distinct entities with distinct policies, practices and principles. Each with their own revenue streams. It would be an idiotic move for them to make.

So here's the problem: people look at an organization like the UFC, with all the ostentation of its recent success, and come away with a skewered perception. Sure, they put on great fights nearly every week, and sure, the fans regularly get the best matchups - but it's a complete monopoly. Meaning that the money only flows in one direction. How else can they put on those types of cards, at that type of rate? It's great for the fans, I won't deny that, but the fighters are left earning peanuts.

Don't get me wrong. I love MMA as a sport. I even called several events for the popular promotion, bodogFIGHT.

Marty Corwin, my producer for twenty years with Don King and for another ten or twelve years with Bob Arum, who could almost read my mind on the air, called me out of the blue one day and said, 'Colonel. I'd like for you to replace Lon McEachern on an MMA telecast up in Vancouver.'

'Marty,' I replied, 'I don't know anything about that shit!'

'Don't even worry about it,' he reassured me. 'You'll have a great co-commentator to lean on, and we've also got Royce Gracie doing color.'

For those unaware, the Gracie family are the godfathers of Brazilian Jujitsu, and therefore MMA royalty. They've got schools all over the world, including New York and London, with millions of members. That's a thriving business. Royce himself competed at UFC-1 where he choked out everybody (including a boxer), announcing the heretofore unknown martial art to the world. I was ignorant of the sport of MMA, sure, but I certainly knew who this guy was. And I was genuinely thrilled to be meeting him.

Royce, for his part, wanted to know everything about Muhammad Ali. He was an Ali groupie, so he was very interested in what I had to say. I found him to be polite and playful and a real good listener. We worked for three days straight to tape the entire season for bodogFIGHT, which was shown all over the world, so we had plenty of time to get to know each other and strike up a friendship. I would bust his balls on the air by saying, 'All you talk about is the Brazilian fighters - because you trained them all, you bastard!' Of course, the Brazilian Jujitsu guy would usually submit the other guy in under three minutes!

When he asked me, during a car ride, what had made Ali such a great fighter, I told him, 'Speed, conditioning, and footwork.' And that made perfect sense to a Jujitsu guy like Royce, a great athlete himself. He especially loved to hear about Ali's work ethic, listening for hours while I relived my memories of 'The Greatest'. Coming from such a different background, he actually taught me a lot as well. So I have no prejudice against MMA. I'm just a straightshooter, and I happen to believe that the comparisons between MMA and boxing are naively misinformed - if you want to be polite about it. If you don't, they're complete garbage! The fact of the matter is, the UFC has been around for about 25 years, while we've been around since the 1800s. Trust me when I say then, boxing isn't going any place soon.

Historically, every ten or fifteen years, there's a turnaround. Right now, we're in a great era of prize fighters. The guys are bigger, stronger and faster than ever before. As is the case with nearly every sport, advances in sports science (nutrition, supplementation, recovery methods etc.) and overall standards of living have pushed the athleticism of modern-day boxing to new heights. Nobody in their right mind would believe that Pancho Gonzales, for example, would beat Novak Djokovic in a tennis match played today. So what makes boxing any different? Sure, individual fighters of yesteryear - and I'm talking about the great champions like Joe Louis, Ray Robinson and Archie Moore - might have been able to hold their own against the champions of today, but the rest of the field? No friggin' way.

That's my take anyway. Feel free to disagree. But what nobody can deny is that the sport is in good hands with the current crop of fighters - especially in the heavyweight division. The big 'tinker' from the UK in particular, is an exceptional talent. Of course, I'm talking about the current heavyweight champion of the world, Tyson Fury.

Fury demolished our best heavyweight in Deontay Wilder and seems to have the rest of the division running scared. I suppose that's what a dominant champ is supposed to do. After going on a Bob Sheridan drinking binge after winning the title and blowing up to 30 stone, he's rededicated himself to the sport and looks within reach now of establishing himself as an all-time great. Victories over fellow Brit, Anthony Joshua, and the Ukrainian wizard, Alexander Usyk, would get him there in my book. And standing at over seven feet tall, let me ask you - who in history would have had an easy time against him?

The answer: no one.

The sport moves in cycles. Fans panicked when HBO left the boxing business, forecasting its imminent demise. Well, DAZN stepped into the void, confidently and seamlessly, and fighters are now earning more than ever. Not only them, but us broadcasters too! I had a year contract with DAZN, working alongside Ray Leonard, Dave Bontempo, and Barry Thompkins, and not only was I handsomely compensated, but I saw firsthand what a good job they do. Of course, any new enterprise has some teething issues, but in my opinion when passion and commitment are present, success always follows.

I guess we're all nostalgic about the past. However, the status quo in any arena is never permanent, and new doesn't always have to mean worse. I'm an old dog now, nearly eighty years old, and if I can be optimistic about the future, if I can look forward and not back, then I believe everyone else can too.

169

CHAPTER XVIII

'TO PRACTICE YOU NEED PASSION'

My best memory of Muhammad Ali is also my final memory. Perhaps six months before the world lost its greatest sporting hero, as I was arriving back in Las Vegas from New York after calling a fight, I noticed a commotion up ahead. My first thought was that it was some kind of an incident - a kilo of coke found in a suitcase, or a pound of C-4 discovered up an ass crack. These are the sort of things that cross your mind in an airport. But as I got nearer, I discovered the true cause.

Barely visible to the casual eye, perched on a chair, crown covered by a nondescript baseball cap - somehow Muhammad Ali still exuded sheer charisma. I felt it myself straight away as my heart warmed by several degrees. He was seated in the terminal, next to luggage, surrounded by a wall of bodyguards who killed for a living. While nobody was getting anywhere near the Champ, some 40 years after hanging up his gloves, he could still inspire a fascination great enough to attract a heaving crowd.

They all just wanted a glimpse of the great man, to see the legend in the flesh. And I don't blame a single one of them. I'd known the man personally for nearly half a century - and I felt exactly the same.

I probably hadn't seen him for a year. The Parkinson's Syndrome, by all accounts, was really kicking his ass, and he had withdrawn almost entirely from public life - only stepping out for very select occasions. Honestly, seeing him that day, I could tell the end was near. The man I'd known had become impossible to see any longer through the tremors of his illness. Of course, the world had grown used to seeing him look so frail. I had too. But there reaches a point when you wonder just how much further a human body can deteriorate. To my eyes, Muhammad had reached that point.

Sadness crashed over me, but I let the wave disperse at my feet.

Right away, Ali spotted me. I was being flanked by a couple of heavies myself, and as I approached, cutting a straight line through the herd, his eyes widened, and he placed both hands on his belly. Glints of reflected light shone from his irises. Then, as if hearing music disguised from the rest of the room, he began to tap out a rhythm on his midsection with his palms. It took me a moment, but then I caught on to the joke. After about ten seconds, his poker face broke, and he cracked a little smile.

It was priceless.

Muhammad, of course, knew me as a broadcaster in my twenties, back when I was a recently retired pro athlete weighing 190 pounds. Well, many decades had passed since those days, and courtesy of my love of all things bad for me, my weight over the years had climbed both steadily and exponentially.. At one point, I'd even weighed close to 30 stone! I'll be honest, as I stood in the airport that day being heckled by 'The Greatest', I wasn't too far off that hefty figure. Still, I wasn't going to take any shit - especially over my love handles. Reverence is all well and good until somebody starts laughing at your belly! Therefore, without the slightest hesitation, I responded with, 'Ali, you can laugh all you want at my stomach, but look at you. You're a fuckin' dead man walking!'

A moment of stunned silence followed, then Ali - throwing his head back - burst into laughter. He could always take a joke. For most fighters, their power is the last thing to go. For Ali, it was undoubtedly his sense of humor. It was the magic ingredient in his personality, and he kept that right till the very end. I can still hear the rumble of his laughter in that terminal. And while I sometimes wish I had said something more profound, more befitting, I now believe that my final words to Muhammad were just right.

A moment of shared humor can say it all.

Along with Gene Kilroy, his best friend and former aide, and Jerry Izenberg, the legendary author and sportswriter, I'm one of the few people left to have known Muhammad in his heyday - going back to the days of Miami Beach and the 5th Street Gym. Gene had actually wanted me to speak at his funeral. Better than anyone, he understands the unique pocket of time that we inhabited together, the magical quality of our having been in so many of the same rooms where history itself unfolded. As such, it would have been one of the great privileges of my life to speak that day - to have paid tribute to the greatest man of my lifetime. However, I really did have somewhere else to be. That same weekend, after all, I was to be inducted into the International Boxing Hall of Fame in Canastota. The big one!

I had actually been enshrined in five other boxing Halls of Fame by that time. Since then I've been inducted into a seventh. But Canastota was the one I'd been waiting for, the one that everyone involved in boxing waits for. It's the sport's Mecca, like Canton is to football and Cooperstown is to baseball.

Located in a beautiful village in Madison County, New York, lush with freshly mowed lawns and picturesque little trees, the hall itself is brimming with the ghosts of legends past, reaching back over a century. Along with my late wife Annie, who was my number one fan, I had in support my entire military unit from Boston - about twenty-five of them. They all came out for me, the Generals included, resplendent in full regalia. I probably had one of the largest cheering sections in the history of the ceremonies. It made a statement too. Till then, a lot of people in boxing kind of assumed that my military career was bullshit. They don't assume that anymore, thanks largely to that barnstorming turnout in Canastota.

Unfortunately, the organizers had us so busy that I couldn't spend too much time with my boys; but just knowing they were there - and to think they had come all that way to support me - was the greatest thrill of all. Of course, they still made it a fun weekend for themselves, mingling with the stars and getting absolutely shitfaced for the duration. Whenever I see them in Boston, many of them still say to me, 'We'll never forget Canastota, Colonel, but we've been to seven ceremonies now. We're not going to anymore!' Fair enough. That weekend, though, for sure had been a very special couple of days.

It was the Class of 2016, and my fellow inductees included the aforementioned Jerry Izenberg, Harold Lederman, the HBO commentator and judge, Mark Ratner, the former Executive Director of the Nevada State Athletic Commission, Lupe Pintor, the former WBC bantamweight champion, and posthumously, Hector 'Macho' Camacho, the enigmatic three-weight world champion from Puerto Rico who had passed away four years earlier. To name a handful. I was honored as hell to stand beside them.

Marvin Camel, the first world cruiserweight champion, was somebody I spent a lot of time with over that weekend. Marvin - a popular guy in boxing - is still waiting for his induction into the IBHOF, and every year the organizers keep bringing him back hoping that he'll get more votes from the people doing the voting. He'll get the nod one day, I'm certain of that. But Marvin doesn't let the frustration show. He's a wonderful guy, and we had a wonderful time together - reminiscing and breaking balls.

I also had a great time with the big guy from Poland, nicknamed the 'Foul Pole' after he tried to vasectomize Riddick Bowe with about a million low blows in New York and Atlantic City respectively. Of course, I'm talking about Andrew Golota. Andrew is actually a sweetheart of a guy, very quiet, very down to earth, and not in the least bit mental - despite spending a career trying to convince the world he was a nutjob! That's been my experience of the guy anyway. But hey, I've got a couple of screws loose myself, so I'm probably not the best person to judge. All I know is that boxing is full of crazy, wonderful people like Andrew. It's the reason that I'm so in love with the sport.

My absolute favorite person in attendance, however, was Christy Martin - the former female WBC super-welterweight champion. Far more than just the 'Coalminer's Daughter', Christie and I were really, really close friends back in the day. You see, she was on all the cards with Mike Tyson and became very famous because of that - becoming the first female fighter to grace the cover of Sports Illustrated. She's now happily married to one of her former opponents, Lisa Holewyne, and is running boxing promotions all over the South. She was simply a gift to the sport. Every one of her fights, win or lose, was an action fight, and she won several championships over the years. Sure, she came up short against Ali's daughter, but Laila Ali was about six feet tall while Christie was barely 5'4". Had they been male fighters, the match never would have been sanctioned. But hey, she never pissed and moaned about it, so neither will I.

Christy was in attendance for my induction speech, along with all my other dear friends at the ceremony. The room was actually packed, the stage a who's who of the industry. When my moment came around, introduced by the esteemed boxing writer Dan Rafael, formerly of ESPN, I saluted the Generals, who had been whooping and hollering, and I told Dan (only half joking) to stop picking so much on the sport's sanctioning bodies.

Then I spoke from the heart.

'My legacy is not working 1,000 world title fights; it's not 50 years in the business calling the great fights but, in my mind, my legacy is that I tried to protect the sport. In Zaire in 1974, when I heard it was going to be broadcast to a billion people, I felt I had a responsibility to the sport. I love the sport, so I went out of my way to protect the sanctioning bodies, the promoters, the referees and, most importantly, the fighters.

'We hear about the concussion protocol in the NFL but what about our guys, who know they can be maimed every time they get into the ring? I protect my fighters; I love my fighters and I will do everything I can to protect the sport because I love the sport and I will continue to protect the sport.'

I meant every word. As I stood up on the stage, the lights warm on my face, and feeling the emotion of the moment collecting in my throat, I couldn't help *but* cast my mind back over the fifty-plus years I'd spent as a broadcaster. The fights. The friends. The wonderful memories. Everything I myself stood for. And here's what I realized. I'm a boxing groupie through and through. When it comes to this sport I love, absolutely, I'm biased as hell! I never say a negative word about boxing. And do you want to know why? Because in my experience, enough damn people do that already.

So I've got some simple rules.

Firstly, I never criticize judges or referees. I'll correct them alright, but I'll never criticize them as individuals, and I'll *never* criticize them about the legality of what they're doing. I'm a certified judge and referee myself with two of the major sanctioning bodies. I know first-hand the difficulty of their job. Therefore, I'll say that Joe Bloggs should have done something differently, and that - in my opinion - he may have made a mistake, but I'll also stress that he's a great referee in general. A small disclaimer, but very, very important in maintaining relationships. This has always been paramount in my mind. After all, we share the same goal: we want to make boxing the very best it can be. Consequently, the entire community of boxing loves me for being a commentator that never talks negatively about officials - for the simple reason that no greater cloud can hang over a sport than the cloud of corruption.

In this regard, the judges in boxing get an absolutely raw deal. They get crucified, in my view, without justification in ninety per cent of cases. Producing scorecards that please all of the people, all of the time, is very difficult. Damn near impossible actually. The reason being is that the criteria for scoring rounds is partly (or even mostly) subjective, especially when very few punches are landed in a given round. Remember, I go to all the boxing clinics. I'm certified under President Mauricio Sulaiman of the WBC and President Gilberto Mendoza of the WBO. This is just the reality of our scoring system.

As a commentator, I'll make it clear when I think one or more of the judges have made a mistake - of course I will - but I won't knock the judge himself. Never. Because number one, I know that the vast majority of them are doing a fine job, and number two, it's usually the closest fights that provoke the loudest uproars. Those with several nip-and-tuck rounds over which the judges are reasonably split. In boxing we call them swing rounds, and even among the best judges in the world these create problems - usually resulting in scorecards that diverge by five points. And the response? Always the same. Screams that the fix was in, that those well-schooled (and state-approved) judges are all on the take, and that boxing as a sport is rotten to its core. But no! All we have learned from those scorecards is that five of the rounds were extremely close and that neither fighter clearly won any of them. That's it!

So whenever I can, amid the boos and whistles, I explain to a crowd that it's up to the fighters themselves to make sure that every round is definitive. That if they don't, they're leaving it in the hands of the judges and just hoping they'll fall on their side. I really can't stress this point enough. I say it on the air all the time: 'The fighters are responsible for making sure the judges have an easy time scoring a 10-9 round!'

That's my stance, and it ain't changing now.

As far as the actual fighters are concerned, I'm probably - no definitely - even more protective. I'll never say anything against the warriors that have the balls to get into the ring. In my career, I've called five fights in which one of the boxers has died as a result of the match. I've seen the dangers up close and personal and understand that it takes rare courage to be a prize fighter. Especially when you consider that most of them don't make any money - so I admire them unreservedly. Never in a million years would I use my position to take cheap shots and be an asshole at their expense. Sure, I'll point out the things that he should or shouldn't be doing *if* he wants to win the actual fight. I'll explain that, well, if this fighter wants to win, he'd better start tightening up his defense and using his uppercut and left hook. Suggestions that I'm able to provide from going to the old gym three or four times a week and being a student of the sport. You see, I'm probably the only commentator that has spent as much time in the gym as the fighters themselves. I know the sport inside and out.

Emmanuel Stewart from the Kronk Gym in Detroit once told me, 'Colonel, I don't know where the fuck you get your information from, but you're the most knowledgeable sports broadcaster I've ever heard!' Coming from someone like Emmanuel, who didn't give out compliments lightly, that was incredibly high praise. I've earned the respect of my peers for my ability to analyze a fight. This is what sets a Colonel Bob Sheridan broadcast apart from the rest. Jim Lampley, Steve Albert, Al Bernstein, Dave Bontempo, Barry Thompkins - they are all exceptional commentators, maybe even better than me. However, the fact remains that they don't possess the same level of insight into boxing that I do.

My comments are always very specific. I'll be critical of a guy's gameplan, and I'll be critical of his execution of that gameplan if it's not bearing fruit; but I'm not there to shit on anybody - I'm there to sell the fight. People have a misconception that boxing commentators are journalists, and we're not. We're sports entertainers, trying our darndest to keep eyeballs on the screen. I wish others in similar positions of influence would take the same view. I mean, among other absurdities, you've got a situation now where the television networks won't even *acknowledge* the world sanctioning bodies. Talk about impugning an integral part of a sport!

People will say the 'alphabet soup' titles don't mean anything - that they're the devices of a corrupt system and should be abolished. Well, ask the fighters if they should be abolished, especially when the difference between having one of those titles and not is often a multi-million-dollar payday. So they're very important. You can't select on television what you want to cover and what you don't want to cover. It's all part of boxing. You have to talk about it whether you like it or not. So I'm friendly with all the associations because I believe in them. The WBC being the best of the bunch in my opinion. They do a superb job of training their officials and improving standards. Why can't people talk about that?

The truth of the matter is, I understand the power of my position. When you sit where I sit, you have an awful lot of power to influence. And that influence has a direct bearing on the career of a fighter - don't think for a second that it doesn't. On the one hand, I can do nothing but help him; but on the other, with my voice heard by millions around the world, I can completely fuck him up. Which of course I would never do. I maintain a great relationship with everybody in the business, *especially* the fighters. I've never wanted to hurt anyone, much less the guy who gets the shit smacked out of him even when he wins. I may be a self-proclaimed tough guy, but that motherfucker is the real thing!

I've done my best to exhibit this reverence, and I truly mean reverence. I believe that viewers at home have appreciated this aspect of me as much as anything else - that, and the fact that I'm essentially an overgrown child who loves to be the silliest guy in the room. This has always been a part of my personality, my sense of humor, and my sense of fun. Growing up in an era dominated by stuffy broadcasters, I aimed to reflect the average Joe a little more, to be more relatable to the masses. Consequently, I developed my own interview style.

Being acutely aware of the tightly wound atmosphere before any prize fight, I avoided the standard 'Don't even bother asking me because you already know the answer' questions that you mostly see on television. Instead, when visiting a dressing room, I'd ask things like, 'Hey, have you ever committed murder?' Or, if he was a farm boy, 'Hey, have you ever engaged in activities with a sheep?' By doing that, I could loosen the guy up, and he'd open up to me. It worked every time. As I gained more fame and people got to know me better, it became easier to interview the big fighters. They knew that, firstly, I never criticized officials, and secondly, I never criticized a fighter. They also knew that I was a lot of fun.

With that in mind, my wild personality has certainly been a key contributor to my success as a broadcaster. Beyond that, if I were to list the three ingredients that have been integral to my Hall of Fame career, they would be as follows: Number one, you have to have a voice. Number two, you have to know the sport. And number three, you have to prepare. You have to fuckin' prepare! You know how in real estate they say, location, location, location? Well, in broadcasting it's preparation, preparation, preparation. You can never be prepared *enough*. That way you're never nervous going in. On the contrary, you're as confident as can be because you already know more than the audience does - a lot more. And then you just allow yourself to flow. It doesn't make any difference if you're going out to a billion people or you're simply performing for the guys in the truck. You're always doing the same thing.

These days, of course, I'm a doddering old fool, so I spend more time than ever poring over bios in my hotel room. Even for the guys I've called before, I still have to get the height, weight, age, who's working their corner. And those are just the basics. The rest is all the technical stuff. Does he have a good left hook? Does he need to close his stance a little bit? When he throws his right hand, does he drop his left hand? All those little details that most boxing commentators miss, not because they're lazy or incompetent, but because they haven't been trained to see them. So even if I don't know a fighter in the afternoon, by the time I reach the air, I know everything about him. To the last detail.

This commitment to preparation really came in handy on the night that Ali (chasing a ludicrous payday) went over to Japan to fight the wrestler, Antonio Inoki. It was a complete novelty fight, an exhibition, and I was calling it back in the States from screenside - an easy paycheck. Basically, I was there to have a good time. However, about thirty minutes before the start of the fight, as I was getting comfortable at my desk, all of a sudden everything went dark. 'Holy shit!' I remember thinking to myself. Here I was in Las Vegas, the most well-lit city on earth, and the arena lights had blown out and I couldn't even see my own shoes! Moses himself might have been less surprised when he saw the burning bush.

My producers, scrambling around the arena like a team of blind electricians, had no idea what to do. Eventually, they resorted to bringing me janitors and security men for interviews just to keep the conversation going. I would ask questions like, 'Has this ever happened before? Have you ever seen this?' and so on for about an hour.

They held up the fight in Japan after learning that we had a problem on the world telecast. I probably ad-libbed for forty-five minutes straight at that point. I had no choice. It was only my preparation that allowed me to pull it off - and to pull it off in style! You see, I wasn't just babbling or talking nonsense, I actually had some pertinent things to say and, under pressure, was able to reel them off one after the other.

As old Red Barber used to tell me, 'Remember Mr. Sheridan, when you're on a broadcast, and it's an hour long, make sure you have enough material for four hours, because you never know when the lights are gonna go out!'

The 'ol redhead wasn't kidding.

So yeah, I don't really get nervous before fights - because I'm trained to be prepared for absolutely anything. With that said, there is a sense of occasion that grips me from the moment the red light goes on. I'm adrenalized and laser focused. Because I always, always want to do a good job on the broadcast - if only for myself!

After a fight, as the talent, you'll often hear your producer gush - sometimes as if reading from a script - that you were fantastic and you were this and that, and that you really nailed it with the last call, etc. Alright, well, that's all bullshit as far as I'm concerned. That's what I'm supposed to do. It's those other nights when the ship hasn't sailed quite so smoothly that really get my attention.

Nobody has to tell me when I've been below par. I'm my own worst critic, and I know better than anyone when I've been just a little off. Therefore, it's really a wonderful feeling when I'm driving home from doing a fight, or a TV show, or whatever the fuck else, and I'm saying to myself instead, 'Man, you were really on tonight!' 'Man, I could have talked for another three hours!' And this feeling fills you with a warm glow. Those are the nights, of course, that you go out and chase pussy and drink beer.

Those are the nights you can actually pat yourself on the back.

CHAPTER XIX

'HERE IN MY HEART, DEEP IN MY SOUL, SOMEHOW I KNOW'

Before I met Annie, the love of my life, this is how I used to do it. Carousing on the decks of a cruise ship with a fleet of my pals, I'd find the most spectacular piece of ass on board. You know, the one with more jello in her lips than in the rest of her skimpy little body combined. Then, once I'd slammed a round of shots with the boys, the well-rehearsed act would duly commence. My buddies knew what to do. Getting as close as they could, they would start in by saying, 'Oh geez, doc did a great job on my wife's breasts. Absolutely beautiful.' And the girl's head, invariably, would whisk around upon hearing this - damn near giving herself whiplash. 'Dr Sheridan is a pretty private guy,' they'd carry on with, 'because he's got a very exclusive practice in both Beverly Hills and Las Vegas. You probably know ninety-nine percent of his clients, they're all very famous people.' And sure enough, 100% of the time, she'd be over at my table, batting her eyelashes and saying, 'Oh, what do you do for a living?'

'Well, I'm involved with boxing.'

'I heard you were a doctor?'

'Well yeah, I'm a doctor as well.'

And that was all it took. As the guys gathered around, and as the wine flowed, I'd soon enough not only have her eying me up as a potential husband, but I'd also have her tits out examining them! Of course, I was very careful about how I did this - there's a lot of liability there. But finally she'd say, 'How much do you charge?'

And just as easily as that I'd win her over. You see, once you get 'em laughing, you can get away with pretty much anything. Even when they found out I wasn't a doctor, these broads all still wanted to hang out with me - because they always had a great time with me. My mission in life was to have fun every day. If the Colonel was having a good time, so was everybody else. And as a television personality, there was no limit to the fun I could have. Doors opened as if by magic, and I would stroll right on through.

Broads, booze, and travel. These were my holy tenets.

And life was good. Following the infamous 'Bite Fight', my commentary career (and personal fame) had gone from strength to strength, as did my earning power - which pretty much doubled overnight. It's funny how a singular event can end up defining a career. Once the world learned that I had called Tyson-Holyfield II only hours after suffering a moderate to severe heart attack, and that I was accompanied at ringside by a nervous looking cardiologist (as reported on by Howard Manly of the Boston Globe, in some of the best press I've ever received), I acquired a kind of mythical status. Outside of The Rumble in the Jungle, where I'm credited as the only guy (in real time) to have noticed that Ali was using the Angelo Dundee loosened ropes to his advantage, Tyson-Holyfield II is the night for which I'm best known. It was the perfect promotion of my image, my public persona - which actually wasn't too far from reality. Subsequently, the freight train I was on never slowed down for a second. I was living the dream, the life of a rogue, addicted to both my job and my fame, and in my mind, I believed there was nothing missing at all. I really believed that.

Until one evening in sunny Spain, on vacation with my buddies and pissed as a fart, everything changed. In an instant.

We had recently visited Hungary and Bulgaria before arriving in Andalusia for a three-day stay. On our first morning in this Spanish coastal area, we received an invitation to attend an upscale after-dinner event designed to lure money from wealthy individuals. It was a classic cash grab, an opportunity for local entrepreneurs with businesses in the Costa del Sol to pitch for potential investments. Given the allure of this beautiful and highly sought-after part of the world, it wouldn't be a hard sell. Rich idiots are always eager to invest in local ventures. I was even contemplating parting with a few grand myself … although I wasn't overly interested.

Dressed in our finest attire and well-liquored up, we therefore endured over three hours of discussions about prospective apartment blocks and restaurants - or at least, we pretended to listen while sipping top-notch champagne. Then, just as restlessness started to set in, a familiar face approached my table and whispered with a sly smile that one of the businesswomen hailed from County Clare in Ireland - my old stomping ground. Upon hearing this, I shot out of my chair faster than a greyhound out of the gate! Remember, at this stage in my life, I weighed anywhere between 340 and 360 pounds. My tuxedo fit around me only by the grace of God. So, as I sashayed across the ballroom with a twinkle in my eye, aiming myself like a missile towards this poor woman, who was seated primly about four tables over, chatting politely with her circle of ten - she must've been thinking to herself, 'What the fuck is this?!!!'

Of course, the lady in my sight was Anne Kelly, my future bride. Annie had a big hairdressing business, from Malaga to Marbella, with a total of seven shops. And now she was confronted by yours truly.

'I hear you're from County Clare?' says I.

'No,' she answers. 'I'm from Tipperary.'

I think fast. 'Oh shit,' I say. 'I wouldn't trust you!' Then I turn on my heels and stride off.

She's right behind me as I return to my own table.

'Who the hell do you think you are walking away from me?' She looks infuriated.

I say, calmly: 'I have no time for Tipperary women.' Here, I kind of wink at her, watching her face change from insulted to intrigued. It actually becomes a running joke: my dislike of Tipperary folk and her mock indignation. And by the evening's end, we had made plans to meet the next day for a drink.

I couldn't have been more excited. However, once I'd sunk a few early-morning cocktails, my focus (as ever) became a little scattered.

She'd suggested an Irish pub a few miles down the road, which I knew well, and so our first date was set for three o'clock sharp. Well, I started drinking at nine in the morning. Along with my good friend Dick Tedeschi and several others, we'd set out that day to drink the rustic little town dry. The only problem was, Dick, because we had been boozing and whoring for coming up to a week straight, started having - well - a bit of a heart attack. Nothing too serious, but something which was best not to ignore. So, by the time we'd got him to the hospital and waved goodbye, I was coming up to being forty-five minutes late for my meeting with Annie. A major league fuck up! I hauled ass, moving as fast as anyone my size can actually move - certain that I was wasting my time. Thankfully, as I burst through the door, panting like a Labrador in July, she was only just then getting up to leave. 'Fuck this fat fuck,' she was probably thinking. But still, against all odds, I talked her into staying - once I'd explained the situation with Dick - and that night, incredibly, we absolutely hit it off.

I remember coming out with a great - a magnificent - agricultural comment. Because Anne was a big girl herself, not overweight but solidly built, I said to her, in serenade - 'You know Annie, I really like you, because you've got beef to the heels like a mullet covered heifer.'

'Are you calling me a cow?'

'Yes,' I said, flashing a million-dollar smile. 'I'm in the cattle business, and that's the best compliment I can give you!'

'Feck off!' she laughed.

And that was how Annie and I met.

From that point on we started dating, and by the end of the week - after spending every minute together and getting to know each other really well - she had tears in her eyes as we traveled to the airport in Malaga. Both of us were down in the dumps, holding hands and exchanging forced smiles. Then, as we stood at the edge of the terminal, saying goodbye with a few tender kisses, she turned my world upside down.

'I love you,' she said.

I froze up. 'Where did that come from?' I said, genuinely blown away. She smiled shyly and looked down, tickling my nose with her hair. I continued: 'Because I could fall in love with you very easily.'

And so we made an appointment for Anne to come to Boston.

For those two weeks, she was all I could think about. Spending an absolute fortune on long-distance phone calls, I was a love-struck puppy while I awaited her arrival. After all, she was going to be my date for an upcoming military ball, attended by my entire brigade, and I couldn't wait to show her off. However, a couple of days before the shindig, it was my turn to start having 'a bit of a heart attack'. My lifestyle was really beginning to kick my ass. Well into my 40s, I'd somehow degenerated into even more of a madman in recent years, going in twice, three times as hard whenever I was out with the boys. Not surprisingly, this insatiable appetite for the 'fast life' had at last landed me in the hospital, the squeeze in my chest tightening with every breath. It was now questionable whether she would come at all, but I said to Anne, 'No, please come. I'll be alright.' And I couldn't resist adding, 'And by the way, I've only known you for a couple of weeks, and you've already given me a heart attack!'

Thank God Annie always got my humor.

Two days later, as planned, she arrived holding as a gift this huge Spanish bowl that had to weigh fifty pounds. She'd dragged this fuckin' thing with her all the way from Spain. But to be honest, I barely even noticed it. I was just so happy to see her again - now on my side of the Atlantic - that I nearly crushed them both.

Against all the odds, we were going to the ball.

Still recovering from my health scare, I'd of course been given strict instructions not to drink any beer or spirits. However, I was allowed a sip of wine. So, naturally, I start drinking pints of Merlot, and having no food in my stomach, I get absolutely shitfaced! Come five o'clock, I realize that I'm not even dressed in my uniform yet - and need to piss as a matter of urgency. I haul ass back upstairs (where Annie is getting ready) and as I burst into the bathroom, I see that she's sitting on the john. 'I gotta go,' I say. 'I'm gonna piss my pants!' 'Get out of here,' she says in horror. But I'm undeterred. With laser-focus, I unzip my fly and piss a perfect stream right between her legs. 'You're filthy!' she screams, calling me all kinds of names. I compose myself, stumbling into a cabinet as I do. 'Annie,' I say. 'It was either that or I was going to piss on you. Surely, it's better to be pissed off than pissed on.' Then, focusing my eyes, I add, 'And besides that, a family that shits together, stays together!'

She realized then and there that I was a bit of a character - to say the least. She also realized that I was extremely drunk. Nevertheless, I managed to change into my military mess dress with a bow tie at record speed, and taking Annie by the hand, who looked wonderful in a green flowing gown, we set off for the venue. It was our first time stepping out together on American soil; we couldn't have been more excited. However, since nobody had seen me since the heart attack, as we walked into the ballroom, I instantly became the star of the show. I could see in Annie's face that she was kind of bemused, wondering just who in the hell I was. But those stars in her eyes didn't last for long.

I'm getting drunker by the second. Bladdered in fact. And while I'm of the firm opinion that tough guys never dance, about an hour and a half into the evening, just as the room's really starting to spin, I'm being approached by a temptress in a tight gold mermaid dress - giving every guy in sight a boner. 'Hello there,' I remember saying, forgetting all about poor Annie. Then, as the floor beneath my feet pitches left and right, I'm led merrily away to the dance floor. It was a complete spectacle. This broad is grinding up against me and all the girls and wives and lovers are looking over at Annie, saying to themselves, 'What on earth is she doing with this flaming fuckin' wild man?' And they were right. I was a wild man. And Annie, by the same token, was an absolute lady. But she also had a sense of humor. So, rather than getting annoyed and storming off (as most women would be apt to do in similar circumstances), she waits for me to wobble back to the table, weak at the knees, and says simply, 'Oh, you wouldn't dance with me, but you'll drape all over that one?'

I gave her a big smile. 'Well, Anne, I gotta be honest, she's got bigger tits than you!' And that was our relationship.

She was my soulmate. We had a wonderful life together, a wonderful chemistry. And she never tried to change me. She knew I couldn't be changed, not in a meaningful way, but she kept me under control as best she could - mostly for my health. I'd had the heart attack leading up to the military ball (my first), and while we were together, I actually succeeded in having eleven more; so she was very concerned about losing me. But when we decided to get married, we said if we could have three or four or five years together, it would be a great time and that's all we were really hoping to have - purely because of my deteriorating health. Neither one of us expected to enjoy a glorious marriage for twenty-four years.

And boy, how she suffered me! Anne was about 6'1" and a very stylish, modern dresser with hats and everything else. Me, when it came to my appearance, I didn't give a rat's ass. Remember I had to work in a tuxedo all the time, my abundant jowl choked by a shirt and tie for hours on end. So, when I wasn't working, I dressed any way I wanted - mostly in jeans and cowboy boots and a big cowboy hat. As such, out in public, where I drew attention like a flamingo in a paddling pool, she had a real tough time explaining me.

For example, I remember the first time she took me to meet her parents in County Tipperary, in a place called Carrick on Suir. With the music of a nearby river playing in our ears, we arrived at their little house just as the sun was setting. In Catholic families, 6 PM is the time they would have a thing on the radio called 'The Evangelist', where everybody is underneath and praising the rosary for about ten or fifteen minutes. Well, we arrived at six sharp. And you guessed it. Dressed like a cowboy and being about as quiet as a marauding elephant, I strode into the living room right in the middle of the fuckin' thing - whereupon her father (who looked like Pope John Paul II and was perhaps even more holy than the Holy Father himself) shot me down with a look that could have felled an elk from a hundred yards. His first words to me were, 'I don't care what kind of a Colonel you are, get on your knees and pray the Evangelist!' And this was my welcome to the family!

Nonetheless, I always like to tell people this: Annie and I were not only madly in love, but we were also great friends. Our senses of humor just perfectly aligned. We'd have so much fun, so many back and forths, that our bellies stayed constantly warm. Like how, on New Year's Eve, I'd always say to her with a bovine face, 'Annie, uh, you heard I'm nominated for husband of the year. Are you with me or against me?'

'Husband of the year? You gotta be effing joking!'

'Do you love me?'

'It's a bad time to ask.'

'So am I husband of the year or not?

'Who are you running against?

'In your case, I don't think I need to run against anybody!'

Then she would just outright clobber me. Not with an object, mind - but with her best Tipperary scowl! Then the scowl would give way to a buttoned-up smile. 'Ok,' she'd say at last. 'You're husband of the year.' And then she would throw her eyes up to heaven and carry on with whatever it was she was doing.

Losing Annie was the worst thing that ever happened in my life. We never had any children together, given our age, but we had a little dog named Lucy, and we poured all of our love into each other. I never once cheated on Annie. I'd already fucked up one marriage, and I knew she loved me so much. When she got sick, I had to be strong for her sake. That was my job as her husband. But beneath it all - all the positivity, the rock-solid exterior, the pillar I wanted to be for her - I'd been gradually falling apart. Losing someone you care so deeply about to a slow illness is awful. You mourn them while they are still alive. But my Annie was so brave, never for a second losing her sense of humor. Once her chemotherapy treatment began, she even pushed me to put the idle hours I was spending in waiting rooms to good use. And so it was that in my seventies, I went back to school.

Now, you've heard me say that I have a university degree in Veterinary Medicine. Well, here is how it happened.

For family as much as for patients, chemotherapy is a terribly drawn-out process, commandeering huge portions of the day. Instead of just sitting around for hours on end, as Annie pointed out, I could be doing something productive. So, the idea just came to me. With my extensive agricultural background, and love of all animals, I should study to become a vet! It would also be a welcome distraction.

So, without further ado, I started a correspondence course at Florida A&M University. It was wonderful at first because I was so excited. However, I soon realized that the University of Texas was actually a better place to be. At that point, I decided to spend a couple of days a week there studying small animals: feline, canine, swine, goats, and even the more exotic ones like bearded dragons. These became the new objects of my focus, and to be perfectly honest, I even surprised myself with how easily I digested the curriculum. Surrounded by kids practically a quarter of my age, I learned how to take care of these creatures in no time at all!

I loved the learning experience and the feeling of being a student again, feeling a full day younger every time I walked out of class.

Following this, I immediately enrolled in an artificial insemination course up in Montana - a subject I was already well-versed in. Bizarrely, there had been an artificial insemination laboratory in County Clare, just down the way from my farm on the Hill Road. Therefore, by the time I was done studying and learning the language of science (which most professors use to disguise their limited knowledge), I was invited to give lectures at the university and submit papers for peer review. No kidding. My little pastime had turned me into a bona fide academic!

So this was how I coped with Annie's illness. I applied myself to an endeavor and I achieved wonderful success. Honestly, I did it mostly for her, and she was real proud of me too. But nothing really had changed. After a prolonged battle, where everything that could have been done was done, I was inconsolable when my beloved Annie passed away. Friends and loved ones rallied around, but I was beyond anyone's reach; totally broken-hearted. The void I felt was immeasurable. Only on the day of her funeral did I finally take a tentative step back towards the land of the living.

But it was tough beyond belief.

Following her passing, searching for a way to both ease my pain and express my love, I'd gone out and ordered a 100,000-dollar, green marble gravestone for Annie. I had it made in Vermont, which is 3500 miles from Las Vegas, getting it shipped from Pease Airbase in New Hampshire to Nellis Airbase a few miles down the road. Although it took nearly five months to arrive, I was able to give her the biggest, the most expensive monument in a lush celebrity graveyard, and it's beautiful.

The funeral itself was the most bittersweet day of my life. Covid was spreading and only three people were allowed inside the chapel for the service - including the priest. Outside, though, congregated like an audience at an open top opera, was the most spectacular turnout I could ever have imagined. Over three hundred people, compressed into the small grounds, redolent with flowers. Commissioners, every judge and referee from the state of Nevada, the guys from Don King Productions and Top Rank - they all came to pay their final respects. And that's not including Annie's friends.

Annie, besides being a hugely successful hairstylist and beauty consultant, had also been a very talented oil painter. In fact, Pino Coco at the Vatican had at one time wanted to buy one of her works: a truly powerful portrait of Jesus Christ done in black and white, showing his teeth under a crown of thorns, with the only color being a drop of blood on his left cheek. She was very highly regarded for her work. As such, all manner of characters from both communities (art and fashion) had shown up, swelling the capacity of the cemetery. I'll admit, a lump had formed in my throat as I emerged from the church - it was so moving to see all of this love for my Annie. It meant the world to me.

The ceremony was wonderful too. We had pipers and drummers and I got up to sing the Irish national anthem in Gaelic, dressed in my full military uniform. I'd worn the same uniform on our wedding day, almost twenty-five years earlier to the day, and I wanted to pay homage. With the pipes behind me, I didn't sound half bad, my voice carried by a firm breeze that also rippled and twisted the Irish flag - raised to full mast over the grounds. Then it was all over. I thanked everyone and watched them filter out, the green of the lawn gradually emerging from the black.

As I returned to the limousine, I was ready to tune the world out. I'd had enough and just wanted to be alone, politely declining everybody's offer for a drink. The thought of having to perform for a crowd - at that moment - felt preposterous. But only minutes later, speaking on the phone to a priest from the Catholic Church (who couldn't be present due to travel restrictions), I was reminded of something that had an immediate, profound effect. It was as though the Lord himself had consoled me. Holding back my tears as the car pulled off, this man of the cloth simply asked me to remember one small fact - that Jesus Christ himself, for all his glory, had only thirty-three years on this earth. Annie, meanwhile, though she would of course be desperately missed, had been lucky enough to have over twice that many. These words really hit home. I suddenly felt I had the strength to attend the wake, which in any case was being held at mine and Annie's home in Las Vegas. I have never been someone to hide away from the world, and though I had every reason to disappear into my grief, I felt at my back a hand pushing me forwards into a life without Annie. The first step was to join my friends and family, to accept their love and support. They had shown up for me; I now needed to show up for them. I needed to be present.

What happened next, though, I couldn't have predicted in a million years.

Throughout this book, I have spoken about my belief in God, about my commitment to His teachings, and the importance of His grace in my life. Well, on the day that I buried Annie, I'll admit that my faith was severely shaken. That is, until the Lord himself gave me a sign that He was still up there, and that He hadn't yet turned his back on me.

Another phone call, this time from an old associate within a certain government agency who had some incredible - life-changing - news for me.

Now, at this point, I was back at the house having a pint of Guinness, huddled in with my three adopted sons, Dennis, Darren, and Damon - all gown men by this time. I've never actually legally adopted them, but since their father passed away over twenty years ago in a prison cell, convicted of the crime of being a black man in America, I've done my best to take care of them. To this day, we're incredibly close, and I couldn't love them more if they were my own flesh and blood. It was only right, then, that they'd been standing next to me, our elbows touching, as I received the call. Hours after saying goodbye to my wife of twenty-four years, my moon and stars, and now loitering in our kitchen with cigar smoke dribbling out of the corner of my mouth, half cut, I heard the impossible words.

'Colonel, it's legit. He's definitely your son.'

'You're shittin' me!'

'His name is Simon Edwards, he's 41 years old and he lives in England.'

'Right. And his mother is…?'

'A lady by the name of Rosemary Ruane. Do you remember her?'

Nothing further needed to be said.

To say I had mixed emotions doesn't even come close. God takes with one hand and gives back with the other. From feeling as though I had nothing left to live for, suddenly - bam! I had been gifted with a real biological son. It was only a few hours later, as the exhaustion crashed over me like a wave, that I tried to make sense of the news in my own head. To stumble down memory lane, like it was yesterday.

Simon's mother was a very dear friend of mine. A mile or so from my little farm in Bunratty, County Clare, was the Shannon Shamrock Hotel, of which Rosemary - or Rosie, as I called her back then - was the manageress. We were more like buddies than lovers. I was actually seeing somebody else at the time, officially, but Rosie was a great gal, and I would always look forward to seeing her. Eventually, we got to know each other really well, meeting up here and there and occasionally sharing a cheeky kiss. Well, nature being what it is, I guess I knocked her up - unbeknownst to me! At this time, in the late '70s and early '80s, I was winding down my rodeo career and had decided to move back to the United States. Trying to stay on the back of a bucking bull for eight seconds had left me a physical wreck, and beyond that, I was getting really busy with the boxing.

As much as I'd loved my time in Ireland, I knew it was time to say goodbye. I also knew that I was leaving behind a lot. Rosie was a fine-looking woman, and she had a great sense of humor. In fact, it was her wicked sense of humor that first attracted me. 'Bob,' she would say from behind her tumbling curls, as she poured my seventh or eighth pint of the night. 'Don't you have a home to go to? Or do yer just like watching me?'

She could read me like a book.

In the wintertime, it was cold in Ireland, and she'd say, with her wide, irresistible smile, 'Why don't you come down and stay at the Shannon Shamrock?' And so I joined the club at the Shamrock, and I'd go down there to shower and swim and stay in a cozy little hotel. That's when she and I would meet, and we'd either get room service or go for walks together. I guess you'd call it trust. We both felt so comfortable being in each other's company. Rosie, who was very bright, loved entering the pub quiz every Tuesday or Thursday - her face lighting up with every question. Although she didn't get too many answers wrong, when she did miss one, everyone in our little group (especially me) would heckle her mercilessly from the sidelines, all of us roaring with laughter. Rosie, well, she'd be up there shaking her head and wagging her finger, a big grin slapped across her face. But like I said, she was so bright, we really didn't get to do that very often. She was just a really fun person to be around, as were the whole crowd of friends we had in Shannon at that time, all of whom loved a jar and a singalong. This period in my life is crammed with wonderful memories that I cherish to this day.

For years after returning home, I found myself longing for the old country. Rosie was somebody I certainly thought about. Above all, we'd been great friends, so I was truly saddened to hear of her tragic death in 1985. My life had been a whirlwind for so many decades, I'd never got word of poor Rosie's passing; I certainly didn't know that she'd become a mother. For her own reasons, she chose not to tell me about Simon. This is something I now accept. The human mind is a labyrinth. It's not up to me to play guessing games about anything - that's how you go crazy.

However, I am grateful to the good people who adopted my son and raised him as their own. I'd be lying, though, if I said I wasn't envious of them. I've missed so much, and I suppose now that I'll always be playing catch up. Though as I write, I've spent countless hours on the phone with Simon, and I can tell you without question that he's a chip off the old block. Charming, intelligent, and an irrepressible rogue!

Sadly, we've not yet had a chance to break bread. Simon now lives in the Philippines, and due to Covid and some health issues on my side, we haven't yet found the right opportunity to get together. But I really hope we will. Learning of his existence breathed new life into my body when I was all but dead and buried. I will never forget that.

I am also eager to meet my two granddaughters, who I understand are happy, healthy, and doing well in school. But, regardless of what happens, my new family - gift-wrapped and left under my Christmas tree two years ago - will have a permanent place in my heart. The little girls, especially, whether or not we ever get the chance to meet, will continually be in my thoughts and prayers and will forever be an immense source of pride. As I hope, one day, I will be for them.

If I'm lucky, I've got another five years in me - ten max - before I'm pushing up daisies next to my beloved Annie. More than ever, I find myself reflecting on the past, and a recurring thought surfaces. When I first moved to Ireland as a young man, the children I saw scampering about in the leaves, in the mud, must now all be in their fifties and sixties. I ponder this for a long time, and then my thoughts inevitably turn to Rosie - she was in the flushes of youth when I knew her, so beautiful and alive. My heart breaks a little, even knowing that it is what it is - the circle of life.

CHAPTER XX

'THE WORLD HAS CHANGED AROUND ME'

I've been cautioned against sharing this next story, so I'll adhere to that advice - despite my lifelong preference for brutal honesty. But what I can say is this: I recently survived an encounter with true criminals.

Let me be as vague as possible. The event in question involved my red Corvette, a gas station in Victorville, California, and a gang of bikers with malevolent intent. Beyond that, all you need to know is that on the fringes of the Mojave Desert, at half-past one in the morning, I sustained catastrophic injuries as a result of a traffic accident - and I very nearly didn't walk away. Two emergency surgeries to my midsection were necessary, and to date, over two years of rehabilitation have been required to fix the damage done to my body. But that doesn't faze me; I'm tough as old boots and have proven my resilience. What does trouble me - greatly - is that my own government's stupidity nearly cost me my life.

It's a bad joke.

After surviving everything I have, traveling to and spending time in some of the most dangerous places on Earth, it was a gang of thugs in Victorville who nearly did me in - right on my damn doorstep! Let me be crystal clear on this: forget about the punks who came after me on their little bikes; they were just criminals behaving like criminals, and they did exactly what they were supposed to do. Instead, the blame for my near-slaying falls squarely on the Democratic Party in America and their misguided policies. You see, with these blue-ribboned dipshits in power, the borders are wide open. Criminals of every description are flowing into the country daily, including cartel members, and nobody gives a damn.

Here's the reality: the Democratic contingent in the United States, which constitutes half the population, is nothing but a bunch of fools - absolutely stupid. What did they think would happen in these Democratic cities when they defunded the police, removed tens of thousands of cops from the streets, and allowed the lunatics to run the asylum? It was a shitshow to end all shitshows - as predictable as allowing toddlers to play with drawers of knives and vats of acid. Absolute morons. Of course, these places degenerated into Mad Max-style dystopias within hours. Bad people need the deterrent of the law to keep them from doing bad things. Hell, even good people need to be kept in line occasionally. It's why our men and women in blue are so crucial - at all times! And make no mistake, nearly every police shooting in America over the past decade could have been avoided if the perpetrator had simply acquiesced to the police officer - nearly every last one of them.

You can take that to the bank.

Cops operate under the most extreme pressure. They never know what kind of situation they are walking into or whether a given day may be their last. The reality is that, at any moment, they could be faced with the barrel of a loaded gun. It's only their own service weapons (and the authority to use deadly force) that enable them to keep *us* - the public - more or less safe in our beds at night, this now proven beyond a shadow of a doubt by the 'defund the police' horror shows of recent years. Cops put their bodies on the line to keep us protected against the slime of society. To stop murderers from killing and thieves from stealing. But instead of being thankful, these liberal assholes just shit all over them. So, of course, nobody wants to be a cop in the United States anymore, and I don't blame them. It's a thankless job. Despite the obvious lunacy of leaving major cities in America unpoliced just to appease a tiny minority of imbeciles, there are still those calling for the abolishment of law enforcement. Mind-boggling.

It's these same morons who characterized Donald Trump as a racist for wanting to protect our borders. On this matter, too, they are completely full of shit. Crime is up across the board since Trump left office and the Democrats decided to open up all the borders again. States like California, in this period, have been flooded with drug dealers and murderers, while upstanding citizens (like yours truly) have become sitting ducks in their own backyards. If you don't have borders, you don't have countries - simple as that. You can't have people walking across unchecked because you don't know who the fuck is who! The process of vetting *must* take place. Why in the hell is that a controversial statement? Especially in the United States, where everybody wants to blow us up. It's just common sense.

We let in a million people a year legally. Good immigration is great for any country and should be facilitated to the max. But every month we've also got thousands more 'unknowns' just strolling across the border, unobstructed by as much as a jagged rock; and it's exactly what the Democrats want. They want more people in because they want more people on welfare. And they want more people on welfare - and this is the truth of the matter - because they want more people to vote Democrat. Namely, the freeloaders and the criminals. It's all tactical. All these people, Pelosi, the President, the other phony politicians, they want to pull standards down with their policies so that they can prop themselves up. When Trump comes back in, and I fully expect that to happen after the 2024 election, every last one of them will be held to account. Because they are destroying the country!

The situation is only getting worse. Today, in certain parts of the country, it's becoming more dangerous than even Somalia. The cartels are coming in over the border with trailers full of fentanyl, an actual poison used to cut Class A drugs - most notably cocaine. A pinch of fentanyl, no bigger than the size of a baby's fingernail, will kill you faster than you can say 'Fuck Trump!' It's an epidemic. But nobody on the left has enough honesty to admit this fact, much less the balls to do anything about it. So I blame the Democrats explicitly for my near-killing, and for much else besides.

I always tell people this: liberalism is wonderful until they run out of other people's money to spend, then they prop up the banks and start all over again. That's why the economy goes down the shitter every time the Democrats come into power. They just keep taxing, taxing, and taxing, in order to give money away to people that are perfectly capable of working. People don't need to be on welfare. If you have any pride, you want to work. Yet millions upon millions of otherwise intelligent folks love these policies for the simple fact that they equate handouts with compassion. And they're absolutely wrong. Electing our politicians shouldn't be a nice-guy contest, as wonderful as that sounds. Rather, it should be a competency contest that asks only these two questions. Firstly, how will they keep the country strong economically and militarily? And secondly, what will they do to preserve the constitutional rights of the American people for the next four years?

That's it.

I once had the opportunity to meet Trump (before he became President) when he and Don King worked together to promote the Trump Towers in Atlantic City, and I actually thought he was a bit of an asshole. But as President of the United States, I couldn't have been a more ardent supporter. Why? Because unlike nearly all of his counterparts in office, especially those in the opposite party, he's a proven businessman who understands that a country needs to be run like a business. And what do all businesses need to generate first and foremost in order to survive? Yes, that's right, profits! Trump understands this. The Democrats, on the other hand, have proven time and again that they shouldn't even be allowed to run a bath. History shows that they have no idea how to govern. In fact, they're far more interested in stealing peoples' firearms - and violating our Second Amendment right to bear arms - than in doing anything remotely productive. And even on this matter, they have no real clue about what they're arguing for.

Guns don't kill people, people kill people. It's a complete fallacy that fewer guns would mean fewer homicides because the *vast* majority of gun owners - like myself - are responsible gun owners. We carry licenses, go to ranges, and keep them for our personal protection. Adding yet more red tape to the already ridiculously sized tangle is a moronic suggestion that would help precisely no one! All we need to do is enforce the laws we have, and we'll have no problems. And how do we best do that? You guessed it. By having more police officers on the streets, reinforced by stiffer prison sentences.

Simple.

What is lacking today is discipline, respect, ethics, two parent families, and the proper teaching of what is right and what is wrong. You don't have to be a clinical psychologist to teach kids about being a decent human being. My parents and grandparents were ignorant immigrants with no formal education, yet they are etched in my mind as amongst some the brightest individuals I've ever met in my life. So, if you're taken in by gun control and other proposed legislation limiting individual rights, you're just plain stupid! It amazes me how so many people with such high university degrees and higher I.Q.'s can lack so much when it comes to common sense, decency, and ethics. Trump may not be the greatest guy in the world, on a personal level, but his policies are infinitely more principled than those of the modern Democratic Party - and believe me, had he not lost the 2020 election, we'd have no war taking place in Ukraine today, and yours truly would be far less beaten up!

Actually, it all worked out great for me in the end. After all, my surgeon in Las Vegas did me a little favor. While having me under the knife for the repairs to my midsection, he took the opportunity to remove some excess skin at the same time. Which (aesthetically at least) was absolutely necessary. See, I'd lost a shit load of weight over the previous eighteen months - trying to stick around on this mortal coil for a little longer - and had whittled down from 350 pounds to 167 pounds. That's the loss of over half my body mass. I looked like a champion swimmer dressed in a poncho made out of epidermis! So, ever-considerate, Doc offered to give me a little tummy tuck as part of the same procedure, saying he would declare it as being medically necessary. All perfectly legal as far as the hospital was concerned, but something which would save me about forty thousand dollars in expenses.

I lay flat on my back, enjoying the morphine-induced high. 'Do what you think is best, Doc,' was my reply. Consequently, I now look like a million bucks! Doc is one of the few surgeons in America today performing male-to-female transition operations, and his vaginas are described as 'perfect flowers.' I trusted him implicitly, not only with that procedure but also with a host of others.

Getting old ain't easy. As I write this, I'm seventy-eight years old, although my 'stage age' is actually eighty. The logic is simple: with all the plastic surgery I've had for television, I already look pretty damn good for my age. So when I tell someone that I'm actually eighty, they think I look even younger! My face doesn't have a single line, and (no shit) I could probably pass for sixty in a dark room. But really, that's all thanks to the doc. After all, it's what you have to do in the shiny world of showbiz, competing with all these beautiful models - something which pisses me off no end. But in reality, I understand that tits attract an audience, and that father time is undefeated. Nonetheless, you can't allow standards to slip. I'm no spring chicken, but I'm not in the grave yet either.

Everybody came out for my last birthday party - over fifty close friends and family joined me at a swanky seafood joint in Las Vegas - where I celebrated like I was twenty-one years old again. It was just a great time, eating lobster like it was going out of fashion and transfusing alcohol straight into my bloodstream. And the whole thing was organized by my beautiful new fiancée, Jennifer Spinato. Sometimes I really do believe in fate. Jennifer is a nurse who cared for my Annie in the final stage of her cancer. About six months later, following my experience up in Victorville, I happened to run into her again. You see, having been transported from California back to Las Vegas to receive my treatment for a severely mangled gut (the best surgeons, after all, are in the City of Sin), I also had the pleasure - the unbelievable good luck - of being reacquainted with that beautiful, smart, caring nurse who I remembered so well - and who now, poetically, was required to look after me. We hit it off straight away.

When I was with Annie, I'd never so much as looked at another woman - her passing a cloud over my head that refused to part. Each morning following her death, along with our little dog Lucy, I would take a fresh rose to her graveside, arriving at the cemetery much earlier than anyone else, the sunrise still hours away, and talk to my girl. I still loved her more than anything. But while laid up in that hospital, recovering from my wounds and juiced to the eyeballs with opiates, I will admit that, for the first time in a long time, outside of finding out about my son, Simon, I felt I had a reason to live again. I fell for Dr Jennifer (as she's known to me) in a heartbeat. I guess, for her part, she liked my sense of humor and my genuine affection.

We live together now, with her mother and her grandmother, and the four of us are like a happy little family. Her grandmother especially (whom I call Granny) is an absolute hoot. We get on like a house on fire. Granny is one-hundred-and-eleven years old; she smokes more than I do, she drinks more than I do, and I love her. Every night before bed, we go out on the porch together, and I smoke a cigar and she has about four cigarettes. And let me tell you, we don't just kiss, we swap tongues! Her daughter Karen, who I also love dearly - after all, she's going be my mother-in-law - can barely even look.

In truth, though, Granny's only ninety-three years old; because, like me, she possesses a real age and a stage age. While she does, in fact, have Alzheimer's and needs to be reminded occasionally of her own name, due to all the head injuries I've sustained (mostly from falling off bar stools), my short-term memory might actually be worse than hers! It's kind of embarrassing for a guy of my intelligence to forget what he ate for breakfast the previous day, especially when - at eighty years old - I can still reel off the starting line-up for the 1954 Cleveland Indians like it was yesterday. Every last man on the sheet.

So life has changed a bit, but I'm still me. More than anything, I've become a little more eccentric in my old age. Until Annie passed away, I'd been a regular guy who loved a 9 AM jar. Now, I've got piercings, I've got tattoos. I paint my fingernails in all kinds of colors. And my fiancée, Jennifer (the doctor), for my birthday gave me a three-carat diamond to hang from my earlobe - so I look like some big Nancy Boy! But I'm having a great time. In fact, courtesy of my vast collection of tongue rings, Jennifer doesn't even mind that my dick doesn't work anymore - those tiny trinkets, of course, being the great equalizer! Let's just say, she's not with me for my good looks, nor to enjoy an easy, stress-free life. But I do my best to relax her, and you know what? I must be doing something right. After all, she's agreed to marry me, despite my persistent attempts at showing her that I'm a crazy man.

I popped the question while we were on vacation together in Alaska. It was the perfect setting for such a wonderful moment and a place which is also particularly dear to my heart. You see, over the years, I'd spent lots of time up there with Annie. We absolutely loved making the trip, especially with friends. I remember one vacation in particular, with my great pals Georgie Calvert and Marty Corwin (and their lovely wives), and my 7'2" bodyguard, Pancho Limon.

It was a fortnight to remember.

Alaska is the biggest state in the United States - about ten times the size of Texas - and is completely unencumbered by people. In fact, the government actually pays folks to move there. I think less than five hundred thousand people currently populate the vast, mostly uninhabitable terrain. And most of them reside in either Anchorage or Fairbanks - the two largest cities in the state. Nonetheless, it's chockful of wild characters living purposefully outside of the grid; similar to how the United States was pre-civil war. A land just teeming with people wanting to march to the beat of their own drum.

Alaska has everything. The ports are beautiful, the mountains are beautiful, and the landscape is full of exotic wildlife. In the summer, you can drink straight from a stream or a lake; and in the winter, by shooting one or two caribou, or one or two elk - which are abundantly available to good hunters - you can have more than enough meat for the year. That's why most Alaskans own three or four deep freezers. In the springtime, they'll load up on salmon too. Even bear meat is on the menu up there, which when properly cooked (with plenty of oil and garlic), let me assure you, is delicious. You owe to yourself to try bear meat prepared by somebody from Alaska. It's like eating grits in the South.

But really why you travel to Alaska is to marvel at the natural beauty. It's best to go early in the year when you'll see the glaciers cap. That means when big chunks of ice fall off the face of the glaciers and shatter the ocean surface like marbles breaking through glass. It's truly a breath-taking sight which ought to be experienced by everybody at least once in their lives. Well, that year, we'd traveled at precisely the right time.

Georgie, Marty, Pancho, and I spent the first hours aboard our cruise ship doing a full lap of the deck and the interior - with special attention paid to the galley and the bar. In other words, the first thing we did was tip every ship employee in sight. After all, we don't believe in tipping when you get off; we believe in tipping when you get on! We'd learned that in Las Vegas - to grease as many palms as possible, as quickly as possible. If I'd paid twenty grand for the cruise itself, an extra five hundred dollars to ensure great service was neither here nor there. And the payoff was guaranteed!

We had a ball together. Marty, participating in a lumberjack contest, almost cut himself in two with his very first swing - the axe only stopping short of his spine by about an inch. Georgie was admonished about thirty times for smoking in unauthorized places on the ship. I was causing mass confusion everywhere I went because of all the busboys trying to take selfies with me. And Pancho, each time he walked into a room, had everyone on board wondering whether they were looking at a grizzly bear or the last of the Mohicans!

We were indeed an odd group. Finally, on the third or fourth night, the captain sent a dinner invitation to each of our cabins, essentially trying to figure out what kind of people he had on board. In response, I sent him a note saying, 'Captain, I don't think you have enough juice to service us with $1500 bottles of wine, so you'd better come to our table!' Sure enough, his curiosity got the best of him, and he expressed his desire to join us for dinner. A few hours later, we found ourselves obliged to buy a few very expensive bottles of vino! Not that anyone cared about money. We just cared about having fun.

One joke we used to love to play out, straining our eyes towards one of the passing islands, where there was absolutely no wildlife to be seen, was to say, loudly as we could, 'Look at the bear! LOOK at that bear!!!' These words would catch in the swirls of air and travel clean across the deck. This got everybody's attention and would bring them racing over in a tiny stampede, causing the ship itself to list about ten degrees. And keeping up the charade, we'd then go, 'What the hell is that white thing he's got? What's he doing? What, what … It's a rabbit. He's gotta be … he's wiping his ass with the rabbit!'

Those are the type of things we did. Very sophomoric, but also very funny when you're swimming in a sea of assholes with lots of money.

I must confess, sometimes it's odd to think that I'm about to get hitched again. But then I think, why the hell not? I'm in tremendous shape. I've just been promoted to a Five-Star General within the Ancient and Honorable Artillery Company of Massachusetts, where this past June Day they had a huge parade for me in Boston, with a marching band and a swarming crowd of hundreds filling both sides of the street. And as far as my health is concerned, I could well have another ten or fifteen years left in me. That's plenty! The saving grace for me, quite honestly, is that I lost the weight. Frankly, I was a walking time bomb, and I don't mean carrying one in Derry or some other place in Northern Ireland. I mean, I was the perfect candidate for yet another heart attack.

At the last count, it has happened twelve times, and I was working diligently on number thirteen. You didn't need a medical degree to know that I was pushing my luck. After all, I had a strong family history of heart disease, was 100 plus pounds overweight, used chewing tobacco for 20 years, had an extremely high beef diet, and was a drinker. By all rights, I should have been six feet under years ago. I mean, cats only have nine lives; I've had those nine - plus ten, eleven, and twelve! Crazy when I really think about it. But in all sincerity, I owe everything to Dr. Ram Singh and Dr. Kathleen Benson at Desert Springs Hospital in Las Vegas. They've kept me alive for twenty-five fuckin' years, so do you think they're not my friends? I fuckin' love them!

In total, I've had seventeen angioplasties. For these, you're bizarrely awake and perfectly able to watch the procedure taking place on a screen. Sure, you're a little doped up, but you can follow everything they do. It's fascinating. As they traverse the vein, you can clearly see the blockages, and when the balloon goes in, you're watching fatty deposits being pushed to the side like chewing gum. Honestly, after my seventh or eighth one, I decided that they were no longer a big deal. Mostly because technology has got so much better, even over the last ten or fifteen years. It's not how it used to be.

Open heart surgery, on the other hand. Well, I admit, for that I was actually scared shitless! They ended up doing a five-way bypass, and simultaneously, they put a strap around my left ventricle, the one that pumps the blood. If this failed, they informed me, the next step would have to be a heart transplant - and they don't give eighty-year-old guys heart transplants in the United States. So, it was either going to be total success or total failure. Thank God I'm a man of faith.

My belief in God's teachings has unquestionably shaped me as a person and given me steadfast comfort in my darkest moments. I'm not a particularly good Catholic, but I do it the best I can, and I speak to a lot of people about faith and Catholicism, and the importance of the love of Jesus Christ in my life. Honestly, plenty of people don't want to hear that, but if you don't want to hear it, then go fuck yourself. Change the channel. That's my attitude. Because this stuff is really, really important to me. Now more than ever. I pray the rosary every day and I say my prayers every day, because I know that every bit of luck I've had in my life (and I've had plenty) is by the grace of God. My intelligence, my personality, my quickness, these have nothing to do with me. They were all gifts from the man upstairs. And I never take that for granted.

Whenever I've traveled, I've always hung out with local people: the local chef, the local shopkeeper, the local drunk. I've never felt a particular need to hang out with famous people. Firstly, because I'm famous enough myself. And secondly, because most of them think it's down to them - their beauty, their talent, their whatever else. And they couldn't be more wrong. Just like me, they got lucky, and any time the good Lord sees fit, He can snatch it all away in two seconds flat. So, I keep in mind the importance of living a righteous life and of being kind to my neighbors. Especially since Annie passed away, I've become very spiritual, and I embrace the fact that I've been given a second chance on earth. Twelve heart attacks? I should be a goner, without question, and I give all the credit to the Lord for keeping me alive. I believe He has me on a mission to help people, and I feel a driving desire to spread the Gospels around the world. And it doesn't make any difference if you're a Catholic, a Protestant, a Hindu, a Muslim or a Jew - whatever you happen to believe in - love is the whole damn thing. That's what I believe in and it's the Gospel that I'm trying to spread.

When I go to the Vatican, I have a secret service pin from the Holy See, and I can go anyplace I want. Most people don't realize, but all of the Popes are buried under the main altar in the Cathedral - including St. Peter, who was the very first Pope. It's only a small chapel - about twenty feet by thirty feet - and not open to the general public; but I've been there several times. In fact, when Annie passed away, I took a vial with some of her ashes and dropped it right on top of St. Peter himself! Of course, I don't tell many people this story, because if I go around saying that Annie is buried in the Vatican - in the Tomb of St. Peter no less - they really will start saying the Colonel has gone fuckin' nuts!

Well, maybe I have. With all the crazy shit I do, I'm certainly not normal. Annie used to beg me all the time, 'Please, don't go around telling your stories anymore, especially your military stories. They all think you're full of shit!' To which my attitude has always been, well, fuck them. If you think I'm full of shit, then don't listen. But I'm a raconteur, a bounder, a cad, a teller of stories, a singer of songs. I can command a room full of a thousand people. And if I'm not the most interesting guy in the world, I don't know who is!

But in all seriousness, life today couldn't be any better. I've got 47,000 head of cattle in twelve countries around the world. I've just gone into the deer placenta business with my best mate Georgie from Christchurch (deer placenta, if you didn't know, has proven anti-aging properties). I've got my own airplane. I've got all kinds of toys. I drive a Bentley and a Corvette. And here in Las Vegas, the city I adore and that I will never leave, I have the love of a wonderful woman - my bride-to-be. And you know something? It's been one hell of a ride. Never could I have dreamed that my life would take so many twists and turns, so many preposterous pit stops, and that my career as a boxing commentator would reach such heady heights. But, like I've always said, I measure true success by the friends I've made and by the memories I've collected. By this barometer, I'm a millionaire indeed. South Boston may have been my birthplace, but the world has become my home. From Alaska to Zimbabwe

As I write, I'm smoking a Cuban cigar, sipping fine whiskey from a five-hundred-dollar lowball glass, and looking out over the horizon. It's eight o'clock at night, and the air is still warm and inviting. I'm going to stay out here on the porch a while longer. It gives me time to remember, away from the bright lights and fast living of the Vegas Strip. Usually, I don't know where to start. My head is filled to the brim with so many faces, places, and incredible events that it can all be a blur. But then I think about Annie, about our marriage, about all the good times, and the thoughts run clear. I've lived quite an extraordinary life, a blessed life. And in the immortal words of Lou Gehrig, the legendary ballplayer of the 1930s, 'I consider myself to be the luckiest man on the face of the earth.'

SPECIAL THANKS

I have various people who I'd like to thank and pay homage to.

Firstly, to the late great Colonel Bob Sheridan, posthumously, thank you so much for your time, kindness, and the humor with which you shared your life story. To Paolo Caputo, (AKA: Uncle Paulie), the Colonel's manager and my older brother, thank you for being the catalyst for this project and presenting me with this once in a lifetime opportunity. Your tireless work behind the scenes kept it going strong. To Alan Bellman at WEM Media, thank you for your guidance and continuous support. Katie Cunningham, thank you for the hours spent picking through early drafts. Marty Corwin, thank you for your colorful foreword. And to Jennifer Spinato, thank you for all you did behind the scenes supporting the Colonel during his final years in Las Vegas, Nevada.

Without you all, this book would not have been possible.

INDEX

BV - #0062 - 080724 - C0 - 234/156/13 - PB - 9781780916576 - Gloss Lamination

ALL THE KING'S HORSES AND ALL THE QUEEN'S MEN

'A SOLDIERS SONG'

Colonel Bob Sheridan
with Marc Caputo

ALL THE KING'S HORSES AND ALL THE QUEEN'S MEN
'A SOLDIERS SONG'

Colonel Bob Sheridan

1944 - 2023

Edited by Katie Cunningham

A dozen sketches by Dr. Ferdie Pacheco, 'The Fight Doctor'

www.colonelbobsheridan.com

First published 2024 by DB Publishing, an imprint of JMD Media Ltd,
Nottingham, United Kingdom.

ISBN 9781780916576

Printed in the UK

CONTENTS